'ALLAMEH
SAYYED MOHAMMAD HOSAYN
TABATABA'I

ISLAMIC
TEACHINGS
AN OVERVIEW

'ALLAMEH
SAYYED MOHAMMAD HOSAYN
TABATABA'I

ISLAMIC TEACHINGS
AN OVERVIEW

TRANSLATED BY
R. CAMPBELL

'ALLAMEH
SAYYED MOHAMMAD HOSAYN
TABATABA'I

ISLAMIC
TEACHINGS

AN OVERVIEW

TRANSLATED BY
R. CAMPBELL

Design by: F. Farhang

January 2002

Library of Congress Catalog Card Number: 88-62667
ISBN 0-922817-00-6

January 2002

Tabataba'i, Mohammad Hosayn, 1907-1981
Islamic teachings: an overview/ Mohammad
Hosayn Tabataba'i; translated by R. Campbell,--
[s. l: s. n], 2002.
234 p.
Cataloging based on CIP information.

1,Islam - Doctrines. 2.shi'ah - Doctrines.
I.Campbell, Robert, 1947- . II.Title.

BP11.T330493   297
2002
                      M78-21070

Contents

In the Name of Allah, the Merciful, the Compassionate

INTRODUCTION

The present book is an overview of Islamic teachings written in a relatively simple language to offer some understanding to non-specialists unable to engage in deep study of Islamic doctrines.

Writing simply is a valuable method for spreading culture, science, and religion. This style of writing has arisen to make human knowledge available to all — to remove the veil of obscurity and difficulty from specialized and involved scientific and technical subjects and make them readily accessible to everyone. Any subject, however technical, may be so restated that anyone can gain some appreciation of the subject and some understanding in proportion to his or her background and breadth and depth of understanding.

We see this style at its best in the Noble Qur'an. Here the most complex questions in human experience, concerning the most subtle points of metaphysics and human nature, are drawn in the simplest possible language. Here we can only mention one or two examples of the Qur'an's heights of expressiveness: in demonstrating the reality of the Resurrection and life after death, the Qu'ran, in words as terse and easily grasped as they are sound and logical, says, '[*Man*] *asks: "Who will reanimate the bones that have rotted away?" Say, "He will reanimate them Who first produced them*"' (36:78-79). This is very solid reasoning and a well-founded and convincing argument. The power that creates things from nothingness is able to gather a thing after its parts are dispersed and bring it back to life like before.

It is said that Abu Nasr Farabi[1] exclaimed, 'If only Aristotle were alive, then I would have advanced this Qur'anic reasoning, and he would have accepted the doctrine of physical resurrection'. You see how this expression is at once reasonable and simple enough for anyone to understand with a little thought.

Another example is the simple yet compelling way that the Qur'an approaches the much-belaboured question of ontology: '*Does He not know what He has created? He is the subtle, the aware*' (67:14). Can one who has given beings their being not know their nature and design? This brief statement completely clarifies the matter, and specialists find in this verse a compelling analysis of its subject.

The Most Noble Messenger (peace and blessings upon him and his family) and the Imams have followed the lead of God's Book in explaining the most elevated and complex subjects in a simple manner that is at once profound and accessible. Consider where the Qur'an states, '*We never sent a prophet except with the language of his people, so that he might explain to them*' (14:4). The verse states plainly that the prophets restated spiritual truths with precision in everyday language; they well understood just how to present these truths in the idiom of the people of their time; they were aware of their sensibilities; they had mastered their artistic and literary temper; and they expressed their teachings through the prevalent and accepted forms of the people of their age. The teachings of the prophets are one in essence, but there are striking differences in how these teachings have been presented to different societies.

The prophets have been directed to observe the principle expressed in this *hadith*: 'We are directed to speak according to their understanding'.[2] Accordingly, points of Islamic doctrine should be presented in a simple, solid way that all can understand; they should be given the literary and aesthetic embellishments they need to make the most striking and deepest impression.

In accordance with this principle and under the inspiration of the Qur'an and *hadith*, our religious scholars have written short, simple books in everyday language that are likewise sound, logical, and well-written. They have clearly realized that public acceptance of an idea is invariably conditional upon the quality of its presentation, the character of the language in which it is expressed — and this is a point that is often forgotten.

Two basic skills are of necessity involved in realizing this method: first, a thorough knowledge of the subject, and second, familiarity with the principles of writing, literacy and aesthetic standards, and the craft of writing simply. One lacking either one of these aptitudes will doubtless prove unable to produce books of use to everyone; it he tries, he will fail.

Accordingly, to prepare short articles of value to humanity on the great questions of the spirit is a major, technically demanding, and difficult undertaking; one who writes on a science for all has carried out a greater and more demanding task than one who writes for an audience of specialists. Therefore, when we speak of writing simply, let it not be supposed that anyone with a little knowledge of a subject and a little experience as a writer can produce such essays. Rather, this task is more difficult and demanding than scientific and technical writing; it will be recalled that one must master two different specialities to undertake it.

When it comes to promulgating religious culture and especially

Islamic culture, such books are urgently needed: people in our society cannot spend long years studying Islam. Articles must be written to acquaint people adequately with Islamic questions; the vast depth and breadth of these questions must not be allowed to stand in the way of public comprehension.

> If one cannot draw all the sea's water,
> One must drink enough to relieve one's thirst.

Accordingly, researchers who have specialized in and mastered various Islamic questions should also acquire literary skills and master the forms of exposition, so that their knowledge not remain mute, and so that they can convey Islamic culture to contemporary minds.

The book you hold is presented for the sake of this vital end. It was with this mission in mind that the late 'Allameh Tabataba'i brought to bear this extensive and profound knowledge of Islamic teachings and his considerable experience in writing relatively simple and popular works to summarize and interrelate these teachings for a general readership. This is one of a handful of books in this field that can benefit everyone and lend more responsibility to Islamic centers and students.

Centre for Publications
Office for Promulgation of Islam
Howzeh-ye 'Elmiyeh
Qom, Iran

NOTES TO THE INTRODUCTION

1. Abu Nasr Farabi, the Muslim philospher who died circa 960 A.D. — Trans.

2. A Prophetic *hadith* from *Al-Haya'*, third edition, Vol. 1, p.146.

In the Name of God, May He be Exalted

MY LIFE: AUTHOR'S AUTOBIOGRAPHY

The present writer, Mohammad Hosayn Tabataba'i, was born into a family of scholars in Tabriz in 1271 A.H. solar/1892 A.D. I lost my mother when I was five years old, and my father when I was nine. To provide for our support, our guardian (the executor of my father's estate) placed my one younger brother and myself in the care of a servant and maidservant. Shortly after our father's death, we were sent to primary school, and then, in time, to secondary school. Eventually, our schooling was entrusted to a tutor who made home visits; in this way we studied Farsi and primary subjects for six years.

There was in those days no set program for primary studies. I remember that, over the period from 1290/1911 to 1296/1917, I studied the Noble Qur'an, which normally was taught before all else, Sa'di's *Golestan* and *Bustan*, the *Illustrated Nesab and Akhlaq*, the *Anvar-e Sohayli,* the *Tarikh-e Mo'jam*, the writings of Amir-e Nezam, and the *Irshad al-Hisab*.[1]

In 1297/1918, I entered the field of religious and Arabic studies and was occupied with readings of texts until 1304/1925.

Over this same seven-year period, in the field of grammar, I studied *Ketab-e Amsela, Sarf-e Mir,* and *Tasrif;* in syntax, *Ketab-e 'Avamel, Enmuzaj, Samadiya, Soyuti, Jami,* and *Moghanni;* in rhetoric, *Ketab-e Motavval;* in jurisprudence, the *Sharh-e Lama'a* and *Makaseb;* in principles of law, the *Ketab-e Ma'alem,* the *Qavanin,* the *Rasa'il,* and the *Kafaya;* in logic, the *Kobra,* the *Hashiya* and the *Sharh-e Shamsiya;* in philosophy, the *Sharh-e Esharat;* and in theology, the *Kashf al-Murad.* This concluded my reading studies in areas other than philosophy and spiritual science.[2]

In 1304/1925, I travelled to Najaf to attend classes given by the late Ayatollah Shaykh Mohammad Hosayn Esfahani. Under his guidance, I undertook a course in principles of law that occupied about six years and a course in jurisprudence of about four years. I studied jurisprudence for about seven years under the late Ayatollah Na'ini and undertook a course in principles of law under him. I also studied jurisprudence under the late Ayatollah Sayyed Abu'l-Hasan Esfahani. I studied Islamic biography under the late Ayatollah Hojjat Kuhkamari.

In the area of philosophy, I had the good fortune to be able to study under the most renowned philosopher of the time, the late Sayyed Hosayn Badkubi. In the course of the six years I was his student, I studied Sabzavari's *Manzuma,* Molla Sadra's *Asfar* and *Masha'er,* Avicenna's *Shifa,* the *Ethologia,* Ibn Tarka's *Tamhid,* and Ibn Maskuya's *Akhlaq.*[3]

Out of the very great concern the late Sayyed Badkubi took for my education, in order to back up my enthusiasm for philosophy with an acquaintance with a rigorous style of thought, he ordered me to study mathematics. To comply with this order, I attended the classes given by Sayyed Abu'l-Qasem Khansari, a master mathematician. I also studied analytical reasoning and plane and solid geometry under him.

Because of difficulty subsisting, I was obliged to return to Tabriz, my birthplace, in 1314/1935. I lived there for ten-odd years, years I must really count as a period of spiritual barrenness in my life, because I was held back from scholarship and reflection by the unavoidable involvements and social contacts entailed in making a living (by farming).

In 1325/1946, I left behind my situation in Tabriz and settled in Qom, where I resumed my work in scholarship. I have remained there up to the present time, early in 1341/1962.

Naturally, everyone has tasted the sweet and the bitter of life in terms of his own experience. I in my turn have found myself in varied environments faced with all kind of vicissitudes, especially since I have spent most of my life as an orphan or a foreigner, or far from friends, or without means, or in other difficulties. I always sensed, however, that an invisible hand has delivered me from every terrible precipice and that a mysterious influence has guided me through a thousand obstacles toward the goal.

> Though I be a thorn, and though there
> be a flower to grace the meadow,
> I grow by that Hand which nurtures me.

When I began my studies and was occupied with grammar and syntax, I took little interest in them and failed to comprehend very much. I spent four years this way. Then divine favour suddenly reached me and changed me, so that I grew excited over my studies and impatient to learn all there was to learn. I never felt weary or discouraged from my studies or philosophical reflections from that time until the conclusion of my schooling about seventeen years later. I forgot all that is fair and foul in the world and thought the sweet and bitter in events equal. I withdrew from social contact with any except scholars; I cut back food and sleep and life's other necessities to the bare minimum and devoted the rest of my time and resources to scholarship and research. I would often spend the night in study until sunrise (especially in spring and summer), and I would always research the next day's lesson in advance, making whatever exertions were called for to solve any problem that arose, so that, by class time, I would already have a clear understanding of the professor's topic; I never brought any problems or mistakes before the professor.[4]

Short compositions that I prepared while studying in Najaf:

Resale dar Borhan (Monograph on Reasoning)

Resale dar Moghalata (Monograph on Sophistry)

Resale dar Tahlil (Monograph on Analysis)

Resale dar Tarkib (Monograph on Combination)

Resale dar E'tebariyat (Monograph on Ideas of Human Origin)

Resale dar Nobovvat va Manamat (Monograph on Prophecy and Dreams)

Works composed while living in Tabriz:

Resale dar Nobovvat va Manamat (Monograph on Prophecy and Dreams)

Resale dar Asma' va Safat (Monograph on the Names and Attributes)

Resale dar Af'al Monograph on [Divine] Acts)

Resale dar Vasa'et Miyan-e Khoda va Ensan (Monograph on Intermediaries Between God and Man)

Resale dar Ensan Qabl ad-Donya (Monograph on Man Prior to the World)

Resale dar Ensan fi'd-Donya (Monograph on Man in the World)

Resale dar Ensan Ba'd ad-Donya (Monograph on Man After the World)

Resale dar Velayat (Monograph on the Viceregency)

Resale dar Nobovvat (Monograph on Prophecy)

[In these monographs, a comparison is made between rational and narrative forms of knowledge. — *Ketab-e Selsele-ye Tabataba'i dar Azarbayjan* (Geneology of the Tabataba'is in Azarbaijan]

Works composed in Qom:

Tafsir al-Mizan Published in 20 volumes. In this work, the Noble Qur'an is expounded in an unprecedented manner, verse by verse.

Osul-e Falsafe (Ravesh-e Re'alism) (Principles of Philsophy [The Method of Realism].) The Philosophies of the East and West are surveyed in the work, in five volumes.

Annotations to the *Kifayat al-Usul*

Annotations to Molla Sadra, *al-Asfar al-Arba'a* Published in nine volumes.

Vahy, ya Sho'ur-e Marmuz (Revelation, or Mystic Consciousness)

Do Resale dar Velayat va Hokumat-e Eslami (Two Monographs on Islamic Governance and Government)

Mosabeha-ye Sal-e 1338 ba Profesor Korban, Mostashreq-e Faransavi Interviews in 1959 with Professor Corbin, the French Orientalist. Recently republished in one volume under the title *Shi'a* (Shi'ism).

Mosahebeha-ye Sal-e 1339 va 1340 ba Profesor Korban Published in one volume as *Resalat-e Tashayyo' dar Donya-ye Emruz* (The Shi'i Mission in Today's World)

Resale dar E'jaz (Monograph on Miracles)

'Ali wa'l-Falsafat al-Elahiya ('Ali and the Divine Philosophy). Also translated into and published in Farsi.

Shi'a dar Eslam (Shi'ism in Islam)

Qor'an dar Eslam (The Qur'an in Islam)

Majmu'e-ye Maqalat, Porseshha va Pasokha, Bahsha-ye

17

Motafarge-ye 'Elmi, Falsafi, va...[5] (Collected Articles, Questions and Answers, Assorted Scholarly, Philosophical, and other Discussions

Sunan an-Nabi (Ways of the Prophet). Recently published in 400 pages with a translation and study by Mohammad Hadi Feqhi.

NOTES TO THE AUTHOR'S AUTOBIOGRAPHY

1. Various classical works of literature and history. — Trans.

2. Various works in the fields named, not all easily identified. — Trans.

3. Various classical works on philosophy. — Trans.

4. Ayatollah 'Allameh Tabataba'i died in Aban 1360/November 1981. — Trans.

5. By the written permission of the author, this collection of articles has been collected by the Markaz-e Barrasiha-ye Eslami [Center for Islamic Researches] and will when complete be published in two volumes titled, *Barrasiha-ye Eslami* [Islamic Researches] and *Eslam va Ensan-e Mo'aser* [Islam and Contemporary Mankind]. — Publishers of the Farsi edition.

CHAPTER ONE

RELIGION

Religion consists in a set of practical and ethical instructions that the prophets have brought from God for the guidance of mankind.

To accept these beliefs and to carry out these instructions lead human beings to happiness in this world and the next.

Therefore, if we are religious and carry out the instructions of God and the Messenger, we will have good fortune both in this ephemeral world and in the eternal life of the next world.

We know that one is fortunate who has a proper goal in life, who does not lose his way in error, who has good, praiseworthy morals, and who does good works. Living in the midst of the world's tumult, one has a calm, strong heart, full of certainty.

God's religion guides us to this happiness and good fortune, which are unachievable without religion. Religious beliefs reside in man's heart like secret police that follow him everywhere and restrain him from immoral acts and compel him to virtue.

Faith is the strongest and firmest assurance against fear and anguish amid life's ebb and flow. Believers do not give up on themselves or feel abject under any circumstances, because they know themselves to be attached to the limitless power of the Creator of the universe. They are mindful of Him and sheltered by Him in all circumstances; their hearts are calm, clear, and strong.

Religion commands us to achieve moral excellence and to carry out good works to the best of our abilities. Accordingly, religion is divided into three areas:

1. Beliefs

2. Ethics

3. Acts

I must now expand on this brief summary to convince you of these points.

BELIEFS

Our minds and hearts tell us that this world of being with its wondrous system did not come about by itself; such an astonishing world of creation could not arise without being arranged by someone. There must certainly be a Creator who has brought about this vast and glorious universe through His limitless knowledge and power. He must have launched this creation with its intricate system on the basis of set and immutable laws covering all of being. He must have created nothing in vain and excluded no being from the divine laws governing the universe.

Can one believe that a gracious God, given all the kindness and attention He has extended to His creatures, has left man, the masterwork of the creation, on his own? That He has left human society to live by its own wits, when people are for the most part prisoners of desire and liable to stray into misfortune?

Is the answer not clear without being spoken?

Accordingly, He must have sent instructions for human beings through prophets free of any sort of error, so that they could attain to happiness by following those instructions.

We observe that the precious fruits of action according to religious precepts are not fully realized in this world. Neither do those who do good arrive at their reward, nor do those who spread corruption and oppression realize the requital for their actions. We thus understand that there must be another world in which there is a precise accounting for people's acts, so that if someone has done a good deed, that person realizes the reward, and if he has done an evil deed, he will realize the punishment. Religion reinforces these beliefs and other right beliefs in people and puts people on guard against ignorance.

ETHICS

Religion instructs us to choose good qualities for ourselves and to be good-natured — to embellish ourselves with good qualities. It instructs us to be dutiful, sympathetic, humane, kind, loyal, good-natured, cheerful, and fair; to stand up for our rights but not to exceed them; and not to transgress against others' property, honour, or lives. It instructs us to extend the utmost in self-sacrifice in pursuit of knowledge and courtesy, and, finally, to adopt justice and moderation in all our affairs.

ACTION

Religion commands us to carry out acts beneficial to ourselves and our society and to avoid acts of corruption. It also teaches us to perform acts of worship of the Creator such as prayer and fasting, as marks of servanthood and obedience.

These are the provisions and commandments that religion has brought and to which it has summoned; as we see, some of them pertain to belief, some to ethics, and some to action. As has been said, to accept them and put them into action is the only means to happiness, because, as we know, man cannot find happiness without being a realist, adopting high ethical standards

21

in life, and acting in accordance with them.

MUST MAN BE BOUND TO A RELIGION?
The first question to arise here is, what connection has human life to religion and theology? Could not life go on in human society without religion and belief in God? Is it not true that someone is called religious who affirms the existence of a God in the world and carries out special acts to please Him?

It is possible for each individual in a society to be made responsible for determining what is beneficial and what is harmful in accordance with laws of human design, and in such a case human laws would have supplanted divine laws and there would be no further need for religion. If we consider closely, however, we see that the decrees and provisions of Islam prove the contrary to be true, because Islam does not only address worship of God but has also provided commands and provisions covering all aspects of individual and social life. It has surveyed the full extent of human life in a marvelous way and has set forth appropriate provisions for every individual and social activity. Finally, it has secured the happiness of the individual in human society from every standpoint, to the greatest possible degree, as any fair-minded person will affirm. As has been explained, God Most High explains Islam in the Noble Qur'an in accordance with the limited compass of human understanding. We mention some verses here as examples:

1. *'Truly, religion before Allah is Surrender [Islam], and those who received the Book did not differ until after knowledge reached them, through transgression among themselves, and as to whosoever disbelieves in Allah's signs, Allah is swift in reckoning'* (3:19).

The religion to which the prophets have summoned the people consists of divine worship and submission to God's commands. The religious scholars of former times, although they knew the difference between truth and falsity, refused to comply with the truth because of their fanaticism and hatred; they each chose a way of their own. In consequence, various religions appeared on the earth. In truth, this group of people denied God's signs, and God will speedily answer such acts with what they deserve.

2. *'Whoever seeks as a religion something other than Islam, it will not be accepted of him, and he will be a loser in the hereafter'* (3:85).

Whoever searches for and follows another religion than Islam, it will in the end not be accepted from him, and he will not be one of those delivered in the hereafter.

3. *'O you who believe! Enter into submission and do not follow the footsteps of the Devil. Truly he is your open enemy'* (2:208).

O Muslims! Be wholly submitted to God in matters of religion, and, since Satan is your open enemy, do not follow him, but do abstain from adding or subtracting anything to or from religion.

4. *'Fulfill the covenant of Allah when you have made the covenant, and do not break your oaths after making them, and after you have made Allah surety over you. Truly Allah knows what you do'* (16:91).

O Muslims! If you have made a contract, be faithful to that contract, and do not break your word after you have given it and made God your witness, since God knows what you do.

The purport of this verse is that Muslims must act according to and fulfill whatever contract they have made with God and the people.

5. *'Summon to the way of your Lord with wisdom and counsel, and reason with them kindly. Truly your Lord knows best who strays from His way, and He knows best who are under guidance'* (16:125).

Summon the people to God's way by explaining what is true and sound and what is corrupt, with good advice and counsel, and by demonstrating the truth in the best possible manner, because God knows best who has found the way and who is lost.

What this means is that, to advance the cause of the religion, Muslims should speak to anyone in accordance with his or her understanding, in a way that will be useful to that person. If one cannot show someone the way through advice and counsel, one should summon him through debate, set forth as one of the means of establishing the truth.

6. *'When the Qur'an is recited, listen attentively and pay heed, so that you may receive mercy'* (7:205).

When the Qur'an is read, do not engage in conversation but absorb its meaning through your heart, so that you might be embraced by God's mercy.

7. *'O you who believe! Obey Allah, and obey the Messenger and those of you who are in authority, and, if you are in dispute over something, refer it to Allah and the Messenger if you believe in Allah and the last day. That will be better and finer in the end'* (4:59).

Believers! Act in accordance with the commands of God, the Messenger, and the leaders whom God and the Messenger have required you to obey. If you believe in God and the Resurrection, resolve your differences in accordance with the Qur'an's and the Messenger's commands, since this is the best practice for you, with the best outcome.

This means that, in an Islamic society, no other basis for resolving differences exists than those of the Qur'an and the words of the Messenger. Any differences must be resolved on these two bases; if a Muslim has resolved a difference through reasoning, this is because he or she has accepted the Qur'an's direction in reasoning.

8. *'It was by Allah's mercy that you were lenient with them, for if you had been stern and cruel-hearted, they would have dispersed from around you. So pardon them and ask forgiveness for them and consult with them on the matter. When you are resolved, rely on Allah, for Allah loves those who rely on Him'* (3:159).

It was by means of God's mercy reaching you that you were so mild and good-natured. If you had been harsh and cold-hearted, they would have scattered from around you. Thus, pardon people's faults, ask forgiveness for them of God, and consult with them on affairs. Since God loves and supports those who rely on Him, whenever you have resolved upon something, rely on God. Since an agreeable manner, benevolence, and consultation in affairs are means to closeness and affection, the members of society should be attached to their leader, if he is to influence them. God commands the leader of the Muslims to be good-natured and to consult. Since it is possible, however, for people to fall into erroneous ideas, He orders him to form his resolve independently after consultation, and to place reliance on God in all matters, considering that no one can oppose God's will.

God Most High presents Judaism and Christianity, whose scriptures are the Torah and the New Testament,[1] and which have social rules and provisions, in the same way, as where He says:

'*How is it that they come to you for adjudication, when they have the Torah, in which Allah has made judgement?...We revealed the Torah, in which are a guidance and a light by which the prophets who surrendered judged the Jews and the rabbis and the priests... And We caused Jesus, son of Mary, to follow in their footsteps..., and We bestowed on him the Gospel, in which is a guidance and light, confirming what was revealed before it in the Torah...Let the people of the Gospel judge according to what God has revealed within it...We have revealed to you the Book with the Truth, confirming what was revealed before it and a watcher over it. So render judgement between them by what Allah has revealed*' (5:43-48).

The Torah and the New Testament, which the Jews and Christians now hold, confirm this point, in that many legal and penal provisions occur in the Torah, and the New Testament apparently upholds the legal system of the Torah.

CONCLUSION

The foregoing makes it clear that, in Qur'anic terms, religion is a way of life that man cannot avoid. The distinction one can make between religion and a secular social code is that religion stems from God Most High, and the social code is the product of human thought. In other words, religion connects people's social existence with worship of and obedience to God Most High, but in secular social codes, no such connection exists.

BENEFITS OF RELIGION

It is plain from the foregoing that religion has profound powers to reform the individual and society, or rather that it is the sole means of well-being.

A society that is not bound to a religion gives up realism and intellectualism and wastes its precious life on waywardness, superficiality, and negligence. Having abandoned intelligence, it lives an animal existence, short-sighted and mindless. It grows faced with immorality and base behaviour and thus gives up all the distinguishing features of humanity. Not only does such a society fail to reach eternal happiness and ultimate perfection, it also confronts unfortunate and disagreeable consequences of its deviations in this tiny, transient world. Sooner or later, its own neglect will catch up with it, and it will well understand that the only means to happiness is religion and belief in God, and it will regret the consequences of its actions.

God Most High says, '*One prospers who tends it, and one fails who leaves it stunted*' (91:9-10). That is, one who keeps oneself from corruption is saved, whereas one who associates with any sort of illicit pursuit fails to reach his object, happiness and deliverance.

Of course, one must know that human happiness and individual and social prosperity are based upon practice of religious commandments. Apart from that, merely nominal attachment to religion is useless, since what has value is the Truth itself, not summons to the Truth. One who calls himself a Muslim and who, for all his inner darkness, base morals, and ugly behaviour, awaits the angel of happiness, is just like a patient who pockets the doctor's prescription and expects to get well. Certainly no one will get anywhere that way.

God Most High says, *'Those who believe and the Jews, Christians, and Sabeans, in fact all who believe in Allah and the Last Day and do good — their reward is with their Lord'* (2:62). That is, among all those called Muslims, Jews, Sabeans, or Christians, those who truly believe in God and the Resurrection and act according to high moral standards will find a good reward with God.

Considering the meaning of the verse, it could be supposed that any people who believe in God and the Resurrection and act well will be saved even if they do not accept all or some of the prophets but it must be understood that, in *Surah* Nisa,[2] verses 150 and 151, God calls such people unbelievers, saying: *'Those who disbelieve in Allah and His prophets and who seek to make a distinction among Allah and His prophets [like the Jews, who disbelieve in Jesus and Muhammad, or like the Christians, who disbelieve in Muhammad], saying, "We believe in some and disbelieve in others", and seeking a way in between — these are disbelievers in truth, and We have reserved a humiliating torment for them'* (4:150-151).

Accordingly, one will realize the fruits of his faith who believes in all the prophets and acts ethically.

HUMAN CIVILIZATION
If we consider the factors that gave rise to human societies in past ages, it grows clear that man seeks nothing else in life than happiness, and of course this happiness is not possible except when all the necessities of life have been secured.

On the other hand, man, with his God-given understanding, perceives that he can never procure and prepare all the things he needs and so secure the ease and pleasure he seeks when acting alone. He sees that he cannot solve life's problems and attain

27

perfection alone, and therefore of necessity he joins in social life to meet his needs. He sees that cooperation with other individuals is the easiest way to reach his objects, and he secures his needs collectively, meaning that each person is made responsible for procuring and preparing certain of these things and then, when the fruits of everyone's labours are combined, each individual draws on and uses them to the extent of his labours and social status and thus conducts his life.

Thus, we labour in concert with and to the benefit of others to secure our happiness; that is, in reality, all having acted for the sake of each other and having pooled the fruits of their labours, each member of society draws a portion of that pooled labour in proportion to his activity and according to his status.

SOCIETY'S NEED FOR RULES

Since the products of individuals' activity are mingled and everyone wants to make use of them, competition and conflict of interests are inevitable products of this continual encounter and relationship. It goes without saying that material interests normally give rise to various forms of discord, rancour, and loss of amity. In order to preserve individuals' amity, society must have a set of rules which can avert chaos if observed.

It is plain that if there were no rules and laws to manage human society, such chaos would arise that it could not survive for even a day.

Of course, such laws vary according to differences in the level of civilization of peoples and nations and differences in their levels of thought and governmental organization, but no society can ever be without a set of customs and rules that at least a majority of its members respect. Never in human history has there arisen a society without any sort of shared manners, customs, and rules.

MAN IS NOT FREE
VIS-A-VIS THE RULES

Since man performs all his actions through his own choice and election, he experiences a certain freedom of action, and, imagining this freedom to be 'absolute' and unconditional and seeking perfect freedom, he flees from all sorts of limitations and chafes under any sort of prohibition directed at him; finally he experiences any limitation touching him as burdensome and frustrating. In this respect, the rules of society, however few, oppose man's freedom-seeking nature, since they limit him to some extent.

From another standpoint, man also appreciates that if he is unwilling to give up some of his freedom to uphold the rules to maintain society, chaos will arise and eliminate all his freedom and comfort.

If he steals a morsel from someone else, without a doubt others will steal morsels from him, and if he oppresses someone, he will in turn be oppressed.

Accordingly, man gives up a part of his freedom in order to preserve a part of it; he respects the rules of society because he has no choice.

A WEAK POINT IN
THE EVOLUTION OF RULES

What we have said demonstrates a contradiction between man's search for freedom and the rules of society. That is, laws are like a chain to which man is shackled; he would like to break the chain and be free of the shackles. This is the great and constant danger threatening the rules of society and shaking their foundations.

Accordingly, there must always be provided, along with rules and practical responsibilities, another set of provisions, consisting of punishments for those who would oppose the rules to restrain people from opposition by fear, and expectations of rewards to encourage obedience to laws. Of course, it is undeniable that these approaches aid in enforcing the laws to an extent, but they cannot altogether halt opposition and preserve the influence and rule of law, because laws of punishment, like other laws are subject to opposition and are ever threatened by man's freedom-seeking nature: people who hold great power can openly and fearlessly exercise their opposition; they can compel the legal and law enforcement apparatus to comply with their wishes.

Those who have no such power can take advantage of the negligence or weakness of those in power to exercise their opposition in secret or to achieve their ends through bribery and mediation or through friendship or blood ties with the influential members of society. Thus they throw the wheel of society off its axis.

The best evidence for this assertion consists in how every day we witness thousands of instances of such opposition and lawlessness in various societies.

THE ULTIMATE SOURCE
OF THE WEAKNESS OF CIVIL LAW

We must now see where this danger springs from, and how we can tame man's rebellious and freedom-seeking nature and so prevent opposition to the law.

Here is the wellspring of this menace, the major cause of corruption in society, such that even rules cannot prevent it: the normal social processes for creating laws focus on the material side of individuals; they take no account of spiritual values and those individuals' instinctual grasp of those values. Their sole object is harmony and preservation of the system and of an equilibrium in social interaction to keep events from winding up in discord and strife.

What secular law seeks is that its provisions are carried out and that acts in society be controlled. It has no further concern with the interior nature of man and the subjective feelings associated with it, which are the motives behind these acts and the hidden enemies of the rules.

When no attention is paid to the freedom-seeking nature of man (along with a hundred other instincts, such as selfishness and the concupiscence that is the basic cause of corruption), disorder arises in society, and opposition spreads by the day. All civil laws are always threatened by frontal assaults by the powerful or night raids by sneak thieves arising from these instincts, and no law can prevent corruption and avoid opposition.

WHAT DISTINGUISHES RELIGIOUS LAW FROM OTHER FORMS OF LAW

The most recent method of society for upholding the law is to institute criminal law and appoint police. But, as we have noted, this method cannot restrain the rebellious nature and other unruly instincts of man and make socially based rules feasible.

Besides having been instituted, like laws of human origin, in order to preserve order and punish the rebellious and hostile, religion has powerful means at its disposal to overturn and crush any opposing force.

1. Because of the relation it has made between social life and worship of God Most High, religion imparts a sense of responsibility for every individual and social act, such that man feels responsible to God Most High for his every action and inaction.

God Most High surrounds man in every direction through His boundless power and knowledge and knows every thought he harbours and every secret in his heart; nothing is hidden from Him.

Religion entrusts the reins of watchfulness over man not to just the outward policeman but to an inward one who is never neglectful in his work and whose rewards and punishments one cannot evade.

God Most High says, '*Allah comprehends what they do*' (7:47), '*And He is with you whatever you do*', '*And your Lord will repay the words of each in full*' (11:111), and '*Allah has been a watcher over you*' (4:1).

If we now compare one who has grown up in an environment of secular law with one who has grown up in an environment of religion, the superiority of religion will be perfectly clear to us, in that a society of religious individuals who practise their religious duties is a society of people who will be free of any mutual suspicion, since they know that God observes what they do in any circumstance. Accordingly, people at large who live in such an environment plainly have nothing to fear from other people's hands or tongues or even their thoughts, whereas no such security is found through the civil codes of the world. Religion also eliminates mistrust in people.

God Most High says, '*You who believe! Refrain from much suspicion, for even a little suspicion is a sin, and do not spy*' (49:12).

People in a religious environment know peace of mind; they will live a completely pleasant and comfortable life and then attain to eternal happiness.

On the other hand, in an environment governed by civil law, one leaves off an illicit act when he sees the police watching, and may resume it whenever he does not.

2. Any religious person perceives, through the guidance of religion, this truth: his life is not confined to the ephemeral life of this world but extends ahead endlessly; it does not end at death. He sees that the only way to eternal happiness and ease lies in observing the religious ordinances that God Most High has sent by means of His prophets. He knows that religious ordinances are given by an all-knowing and all-powerful Lord who will regard man inside and out at His court and judge his hidden and overt behaviour. Accordingly, it is impossible for him to avoid God's decree by concealing an act.

3. A religious person knows by his religious beliefs that every religious injunction he carries out constitutes an act of obedience to his Lord. Although, as a servant, he may deserve no compensation, he will realize a great reward through the grace

of his Lord. From this standpoint, with whatever act of obedience he carries out, in reality he has, by his free choice, carried out a transaction, in which he has freely and gladly given up some of his freedom, in exchange for gaining God's satisfaction and receiving a fine reward.

A religious person, in following religious laws and ordinances, is engaged gladly in a transaction, and whatever he spends in the coin of freedom he gains back several times over. He sells some goods and buys better goods in their place. But when one who is not attached to religion supposes observance of laws and ordinances to be contrary to his interests and his freedom-seeking nature chafes at giving up some of his freedom, he will break his bonds and regain his freedom by one means or another at the first opportunity.

It must be said that religious law differs from civil law in another way. Religious people avoid sin of their own volition, but subjects of civil law abstain from crime only because of fear. Religion governs the whole being of religious people, but civil law rules only the hands and feet. Religion governs both the outer and the inner being, but civil law governs only the outer being. Religion is not merely a policeman who restrains one from reproved acts; it is a teacher and mentor who teaches virtues and perfections to man. Civil law, however, has only this aspect of policeman.

Suppose the profit of civil law to be one measure, that of religious law is thousands. Therefore, those who strive to eradicate religion and pin their hopes on civil law are like someone who, having cut off his own sound leg, attaches a wooden leg in its place.

It grows clear from what has been said that religion is the finest system for organizing human society; it succeeds at compelling people to observe the laws of society better than any other system.

RECOURSES OTHERS HAVE MADE

The undeveloped countries of the world, which have sought to progress and elevate themselves over the last century, in accepting secular governments but failing to note the points of weakness of civil law and failing to use the power of religion, have experienced misfortune; their public life has fallen into a sort of savagery.

In contrast, the developed and self-aware countries of the world, who have discerned the points of weakness of civil laws, have sought for ways to save these laws from utter collapse and wound up following a different road.

These countries have organized their educational systems in such a way that individuals learn a set of sound ethical principles as a matter of course, so that, when they become productive members of their societies, they regard the law as sacred and beyond opposition.

This kind of education makes the observance of the law habitual and, in consequence, contributes appreciably to preserving the well-being of society and saving the civil legal system from collapse.

But we must understand that this sort of thinking takes two different forms in the societies in which it is cultivated:

1. Beliefs in such things as humanitarianism, charity, and kindness towards the underdog that are founded on realism and without doubt are derived from the revealed religions and to which religion summoned people long before developed societies existed. Considering this, such well-being as developed societies have realized through these beliefs must be counted among the blessings of religion.

2. Vain and delusional beliefs that have no value outside the marketplace of superstitions, such as when people are inculcated with the belief that if they suffer and die for the sake of freeing their country, their names will emblazon the pages of history in

gold letters.

Although such superstitious notions yield practical results (for instance, it may be that someone will show valour in battle and kill many of the enemy under the influence of this propaganda), their detrimental effects are many times greater than their benefits, since people are rendered superstitious and their instinctual realism is cut off, because those who have no belief in God and the Day of Requital see death as nothingness; eternal life and attaining one's desires after death are meaningless to them.

One seeks for religion by one's God-given nature. Over the course of his life, man always searches and struggles to attain his own happiness and seeks for effective ways to meet his needs. Without a doubt, man always seeks means that will always work and never leave him in the lurch. On the other hand, we have no means in the world of nature whose effect is perpetual and that will never be defeated or overcome.

The truth that man innately seeks as a means to his own happiness that will never be overturned, as a support that will never be destroyed, and as a way to relate his life to the whole and bring him inner peace is religion. Only the will of God Most High is never defeated or conquered. Only He will never fail us. Islam is the only way of life that has such a relation to God Most High.

Accordingly, it may be said that human instinctual desire is one of the best proofs of the three principles of religion (*tauhid*, prophecy, resurrection)[3] in that this innate sense that is part of the special makeup of man never errs, just as man never confuses the meanings of friendship and enmity or mistakes his own thirst for satiety.

In truth, man sometimes seeks to fly like a bird or to become a star in the sky. Man seeks a real basis for his happiness, absolute tranquility, or a fully human life from the bottom of his heart. So long as he lives, he will never abandon this thought. If there were no invincible cause (God) in the world of being, man, with his pure nature, would not conceive of one. If there were no absolute, not relative, peace and tranquility (which is the peace of the next world) and if the practice of religion (which has reached us through prophecy) were not founded on truth, no such desire would have left its impress on human nature.

A BRIEF LOOK AT THE HISTORY
OF RELIGIONS

From a religious standpoint, the most reliable source for a concise study of the appearance of religions is the Noble Qur'an, since the Qur'an is devoid of any kind of error, partisanship, or tendentiousness. The Glorious Qur'an treats this subject in summary fashion. It tells us that God's religion, which is Islam ('*Truly to Allah religion is Islam*'), appeared when man first appeared. As the Noble Qur'an explains, today's humanity descends from a single man and a single woman, and the man was named Adam. Adam was a prophet to whom revelations were given. Adam's religion was very simple, consisting of some general precepts, such as that people should think of God, be kind to one another, especially to their parents, and refrain from bloodshed, corruption, and evil.

After the time of Adam and his wife, their descendants lived in the greatest simplicity and harmony. As their numbers grew day by day, they gradually massed and formed a collective life. Then they gradually learned how to live and grew more civilized. As their numbers grew, they divided into various tribes, each of which had leaders whom the members of the tribe looked up to. Even after these leaders died, effigies were made of them and worshipped. This was how idol worship first spread. As we see in traditions passed down by religious leaders and as is confirmed in historical accounts of idolatry, because of the oppression of the weak by the powerful, contradictions arose among people. These fundamental and incidental contradictions led to various forms of social conflict.

With their appearance, these contradictions drew man from the road of happiness and toward misfortune and ruin. They prompted Most Merciful God to raise prophets and send scriptures to resolve them. As God Most High says, '*The people were a single nation, and God sent prophets as bearers of good news and warners, and through them He revealed the Book with the Truth to render judgement between people on that over which they differed*' (2:213).

ISLAM

The pure religion of Islam is the last revealed religion and for this reason the most complete religion. With the coming of this religion, previous religions are abrogated, because with the coming of something complete, there is no further need for an imcomplete form of that thing.

Islam was sent for the sake of humanity by means of our beloved Messenger, Muhammad ibn 'Abdullah (peace and blessings upon him and his family). This gateway to deliverance and eternal happiness was opened to the people of this world so that human societies might leave behind their ages of immaturity and deficient powers of thought to grow ready to acquire their full humanity and the worth to realize sublime spiritual teachings and put them into practice.

Thus, Islam has brought humanity spiritual realities that are appropriate to real human understanding, the high ethical values that distinguish man, and commandments pertaining to every area of human individual and social life. It urges us to put them into practice.

From this standpoint, Islam is a universal and eternal religion. It consists of a set of critical concerns and ethical and practical rules that assure man's happiness in this world and the next if he carries them out. Islam's rules are so composed that any human individual and any human society that carries them out will achieve the best living conditions and the greatest progress toward human perfection possible.

Islam brings its benefits to every person and every society equally: big and small, educated and ignorant, man and woman, black and white, easterner and westerner can enjoy the benefits of this pure religion without distinction. They can thus fulfill their needs in the finest and fullest way, because Islam has founded its culture and rules on the nature of the creation and has considered and provided for human needs. Human nature is structured the same way in all individuals, races, and times; plainly, human societies from east to west are of a kind. That is, all belong to the human species, and big and small, man and woman, educated and ignorant, black and white, and so forth are members of a single family and participate in the basic forms of human life. Various individuals and races have similar needs, and those yet to come are the offspring of this family as well and will inherit these needs.

In sum, Islam is a faith that meets the real and essential needs of man; it is sufficient for everyone and will live on forever.

For this reason, God Most High calls Islam the natural religion and calls upon people to keep human nature alive. The foremost religious figures have called Islam an easy religion that does not treat man severely.

THE IMPORTANCE OF RELIGION
TO HUMAN TRANQUILITY

Just as religion has a special place in relation to other systems for organizing society, so too does Islam have a special place among religions. Islam is more advantageous to human society than any other system. This grows clear with any comparison betwen Islam and other religions or secular systems.

ISLAM IN COMPARISON
WITH OTHER RELIGIONS

Among all religions, Islam is the only one that participates fully in society. Islamic teachings are not like present-day Christian practice, which considers only the people's happiness in the afterlife and is silent about their happiness in this world. They are not like present-day Jewish practice, which applies itself only to the indoctrination of a people. Like the teachings of the righteous among the magi and of certain other religions, Islamic teachings reject the idea that they should confine themselves to a few limited topics.

Islam fosters all people and brings them happiness in the two worlds for all time. Plainly, there is no other way to reform societies and bring people such happiness, since, in the first place, it is useless to try to reform one society or nation alone in the context of international relations that become more interwoven by the day. This is really like trying to purify a single drop of water in a polluted lake or ocean. In the second place, to reform one society and ignore others is contrary to the spirit of reform. Islamic teachings take into account every idea that can occur to man about himself and the world, all the ethical values that can find their way to the human soul, and all of the actions anyone can display to his surroundings.

In regard to the role of ideas in Islam, those ideas that have a realistic basis, the foremost of which is the idea of *tauhid*, belief in the unity of God Most High, are adopted as principles.

Islamic ethics adopts what the sound mind accepts as a firm principle of *tauhid*.

Then Islam legislates a set of practical rules and laws on the basis of ethics to regulate the finer points of human life. In consequence, the responsibilities of every individual and society are made clear: everyone — black and white, urban and rural, man and woman, great and small, servant and master, rich and poor, in ordinary and exceptional circumstances: '*A good word, like a good tree, its roots fast and its branches reaching to the sky*' (14:24).

Whoever investigates the ethical teachings of Islam and Islamic jurisprudence at first hand will discover a boundless sea whose circumference no far-seeing mind can comprehend and whose depth no thought can fathom. Nevertheless, each element has an

39

appropriate relationship to the others, and in sum they form a single entity that fosters humanity and directs it to worship of God. The One God has revealed this entity to His beloved Messenger.

ISLAM IN COMPARISON
WITH OTHER SOCIAL SYSTEMS

If we look carefully at the system of the developed countries of the world, we note clearly that, although the scientific and industrial progress of these societies is astounding, such that they have extended their power to the moon and Mars and greatly expanded their economies, this progress has nonetheless brought about great misfortune for humanity. In less than a quarter of a century, the world has been drawn into wars in which millions of innocent people have been killed. The people of this world are even now threatened with a third world war that would be the death-knell for humankind.

From their first appearance, these systems have, in the name of humanitarianism and liberation, put the brand of slavery on the rest of the peoples of the world and tied the four continents with the chains of colonialism. They have served Europe unconditionally and allowed an insignificant number of people to rule absolutely over the lives and property of hundreds of millions of innocent people.

Of course, it is undeniable that the developed nations enjoy a high material standard of living and have attained many of the ends people have long wished for, such as social justice, cultural and technological advances, and so forth. Numerous misfortunes, however, have overtaken them, the most important of which consists of continual international conflicts and bloodshed. Moment by moment, the future of the world seems enshrouded in ever more bitter and ominous events.

It is obvious that all these sweet and bitter fruits are the harvest of the tree of civilization and the direct consequence of the way of life of these nations and societies that appear to be on the road of progress.

It must be understood, however, that its sweet fruit from which humankind has benefited and which has contributed to the happiness of society has grown from high ethical values found in these countries such as honesty, integrity, responsibility, benevolence, and self-sacrifice, not just from law, since the same laws exist in the undeveloped countries of Asia and Africa as well, which nonetheless fall into greater wretchedness by the day.

The fruit of this tree that leaves such a bitter taste in the mouth and led to such misfortune and drives the developed countries to extinction along with the rest arises from such vices as greed, immoderation, cruelty, selfishness, pride, and stubbornness.

If we carefully study the holy commandments of Islam, we note that Islam commands adherence to the first set of these qualities and rejection of the second set. In general, it summons us to whatever action is right and in the best interest of humanity, making such action the basis of its teachings. Islam warns us against any unrighteous action that would bring about disorder in the peaceful life of humanity, even if it is in the best interests of a particular people or nation.

Several conclusions may be drawn from the foregoing:

1. The Islamic system is superior to any secular system and of more benefit to humanity: '*This is the right religion, but most people do not know*' (30:30).

2. The bright spots and sweet fruit of contemporary civilization all arise from the grace of the pure faith of Islam and from its living traces that have been felt by westerners. Islam began summoning people towards these high ethical principles, which westerners have now surpassed us in putting into practice, centuries before western civilization arose.

The Commander of the Faithful 'Ali (upon whom be peace) told the people from his deathbed, 'Beware, do not behave in a

41

way that others excel you in acting according to the Qur'an'.

3. According to the commandments of Islam, one must make ethics one's primary goal and found laws upon ethical values. To forget ethics and to found laws on material interests will gradually draw a society into materialism, so that people will give up the spiritual values that are the sole superiority of man over other animals and substitute for them the predatory ways of wolves and leopards or the placid grazing of cows and sheep. The Most Noble Messenger (peace and blessings upon him and his family) said in this connection, 'I was sent to perfect the morals of the people'.

NOTES TO CHAPTER ONE

1. In the original, the *Taurat* and the *Injil*. Muslim scholars hold that the present-day scriptures here named are not true to the originals. — Trans.

2. *Sura*: a chapter of the Noble Qur'an. — Trans.

3. The concept of *tauhid* has many implications but centers on belief in divine unity and the unity of the relation between God and His creation. Its opposite, an equally complex idea, is *shirk*, in brief, setting other powers up alongside God, polytheism. Those who practice *tauhid* and *shirk* are known as *muwahhids* and *mushriks*, respectively. — Trans.

CHAPTER TWO

BELIEFS

TO CONSIDER THE ORIGIN
OF CREATION IS NATURAL

Man, by a God-given instinct, seeks for the cause of every occurrence he witnesses. He never thinks it probable that a thing should come into being of itself, without cause, by chance. The driver whose car stalls steps out and checks the probable cause of the problem. It never occurs to him that the machine should stall when everything is in perfect running order. In trying to get the car started, he uses whatever means he has on hand; he never sits waiting for it to start by chance.

If someone is hungry, he thinks of bread; when he is thirsty, he looks for water; and if he is cold, he puts on extra clothing or starts a fire. He never sits assuring himself that chance will intervene. One who wants to erect a building naturally secures building supplies and the services of an architect and workers; he does not hope that his intentions will realize themselves.

So long as man has existed, mountains, forests, and vast oceans have existed on earth along with him. He has always seen the sun and the moon and shining stars moving regularly and ceaselessly across the sky.

Nonetheless, the world's savants have searched tirelessly for the causes for these wonderful beings and phenomena. They have never been heard to say, 'So long as we have lived, we have observed these in their present forms. Therefore, they have come about of themselves'.

This instinctive curiosity and interest in causes impels us to inquire into how the creation arose and into its marvelous order. We are led to ask, did this vast universe, with all its interconnected parts that really form one immense entity, come about of itself, or did it gain its being from elsewhere?

Is this astonishing system that is in effect throughout the universe, governed by immutable laws admitting no exceptions and guiding every thing toward its own unique destiny, governed by a boundless power and knowledge, or does it arise from chance?

PROOF THAT THERE IS A MAKER
When one puts his instinctive realism to work, wherever he looks in the creation, he sees abundant evidence for a Creator and Sustaining Power, because man perceives instinctively that each created thing enjoys the bounties of being and automatically follows a determinate course, eventually giving up its place to other things. They never bring about their own being, invent their own course of development, or play the least role in producing or organizing their way of existence. We ourselves have not chosen our humanity or human characteristics but have been created human and given these characteristics. Similarly, our instinctive realism will never accept that all these things have come about of themselves through chance and that the system of being have arose willy-nilly. Our intuition does not accept that some neatly stacked fragments of brick tumbled

44

together by chance. Thus man's instinctive realism proclaims that the world of being certainly has a support that is the Source of being and the Creator and Sustainer of the universe, and that this limitless Being and source of knowledge and power is God, from whose oceanic being the system of existence springs.

God Most High says, '*He Who gave everything its nature and guided it*' (20:50).

THEOLOGY AND THE NATIONS

Most people today are religious, believing in and worshipping a God Who created the universe.

People of earlier times held the same beliefs; so far as is known from history, most people have been religious and affirmed the existence of a God in the universe. Among religious societies, however, divergent views have existed, each people describing the Source of creation in its own terms. All these people have agreed, however, on this central point, and such other faiths as Christianity, Judaism, and Zoroastrianism join with Islam in this affirmation. Those who deny the existence of a Creator are unable to disprove His existence and always will be, but are honest enough to say, 'We have no proof of His existence', but not to say, 'We have proof of His nonexistence'.

The materialist says, 'I do not know'; he does not say, 'There is no such god'. In other words, the materialist is a doubter, not a disbeliever.

God Most High alludes to this point where He says, '*They say, "There is nothing but our life in the world; we die and we live, and nothing destroys us but time" — when they know nothing but merely guess*' (45:24).

There are signs of religion, theology, and belief and trust in the supernatural in even the oldest traces of early man.

Even in recently discovered continents such as America and Australia, and on islands remote from Europe, Asia, and Africa, indigenous people are found to believe in God and affirm that the creation has a divine source, although history tells of no associations between them and the Old World.

When we consider that people have everywhere and always believed in God, we see that this belief is innate in man, who affirms the existence of a God of creation by his God-given nature. This is how the Noble Qur'an refers to this innate characteristic of man: '*If you ask them who created them, they answer, "Allah!" Yet they shrug Him off!*' (43:87). It further says, '*If you ask them who created the heavens and the earth, they answer, "Allah"*' (31:25).

THE EFFECTS OF CURIOSITY
ON HUMAN LIFE

If we give an affirmative answer to these questions on the Creator of the universe and the Originator of its order, which arise from our instinctive search for reality, and if we affirm an imperishable source for the universe and its wondrous system, we shall see that everything depends upon His invincible will, which rests on His limitless power and knowledge.

In consequence, a kind of assurance will embrace us, and we shall never succumb to complete hopelessness in the face of the hardships and difficulties that we meet with in life and even the problems for which there is no remedy, because we realize that God holds the rein of every cause, however powerful. We shall never submit completely to any cause, and if things should go our way, we shall not grow proud and cocksure or forget our place in the scheme of things, because we shall know that outward causes do not exist in isolation but arise from the command of God Most High. In sum, we shall perceive that we must glorify nothing in the world other than God and submit completely to no other command than His.

One who answers these questions in the negative, however, is deprived of this hope and this sense of realism and, finally, of this natural nobility and courage.

Here we see that nations dominated by materialism are

committing slow suicide, and people who are wholly attached to sense objects and sensible causes may put an end to their lives when the least misfortunes dampen their hopes for happiness. When, however, those who experience the grace of knowing God find themselves on the brink of death, they do not give up hope but find hope and assurance in knowing they have an all-powerful and all-seeing God.

In the final hours of his life, hemmed in by enemy swords, Imam Husayn (upon whom be peace) declared, 'The only thing that makes this ordeal easy for me is that I see God is constantly observing my actions'.

In the course of some verses on this truth, the Noble Qur'an states plainly, *'Those who say, "Our Lord is Allah", and then walk aright — they shall not fear or grieve'* (45:13). It also says, *'Those who believe and whose hearts find tranquility in remembering Allah — truly hearts find tranquility whenever Allah is mentioned'* (13:28).

HOW TO KNOW GOD, ACCORDING TO THE QUR'AN

The infant who reaches for its mother's breast in reality wants milk, and if it grasps something and conveys it to its mouth to eat, its essential object is something to eat, and if it sees that it has erred and grasped something inedible, it throws it away. Just so, whatever object one pursues, one wants the real thing, and, whenever it grows clear that one has erred and is following a mistaken course, one regrets the error and the wasted effort. In sum, man avoids error and tries as best as he can to find the real thing.

Here it grows clear to us that man is a realist by nature and instinct; that is, he spontaneously seeks for what is real and true. No one learned this instinctive tendency from anyone or anywhere. If someone may at times act stubborn and bridle at the truth, this means that he is caught up in error and cannot

47

discern what is true and in his best interest. If this were made clear to him, he would not persist in error.

Then too, at times someone will become mentally ill as a result of passionate desire, so that the sweetness of the truth seems bitter to him. At that point, even though he knows what the truth is, he will not abide by it. He resists even though he acknowledges that the truth deserves observance, that he should observe it. It often happens that, owing to addiction to harmful things (such as tobacco, alcohol, and narcotics), someone stifles his own human instincts and knowingly engages in self-destructive acts.

The Noble Qur'an summons us to realism and observance of the truth. It is very insistent on this point, calling upon people in various expressions to maintain their instinctive realism and observance of the truth.

God Most High says, '*What is there beyond truth but error?*' (10:35). He also says, '*Man is at a loss, except those who believe, perform honourable deeds, encourage truth, and encourage patience*' (103:3).

Plainly, all this divine counsel is intended to show that, if we do not maintain our instinctive realism and strive to observe the truth, we shall not attain happiness but shall say and do whatever strikes our fancy and become entangled in daydreams and superstitious notions. Then we become like domestic animals who have strayed far from their track and are victims of our own desires, waywardness, and ignorance.

God Most High says, '*Have you seen someone who has taken his own passion as his god? Would you act as trustee for him? Or do you reckon that most of them hear or understand? They are just like livestock — indeed, they are even further off the track!*' (25:43-44). In sum, what do you think of such a person? Do you suppose that you could educate or reform him? On the other hand, when one's instinctive realism awakens and his inclination to truth comes into play, spiritual truths will present themselves to him one after another; he will embrace each one as he encounters it and so advance on the road of happiness every day.

QUR'ANIC TEAGHINGS ON THE CREATOR
OF THE UNIVERSE

God Most High says, '*Can there be doubt about Allah, the Creator of the heavens and the earth?*' (14:10). In the sunlight, everything is evident to the eye: we see ourselves, others, houses, streets, towns, mountains, forests, and seas. But in the dark of night, all these evident things grow obscure. Then we understand that the light by which we saw those things did not arise from them but from the sun, which illuminated them through some kind of relation. The sun itself shines and illuminates and discloses the earth and what is on it. If the light arose from those things, they would never give it up.

Man and the other animals perceive things through their eyes, ears, and other sense organs and act through their hands, feet, and other internal and external parts. In time, however, these cease to function and in a sense die.

Witnessing this scene, we judge that the intelligence, volition, and movement living things exhibit do not arise from their bodies but from their spirits and souls; when these depart, the bodies cease to live and function.

For instance, if seeing and hearing occurred solely in the eyes and ears, they would persist so long as these organs existed, but this is not so.

Just like the vast world of which we are a part, and whose existence we could never deny, this being and manifestation cannot be doubted. If they sprang from the living thing itself, it would never give them up, but we see with our own eyes that they cease to be one after the other; they are in perpetual flux and transformation; they change from state to state.

We must therefore conclude that all beings find their being from something else that is their Creator and Producer. As soon as a thing's time of createdness is cut, it disappears into nothingness.

The being whose limitless being supports the manifest universe and sustains all its creatures is called God.

He is a being beyond the reach of nonbeing; if this were not true, He would be like other beings whose beings depend not on themselves, but another.

THE QUR'AN AND *TAUHID*

If someone regards the universe with a pure nature and a calm heart, he will witness evidence of the pure being of the Creator everywhere within it. He will have witnesses to this truth everywhere. Whatever we encounter in this world is a manifestation that God has created, or a quality God has placed in it, or part of the system that governs everything by God's command. Man too is one of these manifestations and a witness to this truth from head to foot, because neither does his being arise from itself nor do the qualities that it exhibits arise from his will. Neither is the program for his life, which proceeds from his first moment of existence, placed in his control, nor can he suppose that this system is a random accident or that his existence and its system arise from the environment of his origin. The being of this environment and the system that governs it are not products of this environment either; they do not come about by chance.

Thus we have no other recourse than to affirm the existence of a source for the creation who produces and sustains all things. It is He Who grants existence to all that exists and Who then guides each thing towards its own particular perfection by a special system.

Since we see a single system in the universe in which things are created interdependent, we must conclude that the Source of creation Who operates its system is One alone.

The Noble Qur'an says, '*If there were gods in it other than God, it would be in ruins*' (21:22). If multiple gods governed the universe, and, as idolators say, each god presided over a different part — earth and sky, sea and forest each having its own god — because of differences among the gods, each part of the universe would have its own system, and the workings of the universe would necessarily fall into disarray. As we see, however, all the parts of the universe are interdependent and exist in complete harmony. All compose a single system. Accordingly, we must conclude that the Creator and Sustainer of the universe is one.

One might imagine that, supposing these various gods are intelligent and know that their differences are drawing the universe into disarray, they would avoid disagreements. This is a debased notion; a god who creates and manages a universe or a part of one would certainly not think as we think.

In explanation, from the first day we open our eyes to the creation and witness the system in effect in it, we form mental conceptions of this system. Then, as we act to satisfy our everyday needs, we gauge our actions against these mental conceptions in order to adjust them to this system. For instance, when we are hungry or thirsty, we eat or drink to satiety, and, when we are cold, we dress appropriately, because we have observed that this is how these needs are met in the world.

Therefore, from this standpoint, our action follows from our thought, and our thought follows from the world. In consequence, our action is two steps removed from the world. However, a god who manages the universe or a part of it acts outside of the world of action, and it makes no sense that he should work according to a premeditated scheme. This point is well worth noting.

GOD MOST HIGH HAS ALL
THE ATTRIBUTES OF PERFECTION
What is perfection? A house is perfect when it meets all the needs of a household. It should have adequate space to seat

guests, a kitchen, a bathroom, and so forth. Insofar as it fails to provide these things, it is deficient.

WHY DOES MAN AT TIMES FAIL TO ACCORD WITH THIS TRUTH?

This truth grows clear to people with the least consideration and is beyond doubt, except that one may at times grow so involved in the day-to-day struggles of living that one has no leisure to consider such ideas as these, and so one neglects them. Or one may be too occupied with the superficial charms of nature and too fond of pleasure to reflect upon and then live by this truth and others like it.

Accordingly, the Noble Qur'an pays great attention to explaining in various ways the manner in which things are created and the system that presides over them. It demonstrates that most people have not developed the mental capacity to consider fine intellectual questions, and this is especially true for those who are enamoured with these superficial charms of nature and fond of life's pleasures.

In any event, man is a part of the creation and never stands apart from the universe and the special and general systems that govern it. Any time he wishes, he can stop to pay attention to the creation and its systems and discern the existence of its Creator and Sustainer.

God Most High says, '*There are signs in the heavens and the earth to those who believe — and there are signs to a folk whose faith is certain in your own makeup and in how animals are propagated. The alternation of night and day, and the sustenance Allah sends down from the sky that revives the earth after its death, and the wheelings of the winds are signs for people who reason*' (45:2-5). The Noble Qur'an contains many verses that summon us to reflect on the creation of natural phenomena, such as the sky, the sun, the moon, the stars, the earth, mountains, seas, plants, animals, and man. It points to the wondrous system that governs all of these phenomena, the system, in fact, that propels the various parts of the universe toward the objects of their creation, their reasons for being. The grain of wheat or the almond falls to the ground to grow into a blooming shrub or fruit-bearing tree. From when the seed enters the womb of the earth and splits open, the embryonic plant emerging and sending its white root into the depths of the earth, to when it reaches its destined form, vast systems are at work that dazzle the reason. The shining sun and stars, the luminous moon and the earth, with their various motions and hidden powers, the mysterious forces that are reposed in that seed, the four seasons, atmospheric conditions, wind and rain, days and nights — all these play a part in the growth of this shrub. They act together as nursemaids to this new form they have cradled until it reaches the zenith of its growth.

A human infant, a much more complex phenomenon than that young shrub, is the product of millions or billions of years of the intricate and orderly workings of the creation. Quite apart from its relationship with the outer world, the everyday life of a human being springs from an amazing system within his being that is many centuries old. The world's scientists have devoted themselves to slowly piercing the veils of this phenomenon, but even now their understanding pales before their ignorance.

Similarly, if an individual has all the natural faculties of man, he is perfect, but if he is lacking one, such as a hand or an eye, from this standpoint, he is deficient.

According to what we have learned, the quality of perfection is something that alleviates a kind of need for being and removes a deficiency. An example is the quality of knowledge, which removes the darkness of ignorance and illuminates the thing known for the knower. Another is power, which enables someone powerful to reach his goals. Others are life, comprehension, and so forth.

Our conscience tells us that the Creator of the universe (that is, He from Whom the being of the universe and its beings spring, Who alleviates any conceivable need, and Who offers every bounty and perfection) has all the attributes of perfection, because it is unrealistic to imagine that one could extend a perfection to others that he lacks.

In the Noble Qur'an, God Most High praises Himself as having all the attributes of perfection and presents Himself as devoid of all imperfection: '*Your Lord is Absolutely Self-Sufficient, the possessor of mercy*' (6:133), meaning that only He is absolutely free of need and able to meet the needs of any needy one. He also says, '*Allah: There is no god other than Him. His are the most beautiful names*' (20:8). The most beautiful qualities belong to God and none other (it is He Who is living, knowing, seeing, hearing, powerful, creative, and beyond need). Therefore, we must understand God Most High to possess all the attributes of perfection and His holy presence to be devoid of every attribute of imperfection. If He possessed imperfections, He would stand in need; then there would have to be a god greater than He to resolve His needs. 'May He be glorified and exalted above whatever is associated with Him'.

GOD'S POWER AND KNOWLEDGE

Consider the way the parts of this vast universe are intertwined, its wonderful workings and the way the systems it contains work together in an orderly way. It is all in motion, and so every kind of phenomenon is progressing toward its special goal in a thoroughly orderly manner. Any intelligent person can see from this that the universe and all it contains depend for their continued existence on an imperishable Being Who has created them through His boundless power and knowledge, and Who has nurtured every created thing and directed it toward its perfection through His special mercy. It is He Whose being is imperishable, and it is He Who knows all things and is capable of all things.

God Most High says, '*His is possession of the heavens and the earth; He brings life and death; and He is capable of all things. He is the First and the Last, the Outward and Inward, and He knows all things*' (57:23). He says in another verse, '*Allah's is possession of the heavens and the earth and all that is between them; He creates what He wills, and Allah is capable of all things'* (5:25).

When we say that someone is able to buy an automobile, we mean that he has what is necessary (sufficient money) to buy the automobile, and if we say that someone is able to lift a hundred-pound stone, we mean that he has the strength to do it.

Overall, power to do a thing means having the means to do it, and, given that the needs of everything in the universe in its existence are met by God Most High, we must say that God Most High has the capacity to do anything and that His pure essence is the source of being. God says in another verse, *'Should He not know what He created?'* (67:14). This means that, since every being depends for its being on the boundless being of God Most High, is it inconceivable that a veil should exist between that being and God, or that it should be hidden from God. Rather, everything is clear to Him; He comprehends and rules everything inside and out.

JUSTICE

God Most High is just, because justice is one of the attributes of perfection, and the God of the universe possesses all of them. Also, He repeatedly praises justice and condemns injustice and oppression in His Discourse. He commands people to justice and prohibits injustice, and how could He be characterized by a thing He has condemned or fail to have an attribute He has praised?

In *Sura* Nisa', He says, *'Allah does not an atom's weight of injustice'* (4:40). He also says, *'Your Lord wrongs no one'* (18:49). Elsewhere He says, *'Allah does not will injustice to His servants'* (40:31). He further says in *Sura* Nisa', *'Whatever good befalls you is from Allah, and whatever evil befalls you is from yourself'* (4:79). He further says in *Sura* Sajda, *'[It is] He Who made all things good that He created'* (32:7).

Accordingly, everything is made absolutely good in itself; it is only relatively and by comparison with others that some things are seen to be ugly, unjust, or defective. For instance, we think of the snake and the scorpion as evil and unfair with respect to man, and of a thorn as unattractive when compared to a rose, but these are all beautiful and marvelous beings in their own right.

It is true that, from the standpoint of religious law, God Most High accounts certain human voluntary acts evil and commands us to abstain from them. These are such sins as *shirk*, disobedience to parents, slaughter of the innocent, wine drinking, gambling, and other acts at variance with our religious duties.

Acts that are designated sins are evil in arising through opposition and rebellion against duty (a negative action); they are not attributed to God; rather, where the responsible party exercises choice, the deed is attributed to that party, and he bears the responsibility and accepts the penalty.

MERCY
When we see someone in need, we help him to the best of our ability. We aid the indigent and guide the blind to their destinations. We call such actions merciful and deserving of praise.

Actions that God enacts cannot be other than merciful, because He benefits all by dispensing His limitless bounty and, in giving, He relieves the needs of all beings, without Himself having need of anyone. As He says, '*My mercy extends to all things*' (7:156).

OTHER ATTRIBUTES OF PERFECTION
'*Your Lord is the Absolutely Self-Sufficient, the Possessor of mercy*' (6:133). Whatever goodness and beauty there are in the universe, and whatever attribute of perfection we can think of are gifts from God Most High to His creatures; in this way, He has satisfied one of the needs of the creation. Of course, if He did not Himself possess this perfection, He would be unable to give it to others; instead, like them, He would be in need of

others. Therefore, God draws all the attributes of perfection from His own being; He has not acquired any of them from others or turned in need to anyone. He is Himself characterized by all the attributes of perfection, such as life, knowledge, and power. No quality of imperfection and need such as impotence, ignorance, death, or difficulty can reach His pure presence.

PROPHECY

Although God Most High is free of need from any standpoint, He has, with His perfect power, brought the universe and its various creatures into being and given them innumerable blessings.

Man, like every other living creature, is under God's nurture from his first moment of existence to his last. Each creature is guided by a special system toward a known object while being given the loving attention it deserves at every moment.

If we contemplate only our own life cycle, that is, from infancy through childhood and youth to old age, our conscience will testify to the complete attention that God Most High gives us. Once we grasp this point, our minds will determine beyond a doubt that the Creator of the universe is more kind to each of His creatures than any person could be. Because of this kindness, He always acts in its best interests and never assents to something that is unwise and to their detriment. The human species is one of God's creations, and we know that its best interests and happiness lie in being realistic and acting well, that is, in having sound beliefs, high ethical values, and good behaviour.

Someone might interject here that man, with his God-given mind, can distinguish good from evil and avoid the pitfalls.

It must be realized, however, that our minds alone cannot untie this knot and guide us to realism and right action. All the undesirable qualities and actions that we see in human society stem from persons who have minds and the power of discernment. Because of egotism, greed, and passion, however, their minds have been overcome by emotions and put at the service of desire. In consequence, they have become lost. Therefore, God Most High must summon and guide us to happiness by another means, one that will never be overcome by desire or err in its guidance. This means is that of prophecy.

THE PROOF OF PROPHECY

It grew clear from our discussion of *tauhid* that, since God Most High created all things, it must be He Who fosters them. To clarify, every phenomenon in the world works, from when it first comes into existence, to obviate its defects and needs one after another and to attain perfection and self-sufficiency to the extent possible for it. It follows an ordered course of continued existence. The One Who orders the thing's course and guides it along from stage to stage is God Most High.

We can draw one sure conclusion in this regard: each species of phenomenon in the world has a unique program that unfolds over its lifetime to govern its behaviour. In other words, every identifiable kind of phenomenon in the world has an identifiable set of roles in life to which God Most High guides it. The Noble Qur'an refers to this truth in this way: '*Our Lord is He Who gave everything its nature, and then guided it*' (20:50). This is true of all aspects of the creation — no exceptions are possible. The heavens above us and the earth below, the elements that compose them all, the compounds that form simple phenomena, all the plants and animals — all are governed by this truth. Man is likewise guided in this way, but there is a difference between man and other things.

THE DIFFERENCE BETWEEN MAN
AND OTHER BEINGS

The earth was created millions of years ago. It put all its hidden forces to work, and, to the extent its various elements allow, it still operates, displaying its effects in its rotation and orbital movement. It thus assures its continued existence; it will continue to act in the same way, not failing to perform any of its functions, until some stronger opposing factor intervenes.

From the time an almond bush sprouts from its seed to its maturity, it performs its functions of feeding and growth (in other words, it follows its course of development). It does not and cannot fail to do so unless some stronger opposing factor intervenes. The same is true of any other phenomenon. Man, however, performs his particular actions by choice, through thought and resolve. How frequently does man fail to perform actions that are to his advantage when no external factor has prevented him, and how often does he do things that are to his detriment, knowingly, with forethought and free choice! Sometimes he refrains from taking an antidote, and sometimes he drinks the poison and kills himself.

Plainly, a being who is created with free choice is under no compulsion to follow divine guidance. That is, the prophets promulgate knowledge given by God of good and evil and of happiness and misery to the people and lead believers to fear God's wrath. The believers are free to embrace what they will of these principles. It is true that man may get an idea of what is good and evil or beneficial and detrimental through use of his mind, but more often than not that mind has given itself up to sensual inclinations and sometimes makes mistakes. This fact demonstrates that divine guidance must be accomplished by some means additional to that of the mind, a means that is wholly free from error. In other words, having led people to understand His commandments in a general way through use of their minds, He must reinforce this understanding by other means.

This means is that of prophecy, by which God Most High teaches His commandments to one of His servants through revelation and assigns him the task of conveying them to the people and making people follow them through fear and hope, encouragement and threats.

God Most High says, '*We inspired you as We inspired Noah and the prophets after him...messengers of good news and warning, so that the people might have no argument with Allah after the messengers'* (4:163-165).

QUALITIES OF PROPHETS

It grows clear that God Most High must teach some of His servants spiritual truths and laws conducive to human happiness by occult means.

One who conveys divine messages is called a prophet, or messenger, of God, and the totality of the messages that he brings from God is called a religion.

It also grows clear that a prophet must:

1. Be devoid of error in carrying out his task. He must be free of lapses of memory or other mental failings so that he can communicate what he has realized to the people without errors. Otherwise, divine guidance would not reach its object, the law would fail to provide its intended universal guidance, and people would not receive the intended effect.

2. Be devoid of sin and offenses in his speech and actions. Otherwise, his missionary work would fail in its effect, because, if someone's actions are at odds with his speech, people accord no value to his words and even take his actions as proof that he is a liar and a charlatan, saying, 'If he spoke the truth, he would act according to his words'.

One may reduce these two points to one and say that, if a mission is to be correct and effective, a prophet must be free of sin and error. God Most High makes reference to this fact where He says, '*[He is] the Knower of the unseen, and He does not express His secret to anyone — except to each prophet He has sent, and He places a guard in front of him and a guard behind, so that He might know if they have promulgated their Lord's message'* (72:26-28).

3. Possess moral virtues such as chastity, courage, and justice. There are all well-accepted virtues, and one who is devoid of any

sort of sin and follows religion completely will never be stained with moral baseness.

PROPHETS IN THE MIDST
OF HUMAN SOCIETY

History makes it clear that prophets have lived among us and roused us to follow God's summons, but history does little to illuminate their lives. Only the life of the Prophet Muhammad (peace and blessings upon him and his family) is preserved for us unambiguously, and the Noble Qur'an, his scripture, containing the sublime goals of religion, has also illuminated the messages and aims of former prophets.

The Noble Qur'an states clearly that God Most High has sent many prophets to the people, all of whom summoned them to *tauhid* and the religion of the truth. It says, for example, '*We sent no prophet before you without inspiring him, saying "There is no God but Me, so worship Me"*' (21:25).

THE PROPHETS OF DECISION
AND OTHER PROPHETS

There are five prophets who possessed scriptures and independent teachings, who are referred to in the verse, '*He has instituted the same [religion] for you that He recommended for Noah and that We inspired in you and commended to Abraham, Moses, and Jesus, saying: "Maintain religion, and do not be divided over it"*' (42:13). These five — Noah, Abraham, Moses, Jesus, and Muhammad (peace and blessings upon him and his family), who brought scriptures and revealed laws — are called the prophets of decision (*ulu'l-azm*), but they are not the only prophets. Rather, there has been a prophet for every people, but only some twenty are mentioned in the Noble Qur'an.

As God Most High says, '*[Among the prophets are] those We have told you of, and those We have not told you of*' (40:78). He also says, '*Each people has a messenger*' (10:47) and '*Each people has a guide*' (13:7).

The prophets who have come after each of the prophets of decision have summoned humanity to those prophets' revealed laws. They continued their predecessors' missions. God raised the Most Noble Messenger Muhammad ibn 'Abdullah (peace and blessings upon him and his family) as the Seal of the Prophets, to promulgate the final commandments and the most perfect religious ordinances, made the Messenger's scripture the last, and, in consequence, appointed His religion to last until the Resurrection and His revealed law to live on forever.

NOAH

The first prophet Merciful God raised and directed to humanity with a scripture was Noah (upon whom be peace).

Noah (upon whom be peace) summoned the people of his day to *tauhid* and monotheism and directed them to shun *shirk* and idolatry. It is evident from the account in the Noble Qur'an that Noah struggled hard to end class distinctions and uproot oppression and that he spread his teachings through appeal to reason, something new to the humanity of that age.

In the course of a long period of confrontation with ignorant and stubborn people, he took a small group under guidance. God Most High sent a flood to eradicate the unbelievers and cleanse the land of their pollution. Noah (upon whom be peace), who had escaped the flood with a number of his followers, laid the foundations of a new religious society in the world.

This great prophet is the founder of the law of *tauhid* and the first person to be delegated by God to struggle against oppression, injustice, and tyranny. Because of this great service he performed for the religion of truth, God Most High has graced him with a special greeting that will live on so long as human life continues: '*Peace be upon Noah among all the people of the world*' (37:79).

ABRAHAM

After Noah's time, a long age passed in which numerous prophets such as Hud and Saleh guided people to God and uprightness. Nonetheless, *shirk* and idolatry made steady advances and finally overcame the whole world. God Most High, in His supreme wisdom, raised Abraham (upon whom be peace) as a prophet.

Abraham (upon whom be peace) is the perfect example of someone who lives in accord with his true nature. With his pure nature, he sought for the truth, he realized that there is One God over the creation, and he struggled against *shirk* and oppression as long as he lived.

As the Noble Qur'an makes clear and the traditions of the Imams of the Messenger's lineage affirm, Abraham spent his childhood in a cave far from the bustle of life and the clamour of the towns. He saw only his mother, who brought him food and water.

One day he emerged with his mother and went to town to visit his uncle Azar. Whatever he saw was new and a source of amazement to him. His pure soul, roused by exposure to thousands of wonders, sought for the origins of the things it witnessed. He saw the idols that Azar and others fashioned and worshipped. He asked what they were, but attempts to explain that they were divine did not satisfy him. He saw some people worshipping Venus, some worshipping the moon, and others worshipping the sun. Since each of these set in a matter of hours, Abraham would accept none of them as god.

After going through these experiences, Abraham (upon whom be peace) openly and fearlessly declared himself a believer in the One God and made clear his disgust with the prevalent *shirk* and idolatry. He no longer considered any course but struggle against them. Without admitting any feelings of inadequacy or fatigue, he struggled and summoned people to *tauhid*.

At last, he made his way to the idol temple and smashed the

idols. This made him the worst of criminals in the eyes of the people, and he was sentenced to be burned alive. God Most High, however, protected him from the flames, and he emerged from the fire unharmed.

Eventually, Abraham emigrated from Babel, his place of birth, to Syria and Palestine, where he continued his mission.

Toward the end of his life, he had two sons: one Isaac, the progenitor of Israel, and the other Isma'il (Ishmael), the progenitor of the Arabs. By God's command, he took Isma'il and his mother to the Hijaz in his infancy and left them in an uninhabited, waterless, lifeless land amid the Tahama Mountains. There he summoned the bedouin Arabs to *tauhid*. Later, he built the Ka'aba and legislated the practice of Hajj, which the Arabs continued down to the time of the Messenger and the advent of Islam.

Abraham is the father of the religion of the true nature. According to the Qu'ran, he brought a scripture and was the first to refer to God's religion as Islam and to its adherents as Muslims. The religions of *tauhid*, which are Judaism, Christianity, and Islam, all trace their origins to him, since their respective founders, Moses, Jesus, and the Most Noble Messenger Muhammad (peace and blessings upon him and his family), are all his heirs and follow in his footsteps in their missions.

MOSES
Moses the son of 'Imran is the third of the prophets of decision, those who brought a scripture and a revealed law. He is a son of Israel, a descendent of Jacob.

Moses (upon whom be peace) had an eventful life. When he was born, the Israelites were living an abject life of captivity among the Copts. Their infants were being beheaded by the order of Pharaoh.

Following instructions given in a dream, Moses's mother had laid him in a wooden box and launched it into the Nile. The current carried it directly to Pharaoh's palace.

Pharaoh commanded that the box be taken and opened; there they found the baby.

At the urging of the queen, Pharaoh spared the child's life, and, since they had no child, they entrusted him to a nursemaid (who was, as it happened, the child's mother).

Moses remained in Pharaoh's court until his early youth. Then, because of involvement in a death, from fear of Pharaoh, he fled to Madyan, where he met the prophet Shu'ayb (upon whom be peace), married one of his daughters, and tended his sheep for some years. Then he took thought for his homeland; he left with his family and servants for Egypt. One night along the road, at Mount Sina, he was chosen as a prophet by God Most High and charged with summoning Pharaoh to *tauhid*. He was also to deliver the Israelites from the Copts and to appoint his brother Aaron as his deputy. When he promulgated his mission and delivered his divine message, however, Pharaoh who was an idolater and displayed his own effigy to the Egyptians as one of the gods, refused to accept the message and did not free the Israelites.

Although Moses (upon whom be peace) summoned the people to *tauhid* for years and enacted many miracles, Pharaoh and his people reacted only with harshness and brutality. Finally, by God's command, Moses (upon whom be peace) led the Israelites from Egypt toward the Sinai by night. As they approached the Red Sea, Pharaoh learned of their departure and pursued them with his army.

Moses (upon whom be peace), through a miracle, divided the Red Sea and crossed it with his people, but Pharaoh was drowned with his army. Later, God revealed the Torah to Moses (upon whom be peace) and established the Mosaic Law among the Israelites.

JESUS, THE MESSIAH

Jesus was the fourth prophet of decision, the fourth prophet to bring a scripture and a revealed code. He was born in a supernatural way: his mother, Mary, was a pious virgin who was engaged in worship in Bethlehem when God caused the Holy Spirit to descend upon her, which brought her the good tidings of the coming of the Messiah and caused her to conceive the Messiah by breathing into her sleeve.

After he was born, he spoke from the cradle in reply to unjust accusations made against his mother and told the people of his prophethood and scripture. Later, as a youth, he began preaching to the people and revived the code of laws revealed to Moses with a few changes. He sent his disciples to all parts to spread his message. In time, as his message was spread, the Jews (from among whom he arose) plotted to kill him, but God saved him, and the Jews wound up crucifying someone else.[1]

It is necessary here to make the point that God Most High affirms in the Noble Qur'an that Jesus was given a scripture called the 'Gospel' (*Injil*), which is not among the gospels that were written after his lifetime, the officially recognized ones being the four Gospels of Matthew, Mark, Luke, and John.

NOTES TO CHAPTER TWO

1. The Noble Qur'an, 4:157, and ancient traditions tell us that the crucifixion of Jesus was in some sense illusory. — Trans.

CHAPTER THREE

THE MESSENGER MUHAMMAD, SON OF 'ABDULLAH

The life history of our honoured Messenger Muhammad ibn 'Abdullah (peace and blessings upon him and his family) is better known to us than those of any earlier prophets. Over the ages, their scriptures, revealed codes, and even personalities have been obscured.

In truth, we have no clear accounts of them except the ones that have come down to us in the Noble Qur'an and the narrations of the Most Noble Messenger (peace and blessings upon him and his family) and his heirs. By contrast, there is extant a full history of the Most Noble Messenger that adequately describes his life.

The Most Noble Messenger of Islam is the last of the prophets that the Most Gracious God has sent for our guidance.

Fourteen centuries ago, the people of the world lived in a state in which nothing remained of the religion of *tauhid* but the name. People were wholly estranged from worship and knowledge of God, and their societies were divorced from justice and humane ways. The glorious Ka'aba had been degraded into an idol temple, and the religion of Abraham, the Friend of God, into idolatry.

The Arabs lived a tribal life, and even their towns in the Hijaz, Yemen, and elsewhere were organized on this basis. They lived in the most degraded and backward state imaginable. In place of culture, immodesty, debauchery, drunkenness, and gambling prevailed among them. They buried their infant daughters alive. Most of them lived by theft, banditry, murder, and plunder of each other's possessions and livestock. To kill and tyrannize were their greatest glories.

It was in such an environment that God raised up the Most Noble Messenger (peace and blessings upon him and his family) to reform and guide the people of the world; revealed to him the Qur'an — which is full of true teachings, knowledge of God, illustrations of the meaning of justice, and useful counsel; and appointed him to summon the people to true humanity and observance of truth.

The Most Noble Messenger was born in 570 A.D. (53 years before the Hijra, or Migration to Medina) in Mecca, to a family that was regarded as the purest and most noble of the Arabs.

His father died before he was born, and his mother died when he was only six years old. After two years, his grandfather and guardian 'Abd al-Muttalib also died, and the Messenger was left in the care of his loving uncle Abu Talib (the father of 'Ali, the Commander of the Faithful).

Abu Talib raised the Messenger Muhammad like his own son. Up to a few months before the Hijra, he worked hard to take care of him and never allowed him to be neglected.

Like other Arabs, the Arabs of Mecca tended sheep and camels; sometimes, too, they made commercial travels to such nearby countries as Syria. They were an illiterate people and attached no importance to educating their children.

The Most Noble Messenger (peace and blessings upon him and his family), like the rest of his folk, did not learn to read or write, but, from his youngest days, he showed many virtues. He never worshipped idols; he never lied; he never stole or behaved treacherously. He abstained completely from malicious or flippant acts. He acted with intelligence and care. These qualities won him the affection of his people in a short time, and he became known as Muhammad the Trustworthy (*al-Amin*). Arabs formed the habit of entrusting their valuables to him and spoke of how trustworthy and capable he was. When he was about twenty, a wealthy Meccan woman (Great Khadija) made him her business agent, and, because of his honesty, correctness, intelligence, and capacity, her business affairs prospered, and she naturally felt attracted to the personality of the man and the greatness that lay behind it. Finally, she proposed marriage to the Most Noble Messenger (peace and blessings upon him and his family). He attended to his spouse's business dealings for years after their wedding.

The Most Noble Messenger (peace and blessings upon him and his family) had good relations with the people until he was forty; he was counted as one of them, except that his morals were exceptionally high; he was never involved in others' dirty dealings; he did not engage in the oppression, cruelty, and drive for status that were prevalent. He won over people by gaining their respect and confidence. When the Arabs rebuilt the Ka'aba, the tribes wrangled bitterly as to which would replace the Black Stone. They decided to ask the Most Noble Messenger (peace and blessings upon him and his family) to arbitrate. He decreed that a cloak be spread, that the Black Stone be placed in the middle of it, and that the leaders each take a corner of the cloak and lift the stone. Then he himself placed it. Thus he brought an end to a bitter dispute without bloodshed.

Although the Prophet worshipped the One God, and not the

idols, before the beginning of his mission, since he did not directly attack the superstitious beliefs of idolatry, the people did not interfere with him, just as practitioners of various religions such as Jews and Christians lived among the Arabs in peace.

THE STORY OF BAHIRA, THE MONK

Once while the Most Noble Messenger (peace and blessings upon him and his family) had not yet grown up and was still living with his uncle Abu Talib, Abu Talib made a commercial trip to Syria, taking the Most Noble Messenger (peace and blessings upon him and his family) with him.

It was a large, heavily-laden caravan. As they entered Syria, they reached a town called Busra and dismounted near a monastery. They pitched tents and rested. A monk named Bahira came out from the monastery and invited the caravan party to dine. All accepted the monk's invitation and entered the monastery, except that Abu Talib left his nephew to look after their supplies.

Bahira asked, 'Have all come?' Abu Talib replied that all had except for a youth, the youngest of the party. Bahira said, 'Bring him as well'. Abu Talib had left the Most Noble Messenger (peace and blessings upon him and his family) standing under an olive tree. He called for him to come in. Bahira looked closely at the Most Noble Messenger (peace and blessings upon him and his family) and told him, 'Come closer, I must speak with you'. He drew the Most Noble Messenger (peace and blessings upon him and his family) aside. Abu Talib joined them. Bahira told the Most Noble Messenger (peace and blessings upon him and his family), 'I will ask you something, and I will swear you to Lat and 'Uzza to answer me'. (Lat and 'Uzza were the names of two idols worshipped by the people of Mecca).

The Most Noble Messenger (peace and blessings upon him and his family) replied, 'Nothing is more loathsome to me than these two idols'.

Bahira then said, 'Let me swear you to the One God that you will answer truly'. The Most Noble Messenger (peace and blessings upon him and his family) responded, 'I always speak truly, I never lie. Ask your question'. Bahira asked, 'What thing do you most love?' He answered, 'Solitude'. Bahira asked, 'What do you most watch and love to watch?' He answered, 'The sky and the stars within it'. Bahira asked, 'What do you think?' The Most Noble Messenger (peace and blessings upon him and his family) remained silent, but Bahira closely studied his forehead, finally asking, 'When and with what thought in mind do you sleep?' He answered, 'When, as I watch the sky, I see the stars and find them in my lap, and myself above them'. Bahira asked, 'Do you also dream?' he answered, 'Yes, and whatever I see in dreams, I also see when I am awake'. Bahira continued, 'What, for instance, do you dream of?' The Holy Messenger·was silent. Bahira also fell silent. After a short while, Bahira asked, 'May I see between your two shoulders?' Without moving, the Most Noble Messenger (peace and blessings upon him and his family) replied, 'Yes. Come and see'. Bahira stood, came close, and removed the Most Noble Messenger's (peace and blessings upon him and his family) robe from his shoulders. He saw a black mole and murmured, 'It is the same'. Abu Talib asked, 'The same as what? What are you saying?' Bahira said, 'Tell me. What is your relationship to this boy?' Abu Talib, who loved the Most Noble Messenger (peace and blessings upon him and his family) like a son, replied, 'He is my son'. Bahira retorted, 'No. This boy's father is dead'. Abu Talib asked, 'How did you know? Yes, this is my brother's son'. Bahira said to Abu Talib, 'Listen. This young man has a resplendent and marvelous life ahead of him. If others see what I have seen and they recognize him, they will kill him. Conceal and protect him from enemies'. Abu Talib asked, 'Tell me, who is he?' Bahira answered, 'In his eyes are the marks of a great prophet, and likewise on his back'.

THE STORY OF NESTURIUS, THE MONK

Several years later, the Most Noble Messenger (peace and blessings upon him and his family) was once again on the road to Damascus, on business for Khadija, taking her goods. Khadija had sent her servant Maysara along with him and instructed her to obey him completely. On this journey too, when they reached Syria, they stopped near the town of Busra, alighting under a tree. There was a monastery near there belonging to a monk named Nesturius, who was acquainted with Maysara. He asked her, 'Who is that resting under that tree?' Maysara replied, 'One of the Quraysh'. The monk said, 'No one has or ever will rest under the tree except one of God's prophets'. Then he asked, 'Do his eyes have a reddish tinge?' She answered, 'Yes. His eyes have always had that quality'. The monk said, 'That is right. He is the last of God's prophets. I wish I might live to see the day he is charged with summoning people to God'.

PROPHECIES FROM THE JEWS OF MEDINA

Numerous Jewish tribes who had read descriptions of the coming prophet had emigrated from their homelands and settled in the Hijaz, especially in Medina and the surrounding area. They were awaiting the appearance of the expected Prophet. Since they were a wealthy people, the Arabs harboured ill feelings towards them and even plundered their properties.

The aggrieved Jews would always say, 'We shall endure your predations and oppression until the expected Prophet emigrates from Mecca and arrives here. Then we will embrace the Holy Messenger and extract our revenge from you'. A major factor in the Medinans' quick acceptance of Islam was their mental preparedness for the news. They embraced the faith, but the Jews later rejected it, because of their stubborn prejudices.

QUR'ANIC REFERENCES TO PROPHECIES
OF THE MESSENGER'S COMING

God Most High refers to these prophecies in several places. In relation to the beliefs of a people from among the people of the book, He says, '*Those who follow the Messenger, the unlettered Prophet, whom they will find described in the Torah and the Gospel, which are in their possession. He will enjoin them to do what is right and forbid them what is wrong. He will make lawful for them all good things and prohibit for them only the foul, and he will relieve them of their burden and the fetters that they used to wear*' (7:157).

He also says, '*When a scripture comes to them from Allah, confirming what they have, although they had been asking for a victory over those who disbelieved — when there comes that which they know [to be the truth], they do not believe in it*' (2:89).

THE PERIOD FROM THE BEGINNING
OF THE MISSION TO THE HIJRA

In that dark environment of the Arabian Peninsula, which one may without exaggeration call a cesspool of misfortune and a focal point of oppression and corruption in a world full of injustice and tyranny, God Most High raised up His Messenger and a mercy to the people of the world. He charged him with summoning the people to *tauhid* and worship of the One God, with calling them to justice, good works, and strengthening of social bonds, and with rousing them to hold to the truth without carelessness or indulgence. He commissioned him to lay the foundations of human happiness on the bedrock of faith, fear of God, cooperation, and self-sacrifice.

The Most Noble Messenger (peace and blessings upon him and his family) was first charged with forming the basis of the mission, and, since he was in an environment full of obduracy, cruelty, and oppression, he first promulgated his teachings only among persons from whom he had some hope of acceptance. Thus, he led a small number to accept the faith, the first of

73

whom was (according to accounts) his nephew and protege 'Ali ibn Abu Talib (peace and blessings upon him and his family). The first woman to embrace Islam was his wife Khadija (upon whom be peace).

After a time, the Most Noble Messenger (peace and blessings upon him and his family) was charged with summoning his close relatives. After a revelation, he invited these (about 40 people in all) to his house and disclosed his divine mission. After that, by the command of God, the Most Noble Messenger (peace and blessings upon him and his family) propagated his mission publicly, and the brilliant torch of divine guidance emerged to light the world.

The Arabs, especially the Meccans, reacted harshly to the mission, especially after it was made public. The unbelievers and *mushriks* answered the pure summons with savage cruelty. They had no reasoned response to it.

The Most Noble Messenger (peace and blessings upon him and his family) was at times called a soothsayer and a magician and at others a madman and a poet. He was mocked and ridiculed. When he tried to summon the people to the newly-arisen religion of Islam or when he engaged in worship of God, they heckled him, they dumped dirt clods, thorns, or straw on him, they struck him, they called him names, and, sometimes, they even threw stones at him. Sometimes they would try to coopt him with false promises of wealth and power in an attempt to break his resolution. But the Most Noble Messenger (peace and blessings upon him and his family) never slackened his efforts in the least,although at times he felt sorry for the people in their ignorance and obstinacy. Many verses of the Qu'ran were revealed in this connection in which God Most High expressed sympathy to the Most Noble Messenger (peace and blessings upon him and his family) and commanded him to persevere. Sometimes, too, verses would be revealed forbidding the Holy Messenger from inclining at all to their words or moderating his efforts.

The Most Noble Messenger's (peace and blessings upon him and his family) followers were also subjected to the torments of the unbelievers; many actually died under torture. At times of extremity, some asked permission of the Most Noble Messenger to set aside what God had decreed and to conduct an armed uprising. The Most Noble Messenger (peace and blessings upon him and his family) would respond, 'God Most High has not commanded me to such a thing; we must be patient'. Under the intense pressure, some also emigrated.

In times, the Muslims' state grew desperate; the Most Noble Messenger (peace and blessings upon him and his family) gave permission for his followers to emigrate to Ethiopia, some days' journey away from the scene of their anguish. A party headed by Ja'far ibn Abu Talib (one of the elect of the Messenger's companions) made the migration. After learning of it, the unbelievers of Mecca sent two seasoned men to the king of Ethiopia with numerous gifts. They sought the extradition of the Mecca migrants. Ja'far ibn Abu Talib addressed the king, his court, the Christian priests, and the nobles; he described the luminous being of the Most Noble Messenger (peace and blessings upon him and his family), explained the sublime principles of Islam, and read from *Sura* Maryam.

Ja'far's irreproachable words moved the king and everyone else assembled there to tears. The king denied the Meccans' request and rejected their gifts. He ordered that every measure be taken to provide for the immigrants' comfort.

After this turn of events, the unbelievers made a pact to cut off relations with the Bani Hashim, the Most Noble Messenger's (peace and blessings upon him and his family) relations and supporters. They completely halted all social and commercial relations with them. A signed proclamation to that effect was posted on the Ka'aba.

The Bani Hashim, the Most Noble Messenger (peace and blessings upon him and his family) among them, were compelled to depart Mecca and to seek asylum in a valley known as Shi'b

Abu Talib. They faced extreme hardship and hunger, and no one dared leave the valley. The days were burning, the nights filled with the wailings of children.

After three years, because of the effacement of the proclamation and numerous complaints from neighbouring tribes, the unbelievers abandoned their pact and the Bani Hashim emerged from their asylum.

About that time, however, Abu Talib, the sole supporter of the Most Noble Messenger (peace and blessings upon him and his family), and Khadija, his dear wife, both died, and so matters became yet more difficult for the Most Noble Messenger (peace and blessings upon him and his family). His life was in danger; he could not appear in public or remain long in one place.

A JOURNEY TO TA'IF

The same year that the Most Noble Messenger (peace and blessings upon him and his family) and the Bani Hashim emerged from Shi'b Abu Talib (the thirteenth year of the prophetic mission), he made a short journey to Ta'if (a town about one hundred kilometers from Mecca). He summoned the people of Ta'if to Islam, but the ignorant of the town poured out from everywhere, called him names, pelted him with stones, and finally drove him out of the town.

The Most Noble Messenger (peace and blessings upon him and his family) returned to Mecca and remained there for a time, but, being in danger for his life, he did not appear in public. Considering that conditions were right for doing away with the Most Noble Messenger (peace and blessings upon him and his family), the leaders of Mecca met to devise a plan at their assembly, known as the dar an-Nadwa. This was the plan: each Arab tribe would elect one man to form a party that would attack the Most Noble Messenger's (peace and blessings upon him and his family) house and kill him. Plainly, by involving all the tribes, they left the Bani Hashim no one tribe from which to seek retribution, especially since a member of the Bani Hashim would be among the attackers.

They resolved upon this plan. About forty men from various tribes were designated to kill the Most Noble Messenger (peace and blessings upon him and his family). They surrounded his house by night intending to strike at dawn and carry out their party's plan, but God's will was superior to theirs and rendered their plan a mere daydream. God Most High sent the Most Noble Messenger (peace and blessings upon him and his family) a revelation informing him of their designs. He ordered him to leave Mecca by night and emigrate to Medina.

The Most Noble Messenger (peace and blessings upon him and his family) told 'Ali (upon whom be peace) of the course of events and ordered him to pass the night in his bed. He made a will to him and left the house by night. On the road, he met Abu Bakr, who accompanied him to Medina.

Some time prior to the migration, some Medinan leaders had met with the Most Noble Messenger (peace and blessings upon him and his family) in Mecca, embracing the faith and also promising to support and defend him with their lives and property should he migrate to Medina.

THE MOST NOBLE MESSENGER'S MIGRATION TO MEDINA

The Most Noble Messenger (peace and blessings upon him and his family) reached a cave in Mount Thawr, near Mecca, by night; he remained hidden there for three days. Then he emerged and continued his journey. Finally, he entered Medina and was received by its people.

The unbelievers of Mecca surrounded his house by night and attacked at dawn. They rushed the Most Noble Messenger's (peace and blessings upon him and his family) bed with drawn swords, but, contrary to what they expected, they found 'Ali (upon whom be peace) there in the Most Noble Messenger's (peace and blessings upon him and his family) place. When they learned that the Most Noble Messenger (peace and blessings upon him and his family) had left Mecca, they searched the vicinity and finally returned discouraged.

The Most Noble Messenger settled in Medina. The people of Medina embraced Islam enthusiastically and sincerely aided the Most Noble Messenger (peace and blessings upon him and his family). Medina took on an Islamic look. The city, then called Yathrib, became known as Medinat ar-Rasul ('The Messenger's City'), or simply Medina. It was the first Islamic town. A minority of the Arabs of Medina, about one third of the population, only outwardly conformed to Islam, out of hypocrisy, for fear of the majority.

The Islamic sun shone over the pure skies of Medina, and its light began to spread. One of its first consequences was that the state of war that had existed between the two tribes known as the Aus and the Khazraj was transformed into a state of peace and amity. The believers of Medina clustered like moths around the prophetic flame, and the tribes in the Medinan domain also gradually embraced the faith. God's ordinances were revealed and put into effect one after another. Every day some form of corrupt behaviour would be eradicated, to be replaced by piety and justice. Slowly the believers in Mecca, who were massively harassed by the unbelievers after the Most Noble Messenger's (peace and blessings upon him and his family) departure, left behind their old homes and lives and fled to Medina. They were warmly received by their co-religionists there.

The Muslims who had remained in Mecca and who gradually emigrated to Medina were known as the *Muhajirin* ('immigrants'), and the Medinan Muslims were known as the *Ansar* ('helpers').

The numerous Jewish tribes in Medina and its vicinity, and in the fortress cities of Khaybar and Fadak, had long heard from their rabbis and scholars of the coming of the Prophet of Islam; they had passed these stories on to the Arabs. When these tribes were summoned to Islam after the Hijra, however, they did not answer the summons. In time, a non-aggression pact with special provisions was concluded between the Muslims and the Jews.

The rapid progress of Islam alarmed the unbelievers of Mecca. Their hatred of the Most Noble Messenger and the Muslims grew by the day, and they sought for a way to scatter them. The Muslims too, especially the *Muhajirin*, felt a deep anger toward the Meccans. They were waiting for divine permission to repay the oppressive unbelievers for what they had done and to free the women and innocent children and hapless Muslims still being tormented in Mecca.

The first battle between the Muslims and the unbelievers, known as the battle of Badr, took place in the second year of the Hijra, in a gulch called by that name between Mecca and Medina. In this battle, the unbelievers had about a thousand fully armed and equipped fighters, and the Muslims about a third as many ill-equipped men. By God's grace, however, the Muslims won a clear victory and crushed the unbelievers. The *mushriks* fled to Mecca leaving heavy casualties, many prisoners, and much gear. It is said that seventy unbelievers were killed in this battle, about half of them under 'Ali's (upon whom be peace) sword, and about seventy were taken prisoner.

In the third year of the Hijra, the unbelievers, led by Abu Sufyan, moved on Medina with about three thousand men (five thousand according to some accounts). They confronted the Muslims outside the city, on a plain called Uhud. In this battle, the Most Noble Messenger (peace and blessings upon him and his family) formed ranks against the enemy with about seven thousand men. The Muslims had the upper hand at the beginning of the battle, but, due to an error on the part of some Muslims, the Islamic army was defeated. The unbelievers swarmed from all sides and caught the Muslims amid their swords.

The Muslims suffered heavy casualties in this battle. About seventy of the Most Noble Messenger's (peace and blessings upon him and his family) companions were martyred, most of them from among the *Ansar*, but also including his uncle Hamza. The Most Noble Messenger himself (peace and blessings upon him and his family) received a wound on the forehead. One of his front teeth was broken, and a *mushrik* who had struck him on the shoulder shouted, 'I have killed Muhammad', and so the Muslim army scattered. Only 'Ali (upon whom be peace), along with several fighters, stood surrounding the Most Noble Messenger (peace and blessings upon him and his family), and among them only 'Ali survived, resisting and defending the Most Noble Messenger (peace and blessings upon him and his family) until the battle was over.

Toward the end of the day, Islamic soldiers who had fled regrouped around the Most Noble Messenger (peace and blessings upon him and his family) and revived the fight. Abu Sufyan's army, however, thought it best to retire to Mecca without endangering their victory.

After the army of unbelievers had travelled some miles, a feeling spread through it that they should have followed through on their victory to take Muslim men and children prisoner and to plunder Muslim property. They discussed making a new attack on Medina, but news reached them that the Muslim army was pursuing them with a view to resuming the battle, and they were quickly frightened into abandoning their plan and hurrying back to Mecca.

What they heard was basically true, because, by God's command, the Most Noble Messenger (peace and blessings upon him and his family) had re-equipped the army with the casualties' arms and sent it against the enemy under 'Ali's (upon whom be peace) command.

Although the Muslims suffered heavy casualties in this battle, in fact it had some positive consequences for Islam and the Muslims. More important than the outcome was that they learned through experience the unfortunate consequences of opposition to the Most Noble Messenger's (peace and blessings upon him and his family) orders.

When the two hostile sides ceased fighting, they agreed to conduct another battle at Badr at that same time a year later. The Most Noble Messenger (peace and blessings upon him and his family) was there with a group of his companions at the appointed time, but the unbelievers failed to appear.

After this battle, the Muslims improved their situation; they furthered their cause everywhere in the Arabian Peninsula except in the region of Mecca and Ta'if.

The third battle between the Arab unbelievers and the Most Noble Messenger (peace and blessings upon him and his family) and the last one in which the opposing forces were led by the Meccans was a fierce confrontation known as the Battle of the Trench (*Khandaq*) or the Battle of the Tribes (*Ahzab*). The unbelievers deployed all the forces and means they had in this battle.

After the Battle of Uhud, the leaders of Mecca, foremost among them Abu Sufyan, concurred that, by putting an end to the Most Noble Messenger (peace and blessings upon him and his family), they could put an end to Islam. They invited other Arab tribes to join them in this enterprise. Although the Jewish tribes had concluded a non-aggression pact with the Muslims, they secretly broke their pact and joined in the scheme.

The upshot was that, in the fifth year of the Hijra, a large and well-equipped army of Quraysh, assorted other Arab tribes, and Jewish tribes marched on Medina.

The Most Noble Messenger (peace and blessings upon him and his family), who already knew of the enemy's intentions, consluted his companions. After much discussion, the proposal of Salman Farsi, an outstanding companion, was accepted: a trench was dug around Medina, and the forces were deployed behind it, inside the city. The enemy force, failing to find a way into the city, was compelled to surround it, and a protracted battle resulted.

It was in this battle that 'Amr ibn 'Abd Wad, one of the best known Arab knights and valiants, met his death at the hands of 'Ali (upon whom be peace). In the end, because of the wind and cold, the Arab idolaters' fatigue at the length of the siege, and a falling out between them and the Jews, they abandoned the siege and broke up.

After the war of the trench, which was instigated by the Jews, and in which the Arab unbelievers participated, the Jews openly disavowed their pact with Islam. By God's command, the Most Noble Messenger (peace and blessings upon him and his family) rebuked the Jewish tribes of Medina and then engaged in a series of battles, all of which ended in Muslim victories. The most important of these was the battle of Khaybar. The site was a fortress heavily defended by seasoned Jewish warriors and well-supplied.

In this battle, 'Ali (upon whom be peace) first killed the famous Jewish champion Marhab Khaybari and scattered the Jewish army. Then he attacked and broke into the fortress, where he raised the banner of victory. These battles in the fifth year of the Hijra marked the end of Jewish power in the Hijaz.

SUMMONING THE KINGS TO ISLAM

The Most Noble Messenger (peace and blessings upon him and his family) had settled in Medina, and, as the Meccan Muslims fled the unbelievers' torments and immigrated to Medina, the *Ansar* did their part to provide them a warm reception.

The Most Noble Messenger (peace and blessings upon him and his family) erected the Prophet's Mosque (*Masjid an-Nabi*) in Medina, and another mosque was slowly under construction. Islamic missionaries were being sent to various places. Pacts were concluded with the Jewish and Arab tribes in and around Medina; Islam was on the advance.

In the sixth year of the Hijra, the Most Noble Messenger (peace and blessings upon him and his family) wrote letters to such rulers as the shah of Iran, the Roman Emperor, the Khadiv of Egypt, and the ruler of Abyssinia summoning them to Islam.

That same year, the Most Noble Messenger (peace and blessings upon him and his family) proceeded to Mecca with a party of believers to perform the 'Umra — the 'Lesser Pilgrimage'. They were not allowed to do this, but a pact was concluded with the unbelievers known as the 'Treaty of Hudayba'. One of its provisions allowed an Arab tribe the freedom to side with either party.

After a while, the unbelievers of Mecca broke the pact. In consequence, the Most Noble Messenger (peace and blessings upon him and his family) decided to conquer Mecca; in the eighth year of the Hijra he advanced on the city with ten thousand fighters. The city surrendered without a fight. He smashed all the idols at the Ka'aba. The people at large of Mecca embraced Islam. The Most Noble Messenger (peace and blessings upon him and his family) ordered the leaders, who had shown so much enmity to Islam and sanctioned such inhumane treatment of the Messenger and his followers in the course of twenty years, to appear before him. Showing great magnanimity, he pardoned them all, displaying no signs of rancour.

After conquering Mecca, the Most Noble Messenger (peace and blessings upon him and his family) conducted mopping-up operations in the vicinity, including numerous battles with Arab idolaters, one of which was the Battle of Hunayn.

This battle, in which the Muslim forces confronted the Hawazan tribe, was one of the most important for the Most Noble Messenger (peace and blessings upon him and his family). Twelve thousand Muslim infantrymen stood against the Hawazan cavalry, numbering several thousand. A fierce fight ensued.

At the outset, the Hawazan forces dealt a crushing blow to the Muslims, to the extent that they all fled except for the Most

Noble Messenger (peace and blessings upon him and his family), 'Ali, who stood across from him holding aloft the banner of Islam, and a handful of others. After several hours, however, first the *Ansar* and then the rest of the Muslims regrouped. They fought hard and defeated the enemy. The Muslims took five thousand prisoners in this battle, but, according to the Most Noble Messenger's (peace and blessings upon him and his family) wishes, they were all released. When some people were unwilling to release their prisoners, the Most Noble Messenger (peace and blessings upon him and his family) ransomed them.

In the ninth year of the Hijra, the Most Noble Messenger (peace and blessings upon him and his family) drew up an army at Tabuk (near the border between the Hijaz and Syria) seeking to battle the Romans, because it had become known that the Roman Emperor had based an army of Romans and Arabs in that area. An encounter known as the Battle of Mu'ta, which had resulted in the death of such Muslim commanders as Ja'far ibn Abu Talib, Zayd ibn Harith, and 'Abdullah ibn Rawaha, had already been fought with the Romans in that region. The Roman army, however, had already left the area. The Most Noble Messenger (peace and blessings upon him and his family) remained there for three days to stabilize local affairs, and then returned to Medina.

During the ten years he lived in Medina, the Most Noble Messenger (peace and blessings upon him and his family) directed about eighty big and small battles besides the ones mentioned here. He personally participated in about one quarter of them.

In the battles in which he participated, unlike commanders who give orders to attack and kill from a place of safety, he fought side by side with his soldiers at the front, but it never occurred that he ordered anyone's killing.

GHADIR KHUMM AND THE QUESTION OF THE SUCCESSION

The last holdout against complete Islamic control of the Arabian Peninsula was the city of Mecca, the site of God's sanctuary and the Ka'aba. The city fell to the Muslim army in the eighth year of the Hijra, and Ta'if fell shortly thereafter.

In the tenth year of the Hijra, the Most Noble Messenger (peace and blessings upon him and his family) set out for Mecca to perform his final, farewell Hajj. After carrying out the rituals of the pilgrimage and imparting necessary teachings to the people, he set out for Medina. On the road, at a locale known as Ghadir Khumm (Ghadir Pond), he ordered the caravan to halt. In the midst of one hundred twenty thousand pilgrims from all over the Arabian Peninsula, he took 'Ali's (upon whom be peace) hand, raised it aloft, and proclaimed him his successor.

With this act, the question of the successor, who was to govern the affairs of the Muslims, guard the *sunna* (the body of customary behaviour based on the Prophet's precedent), and uphold religious customs and laws, was settled for the Islamic society. The intent of the noble verse, *'Messenger! Promulgate what has been revealed to you by your Lord, for if you do not, you will not have conveyed His message'* (5:67), was carried out. The Most Noble Messenger (peace and blessings upon him and his family) died shortly after returning to Medina.

THE MOST NOBLE MESSENGER'S STAY IN MEDINA AND THE ADVANCE OF ISLAM

The mission of the Messenger of Islam in Medina was a very high-profile one, felt throughout the city. People of Mecca, Medina, and tribes near and far embraced Islam in droves, so that Islam came to rule the entire Arabian Peninsula in the course of the Most Noble Messenger's (peace and blessings upon him and his family) ten year stay in Medina.

During these ten years, the Most Noble Messenger (peace and blessings upon him and his family) was occupied with carrying out his charge. Not resting for a moment, he transmitted revelations and communicated to the people the sublime teachings of Islam on spiritual values, morals, and laws that he had received from God Most High through these revelations. He counseled the people and answered their questions. He debated opponents and scholars of other nationalities, especially Jews. He conducted national affairs and kept the ship of state afloat.

Despite all this, he devoted much of his time to worship of God and spent many days of the year fasting; that is, he maintained a fast for about three continuous months — the months of Rajab, Sha'ban, and Ramazan, and also fasted one separate month. Sometimes he would carry out a fast of his own known as the Fast of Communion (*Rawzat al-Wisal*), in which he would take nothing for several successive days and nights. He would also spend time managing his household and procuring its needs, and he also at times worked for wages to secure a livelihood.

God Most High says, '*They want to blow Allah's light out with their mouths, but He is perfecting His light, no matter how disbelievers may dislike it. He is the One Who has sent His Messenger with guidance and the True Religion, so He may have it prevail over every other religion no matter how those who associate [others with Allah] may hate it*' (61:8-9). Plainly, God's promise has been progressively realized from the Most Noble Messenger's (peace and blessings upon him and his family) time to the present, when more than one billion Muslims are found all over the globe.

He also says, '*You are the best community that has been raised up for mankind. You enjoin good and forbid evil, and you believe in Allah*' (3:110).

A LOOK AT THE SPIRITUAL CHARACTER OF THE MOST NOBLE MESSENGER

According to definitive historical documents, the Most Noble

Messenger (peace and blessings upon him and his family) grew up in the most debased possible environment, a sinkhole of ignorance, corruption, and moral rot. He spent his childhood and youth in such an environment and without the benefit of a formal education. Although he never worshipped idols or picked up the degraded morals that surrounded him, he did grow up among such people, and his rather ordinary life gave no hint of his eventful future, one that would scarcely be expected for a poor and unschooled orphan.

The Most Noble Messenger (peace and blessings upon him and his family) lived this way until one night, while he was worshipping with his characteristic calm heart and clear mind, his character was transformed.

His quiet, introverted character was transformed into a celestial character. He realized that the accumulated thoughts and beliefs of thousands of years of human society were superstitions, and that the practices of the world's peoples were a form of cruel oppression. He linked the past and the future and discerned perfectly where human happiness lay. The Most Noble Messenger's (peace and blessings upon him and his family) vision and speech were wholly transformed — thereafter, he saw and heard nothing but reality, and he spoke nothing but divine wisdom and counsel. His outlook took wings and, no longer seeking to reform local, everyday commercial concerns, he aspired to reform the world, to overthrow the millennia-old system of human misdirection and oppression. He launched an uprising to revive the realization of truth, brought about the downfall of world powers, and made light of fearsome opposing forces. He spoke of divine wisdom and deduced all the secrets of being from knowledge of the oneness of the Creator.

He expounded the most sublime ethical values man can attain in the clearest possible manner; he made it clear how they relate to one another. He believed more than anyone in what he said and practised whatever he called upon people to do.

He brought divine laws and ordinances including acts of

worship that express the station of servanthood before the glory of the One God in the most beautiful fashion possible. He brought other laws, covering legal rights and punishments that work together perfectly, being founded on *tauhid* and respect for the high ethical potential of human beings.

The laws that the Most Noble Messenger (peace and blessings upon him and his family) brought, considered in their totality, including rules for worship and commerce, are inclusive enough to cover all the questions of individual and social life that could possibly arise and all the various points that can come up with the passage of time.

The Most Noble Messenger (peace and blessings upon him and his family) himself regarded the laws of his religion as global and perpetual in scope. That is, he believed that his religion could resolve the this-worldy and otherworldly needs of all human societies forever, and that people would need to adopt this practice to secure their happiness. He himself said many times, 'What I have brought you secures your welfare in this world and the next'.

Of course, he did not say this idly, but he was voicing a conclusion he reached after careful study of the creation and consideration of the future of human life. In other words, after, in the first place, achieving perfect accord between his laws and the spiritual and physical nature of man and, in the second place, giving full consideration to the tranformations that were to take place in the future, including the disasters that would befall Muslim society, he adjudged that his religious ordinances would stand to perpetuity.

Predictions by the Most Noble Messenger (peace and blessings upon him and his family) that have been passed down to us through authoritative sources have spoken clearly of general conditions and events from after his death to much later times.

He did all these things in the space of twenty or thirty years, thirteen of which were spent under the scarcely endurable tortures meted out by the unbelievers of Mecca, and ten of which were occupied with war and mobilization for battle, external struggles with declared enemies, internal struggles with hypocrites and obstructionists, management of the Muslims' affairs, reform of their beliefs, morals, and behaviour, and a thousand other involvements.

The Most Noble Messenger (peace and blessings upon him and his family) kept to this course through an indestructible resolution to follow and keep alive the truth. His realistic outlook recognized only the truth and allowed nothing to take place contrary to it, even if it would have advanced his own interests or met with public approbation. What he knew to be true he embraced with his heart and soul and never rejected, and what he knew to be false he rejected and never accepted.

HIS SPIRITUAL CHARACTER
WAS EXTRAORDINARY

If we consider these facts fairly, no doubt will remain to us that the appearance of such a figure under such conditions is nothing short of miraculous and could have no other cause than divine intervention. In this regard, God Most High refers many times to the Most Noble Messenger's (peace and blessings upon him and his family) orphanhood and impoverishment in his early life. He treats the miraculous character He endowed him with as proof that he was worthy of the mission. He says, for instance, *'Did He not find you an orphan and protect you? And did He not find you wandering and direct you? And did He not find you destitute and enrich you?'* (93:6-8). He also says, *'You did not read any scripture before it, and you did not write it with your right hand, otherwise those who follow falsehoods might have doubted'* (29:48). He further says, *'If you are in doubt concerning what We reveal to our servant, then produce a sura like it'* (2:23).

THE PERSONAL CHARACTER
OF THE MOST NOBLE MESSENGER

The sole foundation upon which the Most Noble Messenger (peace and blessings upon him and his family) built his religion as the basis of the world's people's happiness was that of *tauhid*.

According to the principle of *tauhid*, the One Who is the Source of the universe and is deserving of worship is the One God. One can glorify and submit oneself to none other than God Most High.

Accordingly, the practice that should be the norm in society consists in all being brothers and equals, and in people giving unconditional obedience to none other than God. God Most High says, '*Say, "People of the Book! Come to an agreement between us and you that we worship none but Allah, and that we associate nothing with Him, and that none of us take others as lords other than Allah"*' (3:64).

The Most Noble Messenger (peace and blessings upon him and his family) had no other object than to promulgate the religion of *tauhid*. He summoned the people to *tauhid* by showing the best moral qualities and frankest manner and by putting forward the soundest logic. His companions used this same method in expounding his principles, as God Most High instructed him: '*Say, "This is my way: I call upon Allah through insight, I and whoever follows me"*' (12:108).

The Most Noble Messenger (peace and blessings upon him and his family) treated all as brothers and equals and never made exceptions in carrying out religious rules. He made no distinctions between friend and stranger, strong and weak, rich and poor, man and woman, or black and white; he gave each his or her due on the basis of religious laws, saying, 'If my daughter Fatima, who is more dear to me than anyone, were to steal, I would cut off her hand'.

No one had the right to run anyone else's life. People had the greatest possible freedom in matters outside the purview of the law. (Of course, freedom vis-a-vis the law is meaningless not only in Islam, but according to any code of civil law.)

God Most High alludes to this system of freedom and social justice where he says of the Most Noble Messenger (peace and blessings upon him and his family), '*Those who follow the Messenger, the Prophet who can neither read nor write, whom they will find described in the Torah and the Gospel [which are] with them. He will enjoin on them that which is right and forbid them that which is wrong. He will make lawful for them all good things and prohibit for them only the foul; and he will relieve them of their burden and the fetters that they used to wear. Then those who believe in him, and honour him, and help him, and follow the light that is sent down with him: they are the successful. Say, "People! I am the Messenger of Allah to you all..."'* (7:157-158).

It is on this level that the Most Noble Messenger (peace and blessings upon him and his family) claimed no special distinction in his life and that no one having prior acquaintance with him had any advantage over others. He would attend to household chores; he received visitors personally; he would attend to others' needs. He did not sit on a throne or at the head of an assembly. When it was time to travel, he mounted and rode without special ceremonies. If he received some goods, he gave whatever exceeded his essential needs to the poor; sometimes he gave away things he really needed and went hungry. He always lived like the poor and associated with the poor. He would never show any neglect in adjudicating people's rights, but he would go to the greatest lengths to forgive and forget when it came to his own rights. When, during the conquest of Mecca, the leaders of the Quraysh were brought before him, although they had persecuted him to such an extent and stirred up so many plots against him after the Hijra, he showed them no rudeness but forgave them all.

Friend and foe alike pointed to the Most Noble Messenger (peace and blessings upon him and his family) as a moral exemplar. No one equalled him in good manners, cheerfulness, tolerance, humility, and sobriety. The Noble Qur'an praises his nobility of character where it says, '*You have been molded with tremendous character*' (68:4). He was the first to offer greetings when meeting anyone, including women, children, and slaves. One of his companions asked permission to prostrate himself before him. He replied, 'What are you saying! This is the practice of emperors, and my status is that of a messenger and a servant'.

From the point that God Most High charged him with propagating religion and guiding the people, he never neglected his duties for a moment, and he carried them out tirelessly. In Mecca, thirteen years before the Hijra, despite the intolerable problems that the Arab *mushriks* caused him, he engaged in worship and propagation of God's religion continually. During the ten year period following the Hijra, facing ever-growing problems with enemies of the religion and obstructions created by Jews, hypocrites, and pretended Muslims, and meanwhile engaging in more than eighty battles with the enemies of Islam, he conveyed the principles of religion and laws of Islam to the people in all their stunning breadth.

In addition to managing the affairs of the Islamic society, which by then covered the whole Arabian Peninsula, he personally looked into people's petty complaints and needs, without the aid of a doorkeeper.

Regarding the Most Noble Messenger's (peace and blessings upon him and his family) courage and valor, it is enough to note that he arose summoning people to the truth in the face of the whole world of that time, a world ruled by tyranny and prejudice. All the tortures and torments that the tyrants of that day could mete out failed to deter him or make him falter, and he never retreated in a battle.

The Most Noble Messenger (peace and blessings upon him and his family) kept himself very clean and regarded cleanliness as a sign of faith; as he would say, 'Cleanliness is the kernel of faith'. Besides keeping clean and wearing clean clothes, he would dress nicely and meet people with a pleasant demeanor. Whenever he would go out, he would go well-dressed. He was also very fond of perfume.

He did not change his demeanor over the course of his life. He remained modest and humble to the end of his life, and, despite his high status, he never assumed any prerogative that would reflect his value to society.

In his life, the Most Noble Messenger (peace and blessings upon him and his family) never spoke abusively of anyone. He never said anything flippant, laughed loudly, or did anything frivolous. He was very fond of contemplation. He listened carefully to every complaint and protest that was brought before him before responding. He never broke into anyone's remarks. He never disallowed anyone's freedom of thought, but he would make people's errors clear to them and so place balm on the inward wounds.

The Most Noble Messenger (peace and blessings upon him and his family) was very kind and tender-hearted and always deeply moved at the sight of pain and grief. Despite this, he never declined to punish wrongdoers and made no distinctions among persons in carrying out God's laws.

A Jew and a Muslim were accused of a theft that occurred at the home of one of the *Ansar*. A large party of *Ansar* went before the Most Noble Messenger (peace and blessings upon him and his family) and tried to pressure him into punishing the Jew but allowing the Muslim to go free, because the Jews were enemies and because this would preserve the dignity of the Muslims and of the *Ansar* in particular. Because he saw the truth to be contrary to their representations, however, he openly supported the Jew and sentenced the Muslim.

While he was personally ordering the battle lines at the battle of Badr, he reached a warrior who was standing a little in front of the others. The Most Noble Messenger (peace and blessings upon him and his family) used a staff to press against the stomach of that man to make him stand a little farther back, so that the line would be straight. The warrior said, 'Messenger of God! By God, this hurts my stomach — I must retaliate'. The Most Noble Messenger (peace and blessings upon him and his family) handed the man his staff and bared his stomach, saying, 'Have your retaliation'. The man ran forward and kissed the Messenger's stomach, saying, 'I know that I will be killed today; I wanted by this means to touch your holy body'. Later he attacked the enemy and fought with his sword until he was martyred.

The Most Noble Messenger (peace and blessings upon him and his family) always aided the weak and oppressed. He instructed his companions, 'Bring the needs of the needy and the complaints of the weak before me, without fail'.

It is said that his last words were instructions to the people regarding slaves and women. At that he ceased speaking and his eyes were closed to the world. God's blessings be upon him and his honoured heirs.

THE MOST NOBLE MESSENGER'S LEGACY TO THE MUSLIMS

Like other aspects of being, the human world is fated to change and transformation. Also, the pronounced differences that are seen in the makeup of human individuals bring about different sensibilities that in turn result in people's minds varying in their suppleness of thought and sense and their ability to remember.

Accordingly, in the absence of deep roots and faithful and reliable guardians, the beliefs, customs, and rules governing a society would very quickly change beyond recognition. We can best satisfy ourselves on this point by experience and observation.

The Most Noble Messenger (peace and blessings upon him and his family) did two things to preserve his global and perpetual religion from this danger: He bequeathed the people an indisputable document and left them in the hands of righteous guardians in the form of God's Book and his noble heirs, respectively. All the schools of Islamic thought have passed down traditions in which the Most Noble Messenger (peace and blessings upon him and his family) says, 'I am leaving and I leave you two precious trusts: one, God's Book, and the other, my heirs. Never separate the two; as long as you cling to these, you will not lose the way'.

CHAPTER FOUR

THE NOBLE QUR'AN

The Noble Qur'an is the fountainhead of verities and spiritual values in Islam, the scripture and documentation of the prophethood of the Most Noble Messenger (peace and blessings upon him and his family). The Noble Qur'an is the Word of God Most High, a set of teachings that have descended from the Source of glory and the Station of grandeur to the Most Noble Messenger (peace and blessings upon him and his family), to show humanity the way to happiness.

The Noble Qur'an consists of a set of theoretical and practical topics imparted to humanity; when we put these points into practice, happiness in this world and the next is ours.

The Noble Qur'an was gradually revealed over the twenty-three years of the Most Noble Messenger's (peace and blessings upon him and his family) mission, in answer to the needs of human society.

The Noble Qur'an is a book that has no other object than to guide people to happiness. Using instructive explanations, it teaches the right beliefs, sound character, and right actions that are the foundation of human individual and social happiness. *'We reveal a Book to you that explains all things'* (16:89).

The Noble Qur'an presents Islamic teachings in summary form; for detailed explanations of them, especially for explanations of legal questions, it directs people to refer to the Most Noble Messenger (peace and blessings upon him and his family): *'We have revealed the remembrance to you so that you might explain to the people what has been revealed for them'* (16:44); *'We have revealed the Book to you so that you might clarify the matters over which they differ'* (16:64).

One of the objects of the Noble Qur'an is to speak to people in ordinary language and to appeal to their God-given reason, not to call them to blind imitation. It evokes common experiences that we have by our nature and that we cannot avoid or disclaim.

God Most High says, *'It [the Noble Qur'an] is a decisive statement; it is no joke'* (86:13-14). The Noble Qu'ran is a discourse that discriminates truth and falsity, not an idle ramble. It explains matters in such a profound way that its reasoning appeals to all people and will stand for all time. It does not reflect the ordinary way people talk, which considers the few facets of an idea that any one person's thought comprehends and more or less ignores the rest. Rather, it is God's speech, which comprehends everything manifest and hidden and reflects knowledge of every beneficial and harmful consequence.

Thus it is necessary for every Muslim to see realistically and to realize the living truth of God's word through bearing the verses above constantly in mind, not to rely on what others have said and thought. He or she must not turn away from freedom of thought, which is the only faculty unique to man, and which the Noble Qur'an calls upon and reinforces so much. God's Book is a living authority for all people in all times, and could not be addressed to the understanding of a certain few people.

God Most High says, '*May they not act like those who were given the Book previously; the waiting period seemed too long for them, so their hearts were hardened...*' (57:16).

The Noble Qur'an calls upon people to return to their own nature and to accept the truth, meaning that we must first prepare ourselves to accept the truth unconditionally and embrace what we have seen is the truth and of benefit to us in this world and the next, ignoring Satan's temptations and the suggestions of our own desires.

Then we must expose our minds to Islamic teachings; if we find them to be true and see real advantages in accepting and applying them, we will submit ourselves to them and so our way of life and the prevalent customs of society will depend on the rules that our own instinctual nature and inclinations call for.

Finally, this will be a unified system all of whose parts and contents will be in complete harmony with the particular makeup of human beings and wholly devoid of contradictions and conflicts. It will not be the system of conflicting forces that has sprung up in place of spiritual values, or the material values that may or may not be rational.

In characterizing the Noble Qur'an, God Most High says, '*It guides to the Truth and the straight path*' (46:30), and '*This Qur'an guides to that which is straightest*' (17:9). In another verse, He states that the reason for the power and soundness of Islam is its conformance with the created nature of man. Clearly, a practice that answers the natural desires and real needs of man is the best approach to human happiness: '*Set your purpose for religion as an upright person — the nature [arising from] Allah, by which He created man. There is no altering Allah's creation. This is the right religion, but most people do not know*' (30:30). He further says, '*This is a book that We have revealed to you so that you may draw the people from darkness into light*' (14:1).

The Noble Qur'an summons us to the clear path that clearly

leads to the final destination. This path is necessarily the one that gives the right answers to our innate desires and agrees with the outlook of the sound mind that is called the 'innate religion' (*ad-din al-fitri*) in Islam.

A practice, however, that arises through the influence of society, based on caprice and meant to satisfy individuals' lusts and angers is nothing but a descent into darkness; in truth, it is to follow a road that will never reach a destination. The same may be said for a practice of blind imitation of one's ancestors, or one adopted uncritically by a weak, undeveloped country from more powerful nations, without regard to the differences in their situations. God Most High says, '*Is one who was dead and whom We have brought to life and placed a light by which he walks among people like one whose state is as one of darkness from which he cannot emerge?*' (6:122).

At this point we may appreciate the importance and greatness of this holy book to Islam and Muslims. Fourteen centuries have passed since the Noble Qur'an was revealed, and yet it has held an honoured position in the most varied human societies and attracted people's attention everywhere ever since.

The Noble Qur'an is a divine book, the nucleus of the worldwide and eternal religion of Islam. All of the sublime teachings of Islam are represented there in compelling form; from this standpoint, its value is equal to that of God's religion. Beyond this, the Noble Qur'an is God's speech and a miracle of the Most Noble Messenger (peace and blessings upon him and his family) that will live forever.

THE NOBLE QUR'AN IS A MIRACLE

It is established that Arabic is a powerful and versatile language that can express the subjective states of human beings in the clearest and most precise manner possible. No other language approaches Arabic in this respect.

History testifies that the Arabs of the *Jahiliyya* (the time of ignorance, the pre-Islamic period), most of whom were nomads, knowing nothing of urban life and lacking all the finer things in life, were nonetheless capable of a level of eloquence unrivaled in history.

Eloquent discourse was the supreme value in Arab culture, and great respect was paid to beautiful and cultivated speech. Just as the Arabs placed their idols in the Ka'aba, they attached charming and affecting poems by their foremost orators and poets to its walls. While they employed a language of such breadth and so many special tokens and exact rules without any error, they went overboard in adorning their words.

In the days when the verses of the Noble Qur'an were first being revealed to the Most Noble Messenger (peace and blessings upon him and his family) and being read to the people, they created a stir among the Arabs and their orators. The compelling, sweet, and meaningful discourse of the Noble Qur'an so found its way to their hearts and entranced the spiritually aware that the eloquent speeches were forgotten and the fine poems (known as the *Mu'alliqat*, the 'hanging' poems, because of their attachment of the Ka'aba) that had been hung from the Ka'aba were taken down.

God's words were so indescribably beautiful and moving that all hearts were drawn to them; with their sweet form, they sealed the lips of the orators.

On the other hand, these words were most bitter and disagreeable to the *mushriks* and idolaters, because they expounded the religion of *tauhid* and attacked the practice of *shirk* and idolatry with a compelling exposition and unassailable logic. They scorned the idols that people called gods, to which they prayed, and to which they made sacrifices; they called them lifeless, impotent effigies of wood and stone, lacking any special virtue. The savage Arabs, overcome with pride and arrogance, living their lives on the basis of bloodshed and banditry, were called upon to embrace the worship of the Truth and respect for justice and humanity. Instead, they fought back and sought for ways to extinguish this shining torch of guidance, but their ill-conceived efforts brought them nothing but despair.

In the early days of the prophetic mission, the Most Noble Messenger (peace and blessings upon him and his family) was brought before a famed Arab orator named Walid. The Messenger recited some verses from the beginning of the *sura* Ha Mim Sajda. For all his pride and conceit, Walid listened attentively until the Most Noble Messenger (peace and blessings upon him and his family) reached the verse, *'If they turn away, then say, "I warn you of a thunderbolt like the thunderbolt that struck 'Ad and Thamud"'* (41:13). Then Walid's appearance changed, he began shaking uncontrollably and seemed to have lost his senses; the assembly then broke up and the people dispersed.

After that, some people went to Walid and complained, 'You disgraced us in front of Muhammad'. Walid replied, 'No, I swear to God, you know that I fear no one and covet nothing, and you know that I am a literary man and skilled speaker. What I heard Muhammad say was nothing like people's speech. It was so compelling and enchanting, you couldn't call it poetry or prose. It was pithy and profound. If I must judge the matter, I really can't say. Allow me three days to consider'. They came back in three days; then Walid said, 'Muhammad's words are magic and sorcery that put a spell on people'.

Guided by Walid's words, the *mushriks* declared the Noble Qur'an to be magic. They avoided hearing it and forbade the people from listening to it. Sometimes when the Most Noble Messenger (peace and blessings upon him and his family) would recite the Qur'an in the Masjid al-Haram, they would shout and clap so that others would not hear him.

Nonetheless, once people had fallen in love with the eloquence of the Noble Qur'an, they would take advantage of the darkness of night to gather behind the wall of the Most Noble Messenger's (peace and blessings upon him and his family) house and listen to its recitation. Then they would murmur to each other, 'This speech cannot be a human creation'. In this connection, God Most High says, *'We are most aware of what they listen for when they listen to you, and when they discuss in secret, the evildoers will say, "You are only following a man who is bewitched"'* (17:47).

When the Most Noble Messenger (peace and blessings upon him and his family) would recite the Noble Qur'an and summon people to the religion before the Ka'aba, the Arab orators, having to pass by him, would bend over to avoid being seen or recognized. God Most High says of this, *'They double up so that they may hide from him'* (11:5).

ACCUSATIONS AGAINST THE MOST NOBLE MESSENGER

Not only did the unbelievers and *mushriks* call the Noble Qur'an magic, they called the Most Noble Messenger's (peace and blessings upon him and his family) whole mission magic. Whenever he summoned the people to God's way and imparted spiritual truths or counsel to them, they would say, 'He's working magic', although he was offering insights to whose rightness the human mind with its God-given conscience testifies and showing the right road, the plain practice exactly representing the happiness and prosperity of human society. They had no excuse for refusing to accept it; no one can justly call such a teaching magic.

Is it magic to say, 'Do not worship the piece of wood or stone that you yourself have carved', or 'Do not make sacrifices of your sons and daughters; do not follow superstitious practices?' Can one refer to such virtues as uprightness, benevolence, humanitarianism, peacefulness, purity, justice, and respect for human rights as magic?

God Most High speaks in reference to this point: *'If you say that they will be raised up after death, those who disbelieve say, "This is nothing but obvious magic"'* (11:7).

THE QUR'AN LAYS DOWN
A CHALLENGE TO THE *MUSHRIKS*

The unbelievers and *mushirks* being so attached to the superstitious practice of idolatry, were never prepared to accept the summons to Islam and acknowledge the truth. Thus, they called the Most Noble Messenger (peace and blessings upon him and his family) a liar and said that the Noble Qur'an was his own invention.

In order to refute this accusation, the Noble Qur'an challenged the foremost orators to put forward verses equal to the Qur'an's and thus to show that the Islamic summons was groundless. As God Most High says, '*Or do they say, "He has invented it"? No, they will not believe. So let them produce its like if they are truthful*' (52:33-34). He further says, '*Or do they say, "He has invented it"? Say, "Then produce a sura like it and call upon whomever you can besides Allah, if you are truthful"*' (10:38).

The Arab unbelievers and *mushriks*, masters of eloquence that they were, and for all their prideful boasting, shrank from this challenge and so tranformed this literary contest into a bloody struggle. It was easier for them to be killed than to accept defeat and disgrace in the literary arena. The Arab orators failed to contend with the Noble Qur'an, not only those living at the time of the revelations, but also those born in later ages. Failing the test, they had to retreat from the field.

It is human nature that, whenever an artistic masterpiece of great performance appears and attracts popular attention, even if it has no more impact on social life than boxing or tightrope walking, some people will get the idea of equalling or topping it. Thus there have always been people making tireless efforts to outdo this scripture. Failing, as they always do, the orators could not but fall back on the explanation that the Noble Qur'an is magic, since magic can make true appear false and vice-versa, but the moving language of the Noble Qur'an has nothing to do with magic but flows from a natural beauty. Since its words impart teachings and summon to objectives whose reality and truth we understand through our native and God-given intelligence, since it demands that we revere the truth and act in accordance with benevolence, justice, and humanitarianism, values we cannot reasonably reject, they are nothing but the plain truth. The Arab orators could not sustain the argument that the Noble Qur'an simply stands at the pinnacle of human discourse and is unrivaled in beauty, eloquence, and fascination. This is evidence that it is the word of God.

In other words, in the case of every trait or talent, such as courage, or reading and writing and the like, in the course of human history a genius will appear who leads the field. Why should not the Most Noble Messenger (peace and blessings upon him and his family) with his special style occupy the peak of eloquence in the field of Arabic letters, but his words be those of a human being and so open to rivals? The orators contemporary with the Most Noble Messenger (peace and blessings upon him and his family) did not say this, and the opponents of the Noble Qur'an could not claim or prove such a thing. Whatever trait or talent that has been brought to the peak of its development by some genius is finally something arising from the capacities of human beings, a product of human nature. Thus, it is possible for others to follow the road that genius has opened and, through the necessary struggle and effort, to do something like what that genius has done, or something in the same manner but better in at least some respects. In that case, the original genius who opened the road becomes a mere forerunner. For instance, no one can outdo the legendary Arab Hatim Ta'i in generosity, but one can carry out deeds similar to his. One cannot outdo Mir, the Iranian calligrapher, in calligraphy or Mani (the founder of the Manichaen sect) in painting, but, with enough effort, one can write a word in the style of Mir or paint a little picture in the style of Mani.

According to the same general law, if the Noble Qur'an were the finest example of human eloquence (not the word of God), the possibility would exist for others (especially the best-known rhetoricians of the world) through practice to imitate this style in order to produce a book, or at least a *sura*, similar to the Noble Qur'an. In offering the challenge, the Noble Qur'an asks people to produce a discourse like its own, not better: '*If you are in doubt concerning what We reveal to our servant, then produce a sura like it, and call your witnesses besides Allah if you are truthful*' (2:23).

In conclusion, it must be noted that the Noble Qur'an is inimitable in respect not only to its eloquence and wonderful style but also to its contents: it offers real answers to all the needs of humanity. It offers authoritative teachings on the unseen, on spiritual truths, and on other matters to humanity at large. For these reasons, no one will ever succeed in producing anything like it.

CHAPTER FIVE

THE HEIRS OF THE MOST NOBLE MESSENGER

The Arabic phrase *ahl al-bayt* (literally, 'people of the house') both formally and commonly refers to a man's household, the society in miniature within his home: his wife and children, as well as servants; in short, all who live within the sphere of the master of the house.

Sometimes the phrase is generalized to apply to close relatives, such as one's father and mother, one's sister, one's nephews and nieces, and one's aunts and uncles and their children.

But neither of these common meanings is intended when the traditional sources refer to the *ahl al-bayt* of the Most Noble Messenger (peace and blessings upon him and his family). According to the accounts that have reached us through unbroken chains of transmission, both Sunni and Shi'i, *ahl al-bayt* is a blessed name that applies only to the Most Noble Messenger (peace and blessings upon him and his family), 'Ali,

Fatima, Hasan, and Husayn (upon whom be peace). Accordingly, the remainder of the Most Noble Messenger's (peace and blessings upon him and his family) household and relations are not members of his *ahl al-bayt* in this sense, although they would be in common usage. Even Khadija, the most honoured of the Most Noble Messenger's (peace and blessings upon him and his family) wives and Fatima's (upon whom be peace) mother, and Ibrahim, the Most Noble Messenger's (peace and blessings upon him and his family) natural son and greatest glory, do not belong to his *ahl al-bayt*.

According to these accounts and others, the nine of twelve Imams who descend from Imam Husayn (upon whom be peace) also belong to his *ahl al-bayt*. Accordingly, the *ahl al-bayt* are these fourteen, also known as the Fourteen Most Pure. When one speaks of the *ahl al-bayt* of the Most Noble Messenger (peace and blessings upon him and his family), one normally means these thirteen persons who survived or descended from him and are related to him.

These persons, whom I will refer to as the *Heirs* of the Most Noble Messenger (peace and blessings upon him and his family), are recognized in Islam as having many special virtues and stations no one else may hold. Two stations are the most important of these: 1. In accordance with the noble verse, '*Allah wills to remove impurity from you, People of the House, and to purify you thoroughly*' (33:33), they hold the station of purity, and accordingly, no sin can arise from them. 2. In accordance with the noble Prophetic *hadith* known as 'Thaqalayn' referred to earlier, these Heirs are always at one with the Noble Qur'an and never depart from God's Book. Accordingly, they are never in error about the meaning of the Noble Qur'an and the Plain Religion.

These two stations imply that the words and deeds of the Most Noble Messenger's (peace and blessings upon him and his family) Heirs are as authoritative as his own. This is the belief of Shi'a Muslims.

THE DOCUMENTED VIRTUES
OF 'ALI AND THE OTHER HEIRS

Many Prophetic *ahadith* have been transmitted on 'Ali's virtues and those of the other Heirs. I will mention three stories that have reached us.

1. In the sixth year of the Hijra, the Christians of the town of Najran sent a delegation of leaders and learned men to Medina. The members first engaged in disputation and wrangling with the Most Noble Messenger (peace and blessings upon him and his family), but they were defeated, and God revealed the verse known as the Verse of Imprecation (*mubahila*): *'Whoever disputes with you concerning him [Jesus], after the knowledge that has come to you, say, "Come! We will summon our children and your children, and our women and your women, and ourselves and yourselves, then we will pray humbly and invoke Allah's curse upon those who lie"'* (3:61). The Most Noble Messenger (peace and blessings upon him and his family) proposed the imprecation to the delegation from Najran in just the form the verse commanded, that their women and children be brought, and that they invoke the curse of God's torment upon the liars.

The delegation from Najran accepted the imprecation, and it was arranged for the following day. Then a large crowd of Muslims and also the people from Najran stood waiting for the Most Noble Messenger (peace and blessings upon him and his family) to come out, waiting to see with what ceremonies he would emerge and also whom he would bring to the imprecation. He emerged with his arm over Husayn's shoulder, holding Hasan's hand, and followed by Fatima, who was followed in turn by 'Ali (upon whom be peace). The Most Noble Messenger (peace and blessings upon him and his family) instructed his holy company, 'When I pray, say, "Amen!"'.

The Najran delegation was shaken at the sight of this shining company, who projected truth and reality from head to foot and who had taken no refuge save God Most High. The head of the delegation told his companions, 'I swear to God, I see faces that, should they turn to the Divine Presence, all the Christians on earth would perish'. Thus they approached the Most Noble Messenger (peace and blessings upon him and his family) and asked to be excused from the imprecation. The Most Noble Messenger (peace and blessings upon him and his family) said, 'Then embrace Islam!' They replied, 'We have no capacity to fight the Muslims; we shall pay taxes annually and live in the sphere of Islam'. Thus the dispute came to an end.

That 'Ali, Fatima, Hasan, and Husayn (upon whom be peace) accompanied the Most Noble Messenger (peace and blessings upon him and his family) on this occasion shows that 'our children, our women, and ourselves' in the verse refers to these persons alone. To clarify, when the Most Noble Messenger (peace and blessings upon him and his family) said, 'ourselves', he meant himself and 'Ali (upon whom be peace); when he said, 'our women', he meant Fatima (upon whom be peace); and when he said, 'our children', he meant Hasan and Husayn (upon whom be peace).

It grows perfectly clear here that 'Ali (upon whom be peace) stood on a level with the Most Noble Messenger (peace and blessings upon him and his family) himself, and also that the Heirs of the Most Noble Messenger (peace and blessings upon him and his family) were four, since anyone's *ahl al-bayt* consists of those who would customarily be referred to as 'ourselves and our wives and children'. If any other people other than these four were members of the Most Noble Messenger's (peace and blessings upon him and his family) *ahl al-bayt*, he would have brought them to participate in the imprecation.

At this point, too, we must accept that these four are infallible, because God Most High has testified to the infallibility of the Heirs of the Most Noble Messenger (peace and blessings upon him and his family): '*Allah wills to remove impurity from you, People of the House, and purify you thoroughly*' (33:33).

2. The Most Noble Messenger (peace and blessings upon him and his family) is reported to have said, 'My *ahl al-bayt* is like

Noah's ark; whoever boards it is saved, and whoever refuses to is drowned'.

3. It is reported through unbroken chains of transmission that the Most Noble Messenger (peace and blessings upon him and his family) said, 'I leave you two precious things that will never be separated: God's Book and my descendants and *ahl al-bayt*; so long as you cling to these, you will not be lost'.

THE IMAMATE

A governmental organization that is set up in a country to manage the people's public affairs does not function automatically; so long as there are no capable individuals working to manage it, it will not be viable, and people will not reap the benefits of good government.

The same rule applies to any other organization that arises in human society, such as various economic and cultural organizations. They can never dispense with competent and honest managers; lacking them, they will quickly decline. This is a plain, easily perceived truth to which abundant experience testifies.

Plainly, this rule applies to the organization of Islam, which may be called the most far-flung organization in the world. It needs managers to survive, and there must always be worthy individuals to communicate its culture and laws to the people and to enforce its ordinances to the letter in the Islamic society, not allowing any slackening in their observance and preservation.

The position of leadership in religious and civil matters in the Islamic society is known as the *imamate*, and its holder is known as the *Imam*. It is the belief of Shi'i Muslims that God Most High must have designated an Imam for the people after the death of the Most Noble Messenger (peace and blessings upon him and his family) to uphold the culture and laws of the religion and to guide people on the way of truth.

Anyone who studies Islamic ideas in a scholarly way and

considers the matter fairly will see that the imamate is one of the essential principles of Islam. Verses in which God Most High has described the organization of His religion make this point clear.

PROOF OF THE IMAMATE

As was made clear in the chapter, 'The Messenger Muhammad', the care and attention that the Sustainer of the universe lavishes on His creation implies that He guides every creature to a predetermined goal (which is to attain the state of perfection). For instance, a fruit tree is guided to grow, blossom, and bring forth fruit; its life follows a different course than that of a bird, which follows its own special course of development and pursues its own special goal. Thus, each creature is guided along a course uniquely its own to a destination uniquely its own. Clearly, man, too, is one of God's creatures and is guided by the same law.

It is likewise clear that, since human beings find happiness in their lives through exercise of free choice, the special guidance appropriate to man must be supplied through the summons, indoctrination, and religious teachings that are sent by means of prophets, if man is not to plead that God Most High has failed to guide him. Note the noble verse, *'Messengers bearing good news and warning, so that the people might have no case against Allah after the messengers. Allah is ever powerful, wise'* (4:165). It points out that, for the same reason that a prophet must be sent and a summons made to religion, there must be someone as infallible as that prophet to uphold the religion and guide the people after he dies. God Most High must appoint someone bearing similar perfections (apart from revelation and prophecy) in the prophet's place to preserve the culture and laws of the religion intact and guide the people. Otherwise, the program of general guidance would collapse, and people would have an airtight case against God.

ONE CANNOT BE FREE
OF NEED FOR THE IMAM

Just as, due to the errors and failings to which it is prone, reason cannot obviate people's need for God's prophets, neither can the presence of religious scholars and their efforts to promulgate the faith amid the community of believers relieve the people's need for the Imam. As we have seen, people indisputably either observe religion or do not, but the point is that God's religion must reach the people without being altered, degraded, or lost.

Certainly, however pious the religious scholars of the community are, they are not infallible or above sin and error. It is, if generally unlikely, not impossible that they might (however unwittingly) distort some of the culture or laws of the religion. The best testament to this assertion consists of the various schools of thought and divergences in view that have come about within Islam.

Accordingly, it is in all events necessary that an Imam exist to preserve the real culture and laws of God's religion, so that, whenever people find the aptitude, they can turn to this figure for guidance.

WHAT THE MOST NOBLE MESSENGER
SAID ABOUT THE GUARDIANSHIP

In characterizing the honoured Prophet of Islam (peace and blessings upon him and his family), God Most High says, *'There has come to you a prophet from among yourselves; he takes seriously how you have come to grief, is anxious about you, compassionate, merciful towards believers'* (9:128). It is unbelievable that the honoured Messenger, who, according to the Noble Qur'an, held nothing dearer than his community of believers, would overlook and remain silent on a divine precept that had such a central importance for the Islamic society for the whole of his life.

The Most Noble Messenger (peace and blessings upon him and his family) knew better than anyone that the vast and highly organized institution of Islam was not something he was to lead for a decade or two, but that it was to be all-embracing and perpetual and must be managed as long as human life goes on. Thus, he contemplated events thousands of years after his own time and issued the necessary instructions concerning them. The Most Noble Messenger (peace and blessings upon him and his family) knew that a religion is a social organization, and that no social organization can maintain itself for an hour without proper leadership. Accordingly, a leader is necessary who will preserve the culture and laws of the religion, who will keep the wheels of society turning and guide people to happiness in this world and the next. How can it be supposed that he should have taken no interest in the day after the day he would die?

The Most Noble Messenger (peace and blessings upon him and his family) was in the habit of appointing someone to manage the people's affairs in his place whenever he was about to leave Medina for battle or Hajj. Similarly, he would appoint governors for towns that had fallen into Muslim hands and commanders for armed parties heading for battle. At times, he would say, 'Your commander is so-and-so, and if he is killed, so-and-so, and if he is killed, so-and-so'. Given such a method, how can it be believed that, when he journeyed to the afterlife, he named no one to succeed him?

In sum, one who looks deeply into the sublime goals of Islam and of the magnificent figure who brought it to us will, beyond a doubt, affirm that the issues of the imamate and the guardianship (*wilaya*) have been fully resolved and clarified.

THE MESSENGER NAMES HIS SUCCESSOR
In regard to the question of the guardianship and governance of the Muslims' affairs after his time, the Most Noble Messenger (peace and blessings upon him and his family) did not content himself with general discussions. Rather, he directly addressed the question from the first day of his mission, right along with such questions as the nature of *tauhid* and prophecy. What he

did was to proclaim 'Ali (upon whom be peace) the guardian of religious and civil matters and his successor in all Muslim affairs.

According to widely accepted accounts, on the very day that the Most Noble Messenger (peace and blessings upon him and his family) was first charged with public summons to the faith, he called together his relations, and assembled them; there he disclosed, confirmed, and established the Commander of the Faithful 'Ali's (upon whom be peace) position of minister, guardian, and successor. Additionally, during the last days of his life, at Ghadir Khumm, in the midst of one hundred and twenty thousand people, he seized the hand of 'Ali (upon whom be peace) and raised it aloft, saying, 'For whomever I am leader, 'Ali is leader'.

Apart from all this, the Most Noble Messenger (peace and blessings upon him and his family) has referred to the Imams who were to succeed him by number, name, and other qualities.

In a well-known account narrated by both Shi'i and Sunni sources, the Most Noble Messenger (peace and blessings upon him and his family) says, 'The Imams are twelve in number and all belong to the Quraysh'. Then he lists their names one after the other. In another account, he tells Jabir ibn 'Abdullah Ansari, 'You will live to see the fifth Imam; convey my greetings to him'.

Furthermore, the Most Noble Messenger (peace and blessings upon him and his family) specifically appointed the Commander of the Faithful 'Ali (upon whom be peace) as his successor. 'Ali (upon whom be peace) in turn named his own successor, as did each subsequent Imam.

THE INFALLIBILITY OF THE IMAM
These accounts make it clear that, like the Messenger, the Imam must be free of sin and error. Otherwise, the religious summons would be defective, and divine guidance would lose its effect.

THE IMAM'S MORAL VIRTUES

The Imam must possess such moral virtues as courage and valour, chastity, magnanimity, and justice, because one who is infallible must act according to all religious laws, and the religion requires good moral qualities. The Imam must excel all other people in moral excellence, because it would be meaningless for one to lead his moral equal or superior, and certainly that would be inconsistent with divine justice.

KNOWLEDGE OF THE IMAM

Since the Imam is in charge of the religion and the leader of the world's people, it is necessary that he know about everything that bears on human needs and human happiness in this world and the next. That a leader in the sense should be ignorant is contrary to reason and meaningless in respect to general divine guidance.

THE FOURTEEN INFALLIBLE PERSONS

The Most Noble Messenger (peace and blessings upon him and his family), Fatima (upon whom be peace), and the twelve Imams (upon whom be peace) are called the fourteen infallible persons, and, among them, the first five — the Most Noble Messenger (peace and blessings upon him and his family), 'Ali, Fatima, Hasan, and Husayn (upon whom be peace) — are known as the people of the cloak, because the Most Noble Messenger (peace and blessings upon him and his family) once drew a cloak over his head and gathered the four others under it. There he prayed, and God Most High revealed the Verse of Purification concerning them: *'Allah wills to remove impurity from you, People of the House, and purify you thoroughly'* (33:33).

THE IMAMS OF GUIDANCE, UPON WHOM BE PEACE

The Imams of guidance, who succeed the Most Noble Messenger (peace and blessings upon him and his family) as leaders of the people in religious and civic affairs, are twelve in number:

1. The Commander of the Faithful 'Ali ibn Abi Talib (upon whom be peace)

2. Imam Hasan Mujtaba (upon whom be peace)

3. Imam Husayn, Lord of the Martyrs (upon whom be peace)

4. Imam Sajjad (upon whom be peace)

5. Imam Muhammad Baqir (upon whom be peace)

6. Imam Ja'far as-Sadiq (upon whom be peace)

7. Imam Musa Kazim (upon whom be peace)

8. Imam Riza (upon whom be peace)

9. Imam Muhammad Taqi (upon whom be peace)

10. Imam 'Ali an-Naqi (upon whom be peace)

11. Imam Hasan 'Askari (upon whom be peace)

12. The Imam Mahdi or Imam of the Age, Muhammad ibn Hasan (upon whom be peace)

THE CONDUCT OF THE HEIRS

The Heirs (upon whom be peace) are perfect exemplars of the Most Noble Messenger's (peace and blessings upon him and his family) teachings; their conduct is precisely his conduct.

Of course, over the period of two hundred and fifty years from 11 A.H. (the year of the Most Noble Messenger's [peace and blessings upon him and his family] death) to 260 A.H. (the year of the occultation of the Imam Mahdi), during which the Imams associated with the people, the social environment underwent significant changes, as did the outward manner of life of the Imams. They did not, however, abandon the essential object of the Most Noble Messenger's (peace and blessings upon him and his family) method, which consisted in preserving the principles of the religion with their implementations from alteration, and in doing everything possible to educate the people.

The twenty-three years of the Most Noble Messenger's (peace

and blessings upon him and his family) mission fell into three distinct phases. The first three years were a time of secret promulgation; the next ten years were a period of open promulgation, in which, however, the Most Noble Messenger (peace and blessings upon him and his family) and his followers were subjected to intense persecution and likewise lacked the freedom of action to effect clear reforms in society; and the last ten years (after the Hijra) found the Most Noble Messenger (peace and blessings upon him and his family) in an environment where he could most fully realize his goals of putting the truth into practice, dramatically advancing the cause of Islam, and imparting fresh realizations to the people by the day.

Plainly, these three different environments each had their own exigencies and displayed the Most Noble Messenger's (peace and blessings upon him and his family) conduct in varying ways.

The various environments with which the Imams were faced all had something in common with that of the Most Noble Messenger's (peace and blessings upon him and his family) mission before the Hijra. Sometimes they resembled the first three years of the prophetic mission, in which no sort of demonstration of the truth was possible. Then the Imams had to carry out their task with the greatest caution. This is true of the time of the fourth Imam and the end of the period of the sixth Imam. Sometimes they most resembled the ten years prior to the Hijra, when the Most Noble Messenger (peace and blessings upon him and his family) openly promulgated the faith in Mecca, but he and his followers were severely persecuted under a regime to which they could not mount an effective challenge. Then the Imam openly taught religious concepts and promulgated rules, but he was unable to avoid persecution, and new difficulties were created every day.

If there was a time somewhat resembling the period after the Hijra, it was that of the caliphate of the Commander of the Faithful 'Ali (upon whom be peace), and a portion of the lifetimes of Fatima, Imam Hasan, and Imam Husayn (upon whom be peace) — the last of these in particular was all too brief, a time mirroring the days of the Most Noble Messenger (peace and blessings upon him and his family), when the truth showed forth unveiled.

In sum, it may be said that, except as I have indicated, the Imams never had the power of open, radical opposition to the tyrannical rulers and governors of their time. Accordingly, they were obliged to adopt the policy known as *taqiyya* — dissimulation, concealment of their true aims by their speech and actions — in order to avoid giving the governments of their time a pretext for further repressive actions. Even so, their enemies on all sides sought for any possible pretext to extinguish the light of guidance and eliminate all trace of the Imams.

HOW THE IMAMS WERE DIFFERENT FROM THE GOVERNMENTS OF THEIR TIME

The various governments that arose in Islamic society after the time of the Most Noble Messenger (peace and blessings upon him and his family) and called themselves Islamic were all fundamentally at odds with the Heirs (upon whom be peace), and their implacable enmity to the truth is a strand of history that never ended.

To the Most Noble Messenger (peace and blessings upon him and his family), one of the most important virtues of the Heirs was their special understanding of the teachings of the Noble Qur'an and of what is permitted and what is forbidden. This should have been enough to earn them the highest respect and veneration of the Muslim community. But that community has not uniformly extended the respect that their station demands.

Recall that, on the first day that he announced his mission, when he first called upon his relations to embrace Islam, the Most Noble Messenger (peace and blessings upon him and his family) named 'Ali (upon whom be peace) as his successor, as he clearly did toward the end of his life at Ghadir Khumm and on other occasions. After his death, however, people chose others to succeed him; the Heirs (upon whom be peace) were deprived of what was rightfully theirs, and in consequence the rulers of the day saw them as dangerous rivals. They were terrified of them and so tried to assassinate them whenever opportunities arose.

The most profound source of difference between the Heirs and these govenments lay in the fact that the Heirs considered an Islamic State to be obliged to preserve and carry out the divine laws of Islam, whereas, as we can see from their actions, these governments did not consider it necessary to observe these laws fully or to model their conduct on that of the Most Noble Messenger (peace and blessings upon him and his family).

In several places in the Noble Qur'an, God Most High forbade the Most Noble Messenger (peace and blessings upon him and his family) and his followers to alter God's laws and warned them against the least inclination contrary to any of them. The Most Noble Messenger (peace and blessings upon him and his family), too, adopted a mode of conduct fully conforming to these unalterable laws, making no distinctions as to time, place, and person in carrying them out.

To observe these laws and enforce them no matter who was involved was incumbent upon everyone, including the Most Noble Messenger (peace and blessings upon him and his family). The *Shari'ah*, as these laws are collectively known, was in force and effect everywhere.

Because of this prevailing justice and equality, all distinctions among people had been effaced. The Most Noble Messenger (peace and blessings upon him and his family), who was ruler and to whom God commanded obedience, assumed no distinctions in his personal or social life and enjoyed no luxuries. He established no official ceremonies and did not parade his greatness before the people. He did not try to create an atmosphere of glory and awe around himself and was not recognizable by any special emblems from those around him.

None of the various social classes sought to elevate itself above the others through special distinctions. Man and woman, noble and humble, rich and poor, powerful and weak, city dweller and villager, slave and free, black and white all stood on the same footing. Everyone was charged with performing their religious obligations; everyone was free of having to submit to the powerful and to tyrants.

If we consider the matter a little, it grows clear to us (especially concerning all the experience from the time of the Most Noble Messenger [peace and blessings upon him and his family] to the present) that the sole object of the Most Noble Messenger (peace and blessings upon him and his family) in his pure conduct was that the divine laws of Islam be carried out among the people in a fair and equitable way, as well as be preserved from alteration and corruption. The governments that followed, however, did not conform to the conduct of the Most Noble Messenger (peace and blessings upon him and his family) but totally altered his methods. This had the following consequences:

1. Almost overnight, extreme class distinctions returned to the Islamic society, which became divided into two groups: the powerful and the weak. The very lives of the one group and all they possessed became playthings for the other group.

2. The Muslim governments gradually altered Islamic laws and refused to carry out these laws and rules, sometimes in the name of the welfare of Islamic society and sometimes in that of security and State policy. They went further in this course by the day, and matters reached a point at which the organizations that bore the name of Islamic government felt themselves under no compunction to observe and carry out Islamic laws. The fate of laws is plain when there is no proper authority to enforce them.

In brief, the fact that the Muslim governments contemporary with the Heirs (upon whom be peace) tampered with Islamic laws and rules to suit their own short-term interests and the results of this tampering set these governments' conduct completely at odds with that of the Most Noble Messenger (peace and blessings upon him and his family). By contrast, the Heirs (upon whom be peace) recognized that the order of the Noble Qur'an to conform to the conduct of the Most Noble Messenger (peace and blessings upon him and his family) is binding for all time.

This basic contradiction led directly to these governments' relentless attacks on the Heirs (upon whom be peace) and willingness to use any means available to attempt to silence them.

The Heirs (upon whom be peace), too, in accordance with their divine duty, went on working to promulgate the real religion and educate pious people in spite of all the difficulties they faced and the schemes of intransigent enemies.

In order to see the truth of this, it is sufficient to take a look at the historical record and see how large the Shi'i population was during the five years of the Commander of the Faithful 'Ali's caliphate. Of course, this large population had built up over his twenty-five years of seclusion. Similarly, the Shi'is who visited Imam Baqir (upon whom be peace) in huge numbers had been quietly educated by Imam Sajjad (upon whom be peace), and the hundreds of thousands of Shi'is and adherents to the Heirs who were associated with Imam Riza (May God be well pleased with him) were reaping the fruits of spiritual teachings that Imam Musa ibn Ja'far had sown in a dark prison cell.

Finally, through the continued educational efforts of the Heirs, the Shi'is grew from a handful of people at the time of the Most Noble Messenger's (peace and blessings upon him and his family) death to a tremendous number at the end of the Imams' era.

WHAT WAS EXCEPTIONAL ABOUT THE METHOD OF THE HEIRS

As I have noted, the Heirs of the Prophet passed their lifetimes under oppressive conditions and discharged their responsibilities under conditions of *taqiyya* in extremely difficult circumstances. Only four of them were able to operate freely, without *taqiyya*, and that for a very short time. Here I will briefly survey the lives of the Heirs (upon whom be peace).

'ALI

The Commander of the Faithful 'Ali ibn Abi Talib (upon whom be peace) was the first perfect exemplar of the teachings of the Most Noble Messenger (peace and blessings upon him and his family).

'Ali (upon whom be peace) was raised by the Most Noble Messenger (peace and blessings upon him and his family) from early childhood and followed him like a shadow until the very end of the latter's life. He was like a moth before the prophetic flame; the final moment when he was separated from the Most Noble Messenger (peace and blessings upon him and his family) was when he embraced his corpse and laid it to rest.

'Ali has a universal character, and one may venture to say that more has been said about this great figure than about any other figure in history. Scholars and writers — both Shi'i and Sunni, both Muslim and non-Muslim — have written more than a thousand books about his character.

Notwithstanding the vast amount of research that friend and foe have carried out about this figure, no one has succeeded in finding an Achilles heel to his faith or in faulting his courage, chastity, spiritual culture, sense of justice, or other virtues, because he was one to whom everything but virtue and perfection was foreign.

As history testifies, among all those who held power since the death of the Most Noble Messenger (peace and blessings upon him and his family), 'Ali (upon whom be peace) is the only one who acted in accordance with the conduct of the Most Noble Messenger (peace and blessings upon him and his family) over the entire period he held power in Islamic society without deviating from it in the least and who carried out Islamic laws just as they were carried out in the Most Noble Messenger's (peace and blessings upon him and his family) time without any tampering.

After the death of the second caliph, and according to his instructions, a six-member committee was formed to appoint a new caliph. After prolonged discussion, the choice had been narrowed to 'Ali (upon whom be peace) and 'Uthman. The caliphate was offered to 'Ali, on condition that he 'observe the conduct of the first and second caliphs among the people'. He declined, saying, 'I will not advance a step beyond what I know to be true'. Then the position was offered to 'Uthman with the same condition, and he accepted it. After he assumed the office, however, he adopted an altogether different course.

'Ali (upon whom be peace) was unrivaled among the Most Noble Messenger's (peace and blessings upon him and his family) companions in heroism, self-sacrifice, and self-efface-ment in service of the Truth. It is undeniable that, if this self-sacrificing hero of Islam had not lived, the *mushriks* could readily have snuffed out the light of prophecy on any number of occasions: on the night of the Hijra, or at the Battles of Badr, Uhud, the Trench, Khaybar.

From the first day he emerged into society, 'Ali (upon whom be peace) lived very simply. During and after the Most Noble Messenger's (peace and blessings upon him and his family) life and even during the time he was caliph, 'Ali (upon whom be peace) lived, dressed, and ate like the poorest of the poor. He said, 'One holding power in a society should live in a way that consoles the needy and those in distress, not in a way that makes them envious and breaks their hearts'. The day he was martyred, although he ruled the entire Islamic domain, he had only 700 dirhams, with which he was going to employ a household servant.

'Ali (upon whom be peace) worked for a living, doing farm work by preference. He also planted trees and dug canals. Whatever he acquired by these means, as well as his abundant booty from battles, he distributed to the poor. He set aside any land he developed as a trust, or he sold it and gave the proceeds to the needy. One year while he was caliph, he ordered that the income from his trust properties be shown to him and then spent. When it was amassed, it amounted to 4,000 gold dinars.

In all the battles in which 'Ali (upon whom be peace) participated, he never faced a rival without overpowering him. Never did he show his back to an enemy. He said, 'If the whole Arab nation were to oppose me and do battle with me, I would not back down. I have no fear'.

Notwithstanding the fact that no one in history approaches 'Ali in bravery, there was no limit to his kindness, sensitivity, and generosity of spirit. He never killed women, children, or those helpless in battle. He never made captives; he never pursued those who fled. During the Battle of Siffin, Mu'awiya's army took the offensive and occupied the bank of the Euphrates.[1] They cut off 'Ali's army's approach to this vital source of water. When later, through bloody battle, 'Ali's army gained control of the river bank, he ordered that the enemy have access to the water.

While he was caliph, 'Ali admitted everyone without any doorman or other intermediary. He went about on foot, visiting the markets and lanes, enjoining people to be pious and to observe each other's rights. He came to the aid of the indigent and widows kindly and humbly. He sheltered homeless orphans in his own home and personally provided for their needs and educated them.

'Ali (upon whom be peace) poured much energy into promulgating knowledge, which he prized greatly. As he said, 'There is no ailment like ignorance'. During the bloody Battle of the Camel, he was arraying his forces when an Arab approached and asked, 'What is the meaning of *tauhid*?' People expostulated on all sides, 'What kind of time is this for such a question?' 'Ali (upon whom be peace) held them back from the Arab, saying,

'We do battle for the very purpose of establishing such truths'. Then he took the Arab in tow and explained the concept to him in compelling terms while continuing to marshal his troops.

Another story comes to us from the Battle of Siffin that likewise shows 'Ali's (upon whom be peace) extraordinary religious discipline and divine power. While the two armies had surged against each other like two foaming seas and blood was spilling everywhere, he reached one of his soldiers and asked for some water to drink. The soldier brought forth a wooden cup, filled it with water, and proffered it. 'Ali (upon whom be peace), seeing a crack in the cup, said, 'To drink water from such a cup is disapproved in Islam'. The soldier responded, 'In such a situation, standing under a rain of enemy arrows and swords, we have no leisure for such fine points'. The answer he received, in short, was: 'We battle so that just such religious ordinances will be enforced. There is no such thing as major and minor ordinances'.

'Ali (upon whom be peace) was the first person after the Most Noble Messenger (peace and blessings upon him and his family) to approach spiritual realities in the manner of philosophical reflection, that is, by free exercise of reason. He used many technical terms and laid out and organized the rules of Arabic grammar in order to protect the Noble Qur'an from copyists' errors.

The exact scholarship, spiritual culture, and consideration of ethical, social, political, and even mathematical problems shown in 'Ali's (upon whom be peace) discourses, letters, and other documents that have reached us are astonishing.

The wealth of these documents makes 'Ali (upon whom be peace) the best known individual among Muslims to have a full realization of the sublime goals of the Noble Qur'an and the critical and practical concepts of Islam as they should be realized. They testify to the soundness of the Prophetic saying, 'I am the city of knowledge, and 'Ali is its gate'. Furthermore, he combined this knowledge with action.

In short, 'Ali's outstanding character is beyond description, and his virtues are innumerable. Never in history has someone's character drawn the attention of the world's scholars and thinkers to such an extent.

FATIMA, THE MAGNIFICENT, THE MOST TRUE

Fatima was the beloved daughter of the Most Noble Messenger (peace and blessings upon him and his family). She gained her father's deepest affection through her profound knowledge, faith, piety, virtues, and fine qualities.

Because of her knowledge, asceticism, and worship, her father gave her the title of the 'Foremost among Women' (*Sayyidat an-Nisa*). The Most Noble Messenger (peace and blessings upon him and his family) said, 'Fatima's pleasure is my pleasure, and my pleasure is God's pleasure. Fatima's anger is my anger, and my anger is God's anger'.

Fatima was born of Khadija in the sixth year of prophetic mission. She married the Commander of the Faithful 'Ali in the second year of the Hijra and died three months and some days after the death of her father.

In her life, she always placed God's pleasure above her own. She brought up her children and apportioned the household chores between herself and her servant, assigning them one day to herself and the next to the servant. She addressed problems affecting Muslim women and spent her free time in worship. She retained only what was absolutely necessary of her private means, particularly the bountiful income from Fadak (a village near Khaybar), spending the rest in God's way, and sometimes giving her day's provisions to the poor and leaving herself hungry. The extended discourse she gave to the Companions and other Muslims at the Prophet's Mosque, her remonstrations to the first caliph when he had ordered her Fadak properties confiscated, and her other recorded discourses and remarks bespeak a great courageous and constant spirit.

Fatima was the beloved daughter of the Most Noble Messenger (peace and blessings upon him and his family), the wife of the Commander of the Faithful 'Ali (upon whom be peace), and the mother to eleven Imams of Islam. All the descendants of the Most Noble Messenger (peace and blessings upon him and his family) are her descendants. She is accorded the station of infallibility according to the text of the Noble Qur'an.

IMAM HASAN AND IMAM HUSAYN

These two illustrious figures are brothers, sons of 'Ali and Fatima (upon whom be peace). The Most Noble Messenger (peace and blessings upon him and his family) loved them to excess and called them his sons, not bearing to see them uncomfortable or unhappy. He said, 'These two sons of mine are Imams standing up or sitting'. The phrase 'standing up or sitting' is an allusion to Husayn's open claim to the caliphate and uprising and war with the enemies of the faith, and Hasan's abstention from these. He also said, 'Hasan and Husayn are the two leaders of the youths of Paradise'.

In accordance with the testament of his grandfather, Imam Hasan was chosen for the caliphate. The people swore their allegiance, and for six months he had charge of the affairs of the Islamic lands, except for Syria and Egypt, where Mu'awiya held sway. He modeled his conduct on that of his father.

During that period, Imam Hasan raised an army to quell Mu'awiya's revolt, but it finally grew clear to him that the people had been taken in by Mu'awiya and that the heads of his army were in correspondence with Mu'awiya and awaiting Mu'awiya's orders to kill or arrest him. Thus he was compelled to propose a truce.

Imam Hasan made such a truce with Mu'awiya, who failed to abide by its conditions. After the pact was concluded, Mu'awiya came to Iraq. He mounted the pulpit before assembled Muslims and proclaimed, 'I did not fight with you for the sake of the religion, so that you would pray or fast. I wanted to rule you, and now I have obtained my object'. Then he said, 'The pact I concluded with Hasan is now under my feet'.

After the conclusion of the truce, Imam Hasan (upon whom be peace) lived about nine and one-half years under Mu'awiya's domination, in bleak circumstances and under bitterly oppressive conditions. He enjoyed no personal safety, even within his own home; finally his own wife Ju'da poisoned him at Mu'awiya's instigation.

After Imam Hasan's martyrdom, his brother Imam Husayn (upon whom be peace) succeeded him as guide to the people by God's command and in accordance with his last will. But conditions did not change; Mu'awiya was calling the shots and managed to cut off all of Imam Husayn's opportunities.

After about three and one-half years, Mu'awiya died, and the caliphate, which had degenerated into a sultanate, passed to his son Yazid. Yazid, by contrast with his hypocritical father, was drunk with conceit and openly indulged in revelry, indecent acts, and rowdiness. As soon as this vain youth assumed control of Muslim affairs, he ordered his governor in Medina to extract an oath of allegiance from Imam Husayn or else to send back his head. When the governor demanded the oath, Imam Husayn stalled for time. He set out for Mecca with his party by night and sought refuge in God's Sanctuary, which is a recognized place of refuge in Islam. After staying there for some months, he realized that Yazid would not relent, and, unless he gave the oath, he would surely be killed. Then too, thousands of letters had arrived from Iraq over these months pledging support and urging him to rise against the Umayyad oppressors.

Imam Husayn understood from his own experience and from indications and the prevailing social climate that an uprising on his part would not succeed. Nonetheless, he resolved to refuse the oath and to fight to the death. He set out with his party for Kufa in a state of revolt. En route, on the plain of Karbala (about seventy kilometers from Kufa), he encountered a large enemy force.

Imam Husayn had called upon no one to join him in his fateful journey and had expressed to members of his party his firm resolve to meet martyrdom, giving them the choice to part company with him. In consequence, on the day he faced the enemy army, he was accompanied by an insignificant number who were committed and resigned to their fate. Thus the enemy army tightly encircled them without difficulty and cut off even their water. There they were caught between the oath of allegiance and death.

Imam Husayn did not submit to the oath but prepared for death. One day, he and his party fought the enemy from the morning until the afternoon; in that battle he, his sons, his nephews, his cousin, and his other companions were martyred, numbering about seventy in all. Only his dear son Imam Sajjad, who was too ill to fight, remained alive.

After martyring Imam Husayn (upon whom be peace), the enemy force plundered his goods and placed his family in captivity, sending them on from Karbala to Kufa and from Kufa to Damascus along with the severed heads of the martyrs.

During this period of captivity, Imam Sajjad (upon whom be peace) and Zaynab, Imam Husayn's sister, made a series of speeches that laid bare the truth about the Umayyad tyranny for all the world to see. Imam Sajjad (upon whom be peace) gave a notable sermon in Damascus, and Zaynab made a series of public speeches in Kufa including speeches at the Kufan governor Ibn Ziyad's assemblies and a speech in the presence of Yazid in Damascus.

In any event, Imam Husayn's uprising against the unbridled tyranny and injustice of the Umayyads, which, as we have seen, resulted in his and his relations' and friends' martyrdom, the plunder of his worldly goods, and captivity for his wife and child, was a memorable occurrence, the like of which cannot be found in the pages of history. One may venture to say that Islam owes its survival to this event; if it had not happened, the Umayyads would have eradicated all trace of Islam.

WERE THE METHODS OF IMAM HASAN AND IMAM HUSAYN DIFFERENT?

Although the Most Noble Messenger (peace and blessings upon him and his family) has named both of these outstanding figures as rightful Imams, their methods appear to be different. Some have gone so far as to say that the two brothers had such contrasting outlooks that one made peace when he had forty thousand fighting men at his disposal, while the other fought to the death, losing his infant son and companions, when he had only forty (apart from his family) in his company.

A careful scrutiny, however, proves the contrary of this view. We see that, whereas Imam Hasan (upon whom be peace) lived through about nine and one-half years of Mu'awiya's reign without openly opposing him, Imam Husayn (upon whom be peace) too spent about the same amount of time under Mu'awiya's rule after his brother was martyred without rising up in rebellion or open opposition.

Accordingly, one must seek for the real source of this apparent difference in the different policies of Mu'awiya and Yazid, not in any different outlooks of the two great Imams.

Mu'awiya's policy was not founded on immoderation; he did not openly jeer at religious law. Mu'awiya presented himself as one of the companions and a scribe of the revelation. Because his sister was one of the Most Noble Messenger's (peace and blessings upon him and his family) wives, known as the Mother of the Faithful, he called himself the Uncle of the Faithful. He had been carefully groomed by the second caliph, who enjoyed the full trust and highest esteem of the people.

Additionally, Mu'awiya generally appointed companions of the Prophet, who enjoyed the respect and veneration of the people (such as Abu Hurayra, 'Amr ibn 'As, Samra, Yusr, and Mughira ibn Shu'ba), to governmental and other sensitive positions in the nation and thus gained public confidence. Numerous stories were circulated among the people about the virtues of these companions, their privileged religious state, their being forgiven whatever they did, and so forth. Thus, whatever Mu'awiya did, if it could be rationalized and justified, these cohorts would undertake to rationalize and justify it, and if not, they would attempt to silence the protests, first with substantial bribes, and, failing that, by murder: tens of thousands of innocent followers of 'Ali (upon whom be peace), other Muslims, and even companions of the Most Noble Messenger (peace and blessings upon him and his family) were killed.

In everything he did, Mu'awiya maintained a facade of religiosity. He also maintained an attitude of patient forbearance and gained the people's affection and compliance through his mildness of manner. He would even answer verbal abuse and contentiousness with good cheer and generosity; this was the backdrop for his policies.

He extended outward signs of respect to Imam Hasan and Imam Husayn and sent them expensive gifts, but he likewise publicly proclaimed that whoever transmitted a Prophetic saying praising the Heirs (upon whom be peace) would stand to forfeit his life and property, whereas whoever transmitted such a saying praising the companions of the Prophet would gain a reward.

He ordered preachers in Muslim pulpits to curse 'Ali (upon whom be peace) and ordered his supporters to be killed wherever they were found. The order was carried out with such zeal that many of 'Ali's enemies were killed on accusation of being among his sympathizers.

The foregoing makes it clear that for Imam Hasan (upn whom be peace) to lead an uprising could only be to the detriment of Islam; it could have no other result than the senseless spilling of his blood and that of his supporters. It is even conceivable that Mu'awiya would have employed people associated with him to kill him and then put on a show of bereavement to appease public sentiment. Then he could conduct a massacre of Shi'is in supposed reprisal and revenge for the Imam's death, such as he had before in the case of 'Uthman.

Yazid's political style, however, bore no resemblance to that of his father. He was a self-satisfied abandoned youth who knew no logic but force and gave no thought to public opinion.

In the first year of his reign, he massacred the descendants of the Most Noble Messenger (peace and blessings upon him and his family).

In the second year, he sacked Medina and left his soldiers free to kill and plunder for three days.

In the third year, he destroyed the Ka'aba.

Thus Husayn's uprising won an ever-deepening and more openly expressed public sympathy, which at first took the form of bloody revolts and gradually led to a vast number of Muslims acting on their native love of the truth and emerging as adherents to the Heirs.

This was why Mu'awiya had enjoined Yazid not to act against Husayn (upon whom be peace). But do you suppose that Yazid's intoxication and egomania would allow him to see where his own self-interest lay?

IMAM SAJJAD

Imam Sajjad (upon whom be peace) followed two different methods at different periods of his Imamate, both of which correspond to methods generally pursued by other Imams.

Imam Sajjad (upon whom be peace) participated in Imam Husayn's uprising and accompanied his father to Karbala, being a witness to the tragic event. After his father's martyrdom, he was made captive and taken from Karbala to Kufa and from Kufa to Damascus. Throughout his captivity, he never resorted to *taqiyya* but always spoke out and made the truth known. His speeches and protests on necessary occasions made manifest the worthiness and glory of the Most Noble Messenger's (peace and blessings upon him and his family) Heirs, the cruel injustice suffered by his father, and the enormities perpetrated by the Umayyad regime. They opened the floodgates of popular sentiment.

After he was released from captivity and returned to Medina, however, moving from a dangerous environment to a peaceful one, he secluded himself, closed his door to strangers, and occupied himself with worship and with quietly educating persons who followed the true way. Over the thirty-five years of his residence there, he directly or indirectly educated a large number of people and imbued them with Islamic culture.

All the invocations that Imam Sajjad delivered from the pulpit in his celestial style have been collected into a work called *Safihe-ye Sajjadiya*. They include all the sublime teachings of Islam.

IMAM MUHAMMAD BAQIR

It was possible to an extent to promulgate the religious sciences during the Imamate of Imam Baqir. Because of the exertions of the Umayyads, Prophetic sayings about the Heirs had been generally lost. Although thousands of sayings would be needed as the basis of law, barely five hundred of those transmitted by the companions had survived.

To make a long story short, as a final outcome of the events at Karbala, and because of Imam Sajjad's thirty-five years of exertions, there was a host of Shi'is in society, who were in desperate need of guidance in matters of Islamic jurisprudence.

And since, because of internal dissension and the general softness and inadequacy of its leadership, the Umayyad dynasty was crumbling, the fifth Imam was able to make use of the time to promulgate the sciences imparted to the Heirs and Islamic jurisprudence. He trained many fine scholars in the traditions of his school of thought.

IMAM JA'FAR SADIQ

In the era of the sixth Imam (upon whom be peace), the times were even more propitious for the dissemination of the Islamic sciences. For one thing, in consequence of Imam Muhammad

Baqir's promulgation of authentic Prophetic sayings, and because of the outreach efforts by his students, the people better understood their need for authentic Islamic culture and were hungry to hear these sayings.

For another thing, the Umayyad dynasty had fallen, and the 'Abbasid dynasty had not yet fully established itself. Also, the 'Abbasid clan was still displaying friendship toward the Heirs, since they had ridden the wave of anti-Umayyad sentiment to power, invoking the cruelties borne by the Heirs and the blood of the martyrs of Karbala.

Imam Ja'far (upon whom be peace) undertook to promulgate various sciences, and scholars swarmed to his door from all over to pose questions about various facets of Islamic culture, ethics, and the lives of the Prophets and the Imams, and to hear his answers, to gain the benefit of his wisdom and counsel.

Imam Ja'far (upon whom be peace) held discussions with people in all walks of life and debated representatives of various sects. He fostered students in the various sciences and published hundreds of books containing Prophetic sayings and scholarly studies that are collectively known as the *Usul*.

Making use of the brief respite available to him in that suffocating time, he trained thousands of students and disclosed priceless treasure-hoards of Islamic sciences and culture. More than forty thousand scholars availed themselves of this abundant source of learning.

Imam Ja'far instructed his students to write down his teachings and commit his own writings to memory. He said, 'A time of disorder will come and many works will be lost. Then you will need these books and writings; they will be the only source to which Muslims can refer for questions of science and religion'. Accordingly, his students brought pen and ink and wrote down whatever they heard in his assemblies.

Imam Ja'far spent every hour of his life (except when resting) teaching in public or private and making his boundless wealth of knowledge available to everyone.

In sum, the wonderful discourses and invaluable guidance lifted the curtain of ignorance and re-established the true religion of the Most Noble Messenger (peace and blessings upon him and his family). For this reason, he is regarded as the founder of the Shi'i path, which since his time has been known as the Ja'fari school of thought.

IMAM MUSA KAZIM

After overthrowing the Umayyad government and seizing the caliphate, the 'Abbasids homed in on the descendants of Fatima and threw all their might into eradicating the progeny of the Most Noble Messenger (peace and blessings upon him and his family). They beheaded them, they buried them alive, they buried them in the foundations of buildings. They burned down the sixth Imam's house, and they summoned him to Iraq for interrogation a number of times. Accordingly, toward the end of the sixth Imam's life, the necessity for *taqiyya* grew more stringent, and, since he was under close surveillance, he admitted only a few elect Shi'as. Finally, he was martyred — poisoned — by order of the second 'Abbasid caliph, Mansur. Thus the tenure of the seventh Imam, Imam Musa Kazim (upon whom be peace) began under the most intense and mounting pressure from his enemies.

Despite the most stringent need for caution and *taqiyya*, he engaged in promulgating the religious sciences and made many Prophetic sayings available to the Shi'as, to the extent that he left more teachings on jurisprudence than any other Imam, with the exceptions of the fifth and sixth Imams. Because of the stringent conditions, most of the accounts he transmitted were attributed to such fictitious figures as 'the Scholar' and 'Abd as-Salih', not explicitly to Imam Musa.

Imam Musa (upon whom be peace) was contemporary with the four 'Abbasid caliphs Mansur, Hadi, Mahdi, and Harun. They kept him under continual pressure. Finally, Harun ordered him imprisoned. For years, he was tranferred from prison to prison, and he was in prison when he was finally poisoned and martyred.

IMAM RIZA

Anyone who gives informed and fair consideration to the history of those times will perceive that, however much the Heirs (upon whom be peace) were tortured and oppressed by the caliphs of their time and by other enemies, the numbers and conviction of their followers grew in proportion. To these people, the caliphate was nothing but a vile and tainted institution.

These caliphs half-consciously accepted this perception and were actually incapacitated by it. After Ma'mun, the seventh 'Abbasid caliph and a contemporary of Imam Riza (upon whom be peace) murdered his brother Amin and assumed office, he conceived a scheme for ridding himself of this psychological torment and for putting a stop to the spread of Shi'ism at one stroke, without using force.

To implement this object, he proposed to appoint Imam Riza (upon whom be peace) his successor, so that the Imam would be tainted in the eyes of the Shi'a by the decadent institution of the caliphate. Thus belief in the greatness and purity of the Imams would be expunged from their minds. The special character of the Imamate, the basis of the Shi'i school of thought, would cease to exist, and so the sect would disintegrate all by itself.

Such a policy would have another beneficial consequence, that of putting a stop to the continual uprisings of Fatima's descendants aimed at overthrowing the 'Abbasid caliphate. After seeing the transfer of the office to their own line, they would naturally refrain from further bloody uprisings. Of course, after implementing this policy, Ma'mun would find it easy to dispose of Imam Riza (upon whom be peace).

Ma'mun offered the Imam first the caliphate directly and then the succession. After encouragement, urging, and finally threats,

Imam Riza (upon whom be peace) agreed on condition that he be excused from dismissals, appointments, and other involvements in matters of State.

Making the most of this circumstance, the Imam extended guidance to the people, imparting priceless elucidations of Islamic culture and spiritual truths (in which Ma'mun evinced a strong interest), which have survived in numbers roughly equal to those reaching us from the Commander of the Faithful (upon whom be peace) and in greater numbers than those of any other Imam.

One of the special graces of the eighth Imam lay in the fact that Shi'as brought many sayings attributed to the Heirs to him, and he identified and rejected numerous fabricated accounts that had been introduced by ill-intentioned people.

An official journey the Imam made as the designated successor from Medina to Marv excited an amazing outpouring of popular support all along the way, especially in Iran. People thronged around him night and day, sometimes having travelled great distances, to learn religious law and culture.

The Imam's unprecedented popularity indicated to Ma'mun that he had made a serious miscalculation. In order to mend the breach in his policies, he martyred the Imam by having him poisoned and so returned to the long-time policies of the caliphs toward the Heirs and their adherents, the Shi'as.

IMAM MUHAMMAD TAQI, IMAM 'ALI AN-NAQI, AND IMAM HASAN 'ASKARI

These three great Imams all lived under much the same conditions. After the martyrdom of Imam Riza (upon whom be peace), Ma'mun summoned the Imam's only son, Muhammad Taqi, to Baghdad. He treated him kindly, giving him his daughter in marriage, and kept him there with full honors.

Although this behaviour appears friendly, Ma'mun was pursuing his same policy by keeping the Imam under close surveillance in every respect. Likewise, the residence of Imam 'Ali an-Naqi and Imam Hasan 'Askari in Samarra, then the 'Abbasid capital, was in fact designed as a detention.

The total time these three great figures held the Imamate was fifty-seven years. During their time, the number of Shi'i Muslims in Iran, Iraq, and Syria reached the hundreds of thousands and included thousands of trained collectors of traditions. Nonetheless, very few sayings are attributed to these three Imams. They did not live very long lives, either — the ninth Imam was martyred at the age of twenty-five; the tenth, at age forty; and the eleventh, in his twenty-seventh year. This fact shows the crippling level of control the opposition was subjected to in those times. These Imams were not free to carry out their function. Nevertheless priceless sayings on the principles of religion have reached us from them.

THE IMAM OF THE AGE
AND PROMISED MAHDI

In the time of Imam Hasan 'Askari, the caliphate adopted a resolution to get rid of his successor by any means possible and so to put an end to the Imamate and, in consequence, the Shi'i sect. Imam 'Askari was put under an even stricter watch for this reason.

Accordingly, the birth of the Imam of the Age (upon whom be peace) was concealed, and he was kept hidden until he was six (so long as his father was alive). No one ever saw him except for a few select Shi'as.

After his father was martyred, by God's command he went into occultation, during a period known as the 'Lesser Occultation' (al-ghaybat as-sughra). During this period, four special deputies in succession would answer the questions of the Shi'as and resolve their problems. After that, the Imam went into the 'Greater Occultation' (al-ghaybat al-kubra), until a day when, by God's command, he will reappear to fill the world with justice as it is now filled with oppression.

Numerous traditions of the Most Noble Messenger (peace and blessings upon him and his family) and the Imams (upon whom be peace) have reached us by way of both Sunni and Shi'i traditionists on the personal characteristics of the Mahdi and the nature of his occultation. Also, numerous prominent Shi'as had the opportunity to meet with the Imam Mahdi, witness his beauty, and hear from his father the good news of his Imamhood.

Apart from this, in considering the topics of prophecy and the Imamate, we reached the conclusion that humanity can never lack for God's religion or for an Imam to safeguard it.

WHAT ETHICAL CONCLUSIONS MAY WE DRAW?

What we may conclude from such a brief survey of the history of God's prophets and religious leaders is that they were realistic men who would make any sacrifice to realize the truth, and who called upon all people to do likewise.

In other words, they strove to bring human individuals and societies to their just fruition. They sought to free people from the grip of ignorance and superstition and to grace them with correct ideas and beliefs. They wanted to see a humanity that was stained by the temperament of beasts, like predators that rend each other to fill their stomachs, elevated to the true nature of humanity and realizing it in their everyday lives to earn their true happiness.

These leaders, in other words, did not pursue their own individual happiness but devoted their lives to opening the road to happiness for human society. That is, they found their own happiness (which is everyone's real object) in working for the good of all, and they sought to help others to attain this same level, so that each would want for everyone what he wanted for himself, and not want for others what he did not want for himself.

It was through their relentless quest for reality and pursuit of the truth that these great figures realized how crucial it is for humankind to carry out the great mandate of universal compassion and all the lesser mandates that spring from it. They were especially endowed with the quality of self-sacrifice and unsparingly sacrificed their wealth and persons for the sake of the truth. They struck at the roots of every vice that springs from malevolence. They abstained from miserliness, shunned self-satisfaction, refused to lie, slandered no one, and made designs on no one's wealth or position. I treat these qualities and their consequences in the chapter on 'Ethics' below.

NOTES TO CHAPTER FIVE

1. Mu'awiya: the first caliph of the Umayyad dynasty (661-680 A.D.). For more on his and his successor's reigns, see pp.129-135. — Trans.

CHAPTER SIX

THE RESURRECTION

The resurrection is one of the three central principles of the holy religion of Islam, in which belief is incumbent. Everyone without exception knows the difference between the beneficent and the maleficent through his God-given conscience. Everyone knows that to do good is well and necessary (if not everyone carries this out) and that to do evil is undesirable and avoidance-worthy (if not everyone actually avoids it). There is no doubt that the good and evil of beneficence and maleficence are in the nature of consequences of these two qualities. There is likewise no doubt that the day never comes in this world when the beneficent and maleficent experience full consequences of their good and evil deeds. We see with our own eyes how many beneficent people spend their lives in utterly miserable circumstances, and how many evildoers, absolute criminals and scoundrels, have prosperous and successful lives built on their vile and shameful conduct.

Accordingly, if man had no future existence in any world other than this one, in which his good and evil acts would be reckoned and he would receive an appropriate requital, the idea that good deeds should be carried out and that bad deeds should be avoided would never have occurred to him.

One must not suppose that the requital for a good deed consists in the deed's contributing to the development of social structures through which people attain happiness so that the doer finally reaps some of the benefits of the deed. One likewise must not suppose that the requital for a misdeed consists in the evildoer's finally being caught up in the social decline to which his act contributed. The powerless may think this way, but when persons have reached the pinnacle of power, they are beyond the reach of the vicissitudes of society. Rather, the more corrupt and disordered is the society, and the worse the lot of the common people, the more these elements prosper. This fact does not prove, however, that these elements have no innate recognition of right and wrong.

One further must not suppose that their requital will consist in seeing their names blackened and their memory cursed. This will only happen after they die and all trace of them is gone, especially of the pleasurable times they enjoyed.

Setting aside these suppositions, there would seem to be no reason left for us to recognize good as good and worth acquiring, and bad as bad and avoidance-worthy. To believe in such a thing would be merely superstitious if there were no such thing as the resurrection. Therefore, we must understand how this pure and unshakable belief that is part of our created nature shows us that God Most High will raise everyone up from the dead and survey their deeds, giving an eternal bounty to the beneficent and giving the evildoers what they deserve. This occasion is called the Day of Resurrection.

VARIOUS RELIGIONS AND SECTS
AND THE DOCTRINE OF THE RESURRECTION

All the religions and sects that call upon people to worship God Most High and that enjoin good and forbid evil hold to the doctrine of a resurrection and an afterlife for man after death. This is because they can entertain no doubts that a beneficent act will have value only when it leads to a reward, and, since no such reward is witnessed in this life, there must be an afterlife in another world after death.

Apart from that, evidence has been found in very ancient burial sites that ancient peoples believed in a life after death and, in accordance with this belief, carried out rituals to secure the comfort of the dead in the other world.

THE RESURRECTION ACCORDING
TO THE QUR'AN

The Noble Qur'an reminds us of the Resurrection in the course of hundreds of verses, seeking to dispel any doubt about it. It cites the Resurrection in many cases to aid visualization and lend immediacy and conviction to explanations of the absoluteness of divine power. It says, for instance, *'Has man not seen how We created him from a drop of semen? Yet he is an open adversary. He makes up something to be compared with Us and forgets how he was created. He even says, "Who will revive [our] bones once they have rotted away?" Say, "The One Who raised them up in the first place will revive them, and He is Aware of all creation"'* (36:77-79).

Sometimes the Noble Qur'an points out God's power through the image of the world's return to life in spring after the death of winter; for instance, it says, *'Among His signs: that you see the earth desolate, but when We send water down upon it, it stirs and sprouts. The One Who revives it is the reviver of the dead; He is capable of anything'* (41:39). Sometimes it seeks to awaken man's God-given nature through logical reasoning to lead it to confess the truth of this concept, as where it says, *'We did not create*

145

heaven and earth and all that is between them in vain. That is the supposition of those who disbelieve. Those who disbelieve should beware of the fire! Shall We treat those who believe and do good works like those who spread corruption on the earth? Shall We treat the pious like the wicked?' (38:27-28). Heaven and earth were not created in vain, for if people came into being only to wander the earth a few days and then die, to be replaced by others who would live the same way, the creation would indeed be a vain plaything, but nothing proceeds from God, the Wise, in vain. The pious cannot be treated like the wicked, because neither realizes the full fruits of their actions in this world. If there were no other world, in which each group realizes the appropriate fruits of their action, the two groups would have the same standing before God, and this is contrary to divine justice.

FROM DEATH TO RESURRECTION

According to Islam, man is a creature composed of body and soul, or body and spirit. Man's body is itself a material composite and subject to material laws — that is, it has mass and weight, its existence is limited in time and place, it is affected by heat and cold and the like, and it gradually ages and wears out. Finally, as God Most High ordains, one day it decomposes and disappears.

The human soul, on the other hand, is not material and has none of these material properties. Instead, it has such spiritual properties as knowledge, feeling, thought, and will, or kindness, malevolence, happiness, pain, hope, and fear. There is no common measure between these properties and the material ones, but the heart, the brain, and the rest of the organs of the body obey the soul and its properties in their innumerable activities. No one organ of the body can be identified as the command center.

God Most High says, *'We created man from an extract of clay. Then We placed him as a drop in a secure place. Then We turned the drop into a clot, then We turned the clot into tissue, and then We turned the tissue into bones and clothed the bones with flesh.*

146

Then We reproduced him as a fresh creation' (23:12-14).

THE MEANING OF DEATH

According to Islam, death does not mean that we cease to exist. It means, rather, that the human soul, which is imperishable, severs its tie to the body, and, in consequence, that the body perishes and the disembodied soul continues its life without it.

God Most High says, *'They say, "When we have sunk deep in the earth, shall we take part in some fresh creation?" Indeed they disbelieve in the meeting with their Lord. Say, "The Angel of Death who has been given charge of you will gather you in. Then you will be returned to your Lord"'* (23:10-11). The Most Noble Messenger (peace and blessings upon him and his family) has said, 'You will not cease to exist, but rather you will be transferred from one dwelling to another'.

THE BARZAKH (*AL-'ALAM AL-BARZAKH*)

Islam holds that we live in a special mode after death. If one has done good deeds, one enjoys riches and happiness, and if one has done evil, one will suffer torment. At the time of the Resurrection, all will be gathered for reckoning. Where we live from death to the Day of Resurrection is called the *barzakh*.

God Most High says, *'Behind them is a barrier (barzakh) until the day they are raised'* (23:100). He also says, *'Do not think of those who are killed in the way of Allah as dead. No, they are living. They will be provided for by their Lord'* (3:169).

CHAPTER SEVEN

MORALS

All the countless resources that we have available today and strive day and night to acquire and use were not originally at man's disposal. They gradually became available for use through human effort.

In any event, from the time of the first human beings to the present, people have ceaselessly used their God-given nature to strive for better means of life. One who does not employ his vital powers or his external or internal organs — his eyes, ears, tongue, hands and feet, or his brains, heart, lungs and liver — will be nothing but a corpse.

Thus man works and acts in various ways not just because he is compelled to do so but because he is human, and because he perceives through his innate intelligence that he must struggle to realize his wishes and to secure his happiness by any means available. Also, people feel that they must carry out a set of appointed tasks whatever their manner of life or environment — religious or secular, under the rule of law or under tyranny, urban or rural. By fulfilling these tasks, they realize the true aims of humanity and create a satisfying life for themselves.

Of course, the value of these tasks, which constitute the sole means to happiness, is the value of humanity itself, which is the most precious commodity conceivable, and which we would exchange for nothing else. Thus to know and to carry out one's duty is the most important practical problem that we face in our lives, because its importance is the importance of man. One who shirks his clear duty or sometimes falls short of performing it confesses his baseness and worthlessness. With his every breach of faith, he strikes a fresh blow against his society and, in truth, himself.

God Most High says, '*Man is at a loss, except those who believe, perform honorable deeds, encourage Truth, and recommend patience*' (103:2-3). He also says, '*Corruption appears on land and sea because of what people's hands have done*' (30:41).

DIFFERENT VIEWS OF DUTY

We have a clear responsibility to discern what our duty is and to carry it out. We shall never find anyone who, speaking from his innate human nature, denies this fact. Since duty is so closely related to human happiness, and since religion propounds a different view of human life than do secular systems, duty under religion will necessarily be different from duty under other systems.

Religion holds that human life is a boundless, endless life not terminating at death. What this endless life realizes after death is the product of the pure and right beliefs, good moral qualities, and pious acts that one has enacted in this world while alive. Accordingly, religion takes into view eternal life in the next world when assigning duties to individuals and societies in this. Religion sets forth its rules in the light of the knowledge and

150

worship of God and service to Him whose invaluable effects will be revealed after death and at the Resurrection.

Secular systems (of whatever sort) consider only the ephemeral life of this world and set out duties for man that aid him in pursuing the material life and benefits that he shares with the other animals. In truth, they arrange an animal life for man that springs from the feelings of grazing animals and their predators. They pay no attention to man's realism and his eternal life, so filled with spiritual values. Thus sublime human moral values are gradually lost to secular societies (as experience shows conclusively), whose moral decline becomes more evident by the day.

Some say that the basis of religion is imitation and the acceptance of a series of duties and rules without question, but that secular systems are able to adapt to the exigencies of the time.

Those who have made this point have failed to note that any laws and rules in a society must be carried out without question. One never observes individuals in a country carrying out its existing laws in a spirit of debate and scientific discussion. No one is excused from observing a law because he finds it unsound. There is no difference between religious and secular codes in this respect.

One can discern the broad logic of the laws of a nation and deduce some (not all) of their particulars by studying its natural and social conditions and researching its general approach to life. This holds for a religion as well; through study of the creation and the natural needs of man, one can discern the broad lines of religious law (the system based on nature) and many of its particulars. The Noble Qur'an and many traditions call us to reasoned reflection and make reference to the sound policy many rules represent. Many traditions have reached us from the Most Noble Messenger (peace and blessings upon him and his family) and the Heirs (upon whom be peace) on the reasoning behind these rules.

KNOWING ONE'S DUTY

As I pointed out at the beginning of this work, the holy religion of Islam constitutes a universal and eternal program for human life in both worlds revealed to the Most Noble Messenger (peace and blessings be upon him and his family) by God Most High. It is to be carried out in human society and to navigate the ship of humanity out of the whirlpool of ignorance and misfortune.

Considering that religion is a program for living, it must necessarily set forth a task for man in this regard that it expects him to carry out. Overall, our life has to do with three things: 1. God Most High, Whose creatures we are, to Whose grace we owe more than to anything else, and toward Whose holy presence we must above all know our duties. 2. Ourselves. 3. Our fellow human beings, with whom we must live and cooperate. Accordingly, by this rule, we have three overall sets of duties: toward God, toward ourselves, and toward others.

MAN'S DUTIES TOWARD GOD

Our duties toward God Most High are our most important duties. We must strive to perform them with a pure heart and will. Our first duty is to recognize our Creator. Since the being of God Most High is the source for the being of every creature, every phenomenon, to know Him enlightens any being capable of insight. Disregard of this intuitive realization is the source for every sort of ignorance, blindness, and indifference to duty. One who remains heedless toward knowledge of the truth and who thus extinguishes his inner vision has no way to attain real happiness.

As we see, people who turn away from knowledge of God and attach no importance to this truth in their lives are wholly lost to human spiritual values and know no other logic than that of grazing animals and predators. God Most High says, '*So shun anyone who avoids mentioning Us and who only wants the worldly life; that will be their range of knowledge*' (53:29).

It must of course be recalled that knowledge of God is a

152

necessity for man as a realistic and instinctively rational being. Wherever in the creation he looks with his God-given mind, he witnesses signs of God's existence, knowledge, and power. Accordingly, man does not create his knowledge of God, but rather he pays attention to this plain and unconcealable truth and answers his own conscience — which is summoning him to God at every moment — affirmatively, expelling all doubt from his heart by holding fast to this knowledge.

WORSHIP OF GOD

Our first duty is to know God, and our second is to worship Him. As we come to recognize the Truth, it grows clear that our happiness, our sole object, lies in carrying out the program that Merciful God has set out for our lives and promulgated through His prophets. Therefore, service to God and obedience to His command is the one duty before which all other duties shrink to insignificance.

God Most High says, '*Your Lord has decreed that you worship [and obey] none but Him*' (17:23). He also says, '*Did I not charge you, progeny of Adam, not to worship Satan — for he is your open enemy — but that you worship Me? This is the straight road*' (36:60-61). Accordingly, it is our duty to recognize our status of servanthood and need, to consciously recollect the boundless greatness of God Most High, and to obey His commands, knowing that He comprehends our beings in every respect. We must not worship anything other than God Most High, and we must not extend obedience to anyone but the Most Noble Messenger (peace and blessings be upon him and his family) and the Imams of Guidance (upon whom be peace), to whom God Most High has commanded obedience.

God Most High says, '*Obey Allah, and obey the Messenger and those among you who hold command*' (4:59). Of course, in obeying God and those who hold command in religion, the Imams, one must hold everything related to God in total reverence. One must recall the holy name of God and the names of those in command of religion with the proper courtesies. One must strive to do honour to God's Book (the Noble Qur'an), the Holy Ka'aba, mosques, and the shrines of the Imams. As God Most High says, '*Whoever glorifies Allah's ceremonies should do so from heartfelt heedfulness*' (22:32).

MAN'S DUTIES TOWARD HIMSELF
Whatever method man adopts in his life, whatever road he follows, he seeks, in truth, only his own happiness. Since knowing what constitutes happiness for a thing derives from knowing the thing itself (until we know ourselves, for instance, we shall not know our real needs, which we must satisfy to attain happiness), man's essential task is to know himself, so that he can see what constitutes his happiness. He can thus use the means he has available to relieve his needs and avoid throwing his precious life, his only asset, away.

The Most Noble Messenger (peace and blessings be upon him and his family) has said, 'Whoever knows himself knows his God'. The Commander of the Faithful 'Ali has said, 'Whoever knows himself has attained the highest level of spiritual knowledge'. After man attains self-knowledge, he realizes that his greatest task is to honour his essential humanity. He must not crush this radiant essence; he must strive to maintain his outer and inner health, so that he may attain to an eternal life of enjoyment. The Commander of the Faithful 'Ali has said, 'If one honours oneself, sensual temptations will appear mean and trivial'. Our being is composed of two things: body and soul. It is our duty to strive to keep both sound and resilient. The holy faith of Islam has issued precise instructions sufficient to enable us to keep body and soul healthy.

PHYSICAL HEALTH
The holy faith of Islam has adequately covered the issue of physical health through a series of rules such as prohibitions against eating blood, carrion, the flesh of certain animals, or poisonous foods, prohibitions against drinking alcoholic beverages or impure water, prohibitions against gluttony and

self-inflicted injury, and other prohibitions too numerous to name here.

Cleanliness is one of the most important aspects of health. The pure faith of Islam has accordingly given great attention to this principle, greater attention than any other religion has given to it. The Most Noble Messenger (peace and blessings be upon him and his family) has said, 'Cleanliness is part of faith,' and cleanliness could receive no greater commendation.

Numerous injunctions to bathe have reached us from great religious figures. Imam Musa Kazim (upon whom be peace) has said, 'Bathing every other day makes one beefy and strong'. The Commander of the Faithful 'Ali has said, 'What a fine edifice the bathhouse is, that removes man's impurities'.

Beyond offering general injunctions to cleanliness, Islam commends specific acts of hygiene, such as trimming the nails, shaving superfluous head and body hair, washing one's hands before and after eating, combing the hair, rinsing the mouth and cleansing the nostrils, sweeping out one's house, and cleaning up walks, doorways, areas under trees, and so forth. Additionally, Islam has decreed that acts of worship must always be accompanied by cleanliness; for example, the body and clothing must be cleansed of filth. Several times each day, one must prepare for ritual prayer by performing the cleansing known as *wuzu*. The ritual bathing known as *ghusl* may be required for prayers and fasting. Since water must reach the skin without being blocked by oil or dirt on these occasions, the necessity for the body to be clean is clearly implied.

The blessed *sura* Muddaththir was one of the first to be revealed to the Most Noble Messenger (peace and blessings be upon him and his family) at the beginning of his mission. In its fourth verse, God Most High commands that clothing be kept clean, *'Purify your clothing'* (74:4). It is incumbent that one's clothes be clean in the special legal sense at time of prayer, but it is commendable to keep oneself clean and free of filth whatever one is doing; each of the infallible Imams (upon whom be peace) have enjoined this on various occasions. The Most Noble Messenger (peace and blessings be upon him and his family) has said, 'Whoever puts on clothes should keep them clean'. The Commander of the Faithful 'Ali has said, 'To clean one's clothes dispels grief and sorrow and also renders one's prayers acceptable'. Imam Sadiq and Imam Kazim (upon whom be peace) are related to have said, 'To have ten or twenty shirts into which to change is not excessive'.

In addition to keeping their persons and clothing clean, Muslims must dress well and maintain a good appearance in public. Hazrat Ali has said, 'Wear costly clothing and adorn yourself, because God is beautiful and loves beauty, but [your clothing] must be lawfully acquired'. He then cited this verse, '*Say, Who has forbidden Allah's adornments that He has provided for His servants, and the wholesome things that He provides?*' (7:32).

Our mouths, in consuming food, become contaminated with food particles, with cling to the bases of the teeth, the surface of the tongue, and other parts of the mouth. Fermentation, decay, and other chemical reactions involving these particles can produce evil odors and even poisons that can be assimilated along with one's food. Besides, an afflicted person's breath can foul the air and vex other people in a gathering. Accordingly, the revealed law of Islam calls upon Muslims to brush their teeth and rinse out their mouths with clean water at least daily, and recommends this particularly before *wuzu*.

The Most Noble Messenger (peace and blessings be upon him and his family) has said, 'If I did not fear the hardship it would cause, I would make it obligatory for all Muslims to brush their teeth'. He said on another occasion, 'The angel Gabriel always commended brushing one's teeth; I even supposed it would eventually be made obligatory'.

People must breathe, and the air generally found around human habitations is not free of dust and pollutants. Of course, to breathe such air can harm the respiratory system. To avoid such harm, Merciful God has caused hairs to grow within the human nose to prevent dust from reaching the lungs. Nonetheless, dust sometimes accumulates in the nose and prevents its hairs from fully performing their function. The holy law of Islam has accordingly commended Muslims to rinse their nostrils several times before performing *wuzu*. By drawing clean water into the nose, one preserves the health of his respiratory system.

SPIRITUAL HEALTH
Man perceives the worth of good qualities and their importance for the individual and for society through his God-given conscience. Accordingly, no one is found in human society who does not praise moral virtues and venerate one who possesses them.

The importance man gives to moral virtues needs no explaining, and Islam's extensive moral commandments are plain to anyone. God Most High says, '*A soul and He who tempered it, and filled it with its [sense of] iniquity and its [sense of] duty — whoever purifies it will prosper, while whoever stunts it will fail*' (91:7-10).

Imam Sadiq (upon whom be peace) has said in explication of this verse, 'God has shown man what is good and must be done and what is evil and must be foregone'.

LEARNING
To possess knowledge is a spiritual virtue, and the superiority of the wise over the ignorant is as plain as day.

Man is distinguished from the other animals by his power of reason and wealth of knowledge. Other animals have each their own fixed repertoire of instincts, by which they meet their needs in a stereotyped fashion. They can never hope to progress, and they cannot blaze new paths for themselves or others. Only man adds daily to his stock of knowledge and enriches his material and spiritual life through discovery of natural and supernatural laws, studying past ages and laying the foundation for his own and others' futures.

Islam does more to encourage people to acquire knowledge than

157

any other ancient or modern social system, than any other religion or legal code. In order to found a radically new culture, Islam has made it incumbent for every Muslim man and woman to acquire knowledge. The Most Noble Messenger (peace and blessings be upon him and his family) and the Imams (upon whom be peace) have left us numerous injunctions in this regard. The Most Noble Messenger (peace and blessings be upon him and his family) has said, 'To acquire knowledge is incumbent upon every Muslim'. These accounts speak of knowledge (*'ilm*) in the most inclusive possible sense, including all the branches of knowledge. To acquire knowledge is incumbent on everyone, without regard to gender or nature.

The Most Noble Messenger (peace and blessings be upon him and his family) has also said, 'Strive to acquire knowledge from the cradle to the grave'. Each religious obligation is associated with a time. All of them call for maturity; that is, one is required to observe them only upon reaching maturity. Some religious obligations lapse with old age and infirmity. To acquire knowledge, however, is incumbent on us from the day we are born to the day we die, through all the so-called stages of our lives. According to this principle, a Muslim must pursue learning throughout his life and add to his or her stock of knowledge every day of it. The above-quoted tradition has extended the time for this obligation and rendered it universal.

The Most Noble Messenger (peace and blessings be upon him and his family) has further said, 'Seek knowledge, though it be in China', and 'Knowledge is the most precious of things, which the believer has lost. He will pursue it even if he must seek it in China'. In accordance with this command, each Muslim is charged with acquiring knowledge, even if he or she must travel great distances. In the end, one must be prepared to pay any price to recover what one has lost.

Another saying of the Most Noble Messenger (peace and blessings be upon him and his family) maintains, 'Wisdom is the cherished goal of the believers; he will acquire it wherever he finds it'. The only condition to acquiring knowledge is that it be useful to society.

Islam strongly encourages study of the secrets of creation and contemplation of heaven and earth, human nature, history, and the relics of past peoples (philosophy, mathematical and natural sciences, and other areas), as well as study of moral and legal questions (as they appear in Islamic moral and legal philosophy) and development of technologies that contribute to human welfare. The following account illustrates how highly the Most Noble Messenger (peace and blessings be upon him and his family) valued knowledge. When some unbelievers fell captive to the Muslims during the battle of Badr, he ordered heavy ransoms be demanded to free them, except that some prisoners who knew how to read and write were exempted, on condition that each of them teach the art to ten young Muslims. This was the first adult education program known to history, a great honour to Muslims. It is noteworthy that the Most Noble Messenger (peace and blessings be upon him and his family) commanded something that has not been witnessed in history before or since: that knowledge be accepted in place of booty, not along with it. No one in the world has seen a victorious commander accept instruction for the young in place of ransom and booty.

The Most Noble Messenger (peace and blessings be upon him and his family) visited these classes personally. He called together those who knew how to read and write and ordered that the youths be tested to see what progress they had made. Whatever youths showed the most progress through these tests were given the greatest encouragement. One historian records that a woman named ash-Shifa', who had learned to read and write in pre-Islamic times, used to come to the Most Noble Messenger's (peace and blessings be upon him and his family) house and teach reading and writing to his wives. He praised and encouraged her for her efforts.

THE IMPORTANCE OF STUDENTS

The significance attached to reaching any goal and the associated effort are in proportion to the goal itself. Since, as anyone knows by his God-given nature, nothing is more important in human life than knowledge, it follows that no one is more valuable than a student. Islam, as a religion founded on our true nature, maintains such value for students. The Most Noble Messenger (peace and blessings be upon him and his family) has said, 'One who pursues studies is beloved of God'.

Although *jihad*, struggle for the sake of faith, is one of the pillars of faith, and although the Most Noble Messenger (peace and blessings be upon him and his family) or the Imam has given orders to wage war, in which Muslims at large must participate, those who are studying the religious sciences are excused from this duty. There must always be a sufficient number of Muslims acquiring knowledge at places of learning. God Most High says, *'The believers should not all go out to fight. Of every troop of them, a party should go to study religion, so that they may admonish their folk when they return to them, so that they may beware'* (9:122).

THE IMPORTANCE OF TEACHERS

The teacher is the shining light of learning who dispels the shadows of ignorance and illiteracy from the world. It is the teacher who leads the inwardly blind and ignorant to see and know, and who guides them to the Holy Land and Paradise of happiness. Thus Islam holds that teachers must be respected and obeyed as the holiest and most respected people in society. To demonstrate their deservedly high status, it is sufficient to cite the sage remark of Imam 'Ali: 'Whoever has taught me a word has made me his slave'. He has also said, 'There are three sorts of people: first, scholars of divinity; second, those who acquire knowledge for the sake of delivering themselves and others; and third, those who sit like flies on livestock and buzz around with every gust of wind [or, by other accounts, "who swarm to wherever they smell a foul odor"]'.

RESPECT FOR SCHOLARS

In explaining the worth of knowledge and great stature of scholars, the Noble Qur'an says, *'Allah will raise those of you who believe and those who have knowledge to high degrees'* (58:11). The Most Noble Messenger (peace and blessings be upon him and his family) valued scholars to such an extent that he said, 'The death of a tribe is easier to bear and less harmful than the death of one scholar'.

Similarly, God Most High says in another verse, *'Are those who know equal to those who do not know? But the wise will heed'* (39:9). The verse shows that the learned and the ignorant are never equal. The scholar has an essential superiority over one who is bereft of knowledge. We may gather from this verse that in speaking of knowledge, the Noble Qur'an does not mean knowledge of religion only but refers to anything that enlightens people and aids them in questions of this world and the next.

Imam Muhammad Baqir (upn whom be peace) has illustrated the superiority of scholars over anchorites and ascetics in this way: 'A scholar who puts his scholarship to use is superior to seventy thousand anchorites'. The worth of any given person in the eyes of the Most Noble Messenger (peace and blessings be upon him and his family) is determined by that person's knowledge: 'The most scholarly person is one who is always using the knowledge of others to add to his knowledge. Man's worth lies in knowledge; therefore, the greater one's knowledge, the greater one's worth, and the less one's knowledge, the less one's worth'.

THE TASKS OF THE TEACHER
AND THE STUDENT

The Noble Qur'an regards knowledge as the real life of man and holds that, without knowledge, a human being is no different from a corpse. Accordingly, the student must make his teacher the focus of his life and consider him the source of his life and gradually realize his real life from his teacher. He must never fail to give him all due honour and respect. Even if the teacher acts harshly and angrily in teaching him, the student must never react with defiance. He should always pay respect to the teacher in his presence and in his absence, while he is alive and after his death.

Correspondingly, the teacher must hold himself responsible for the student's life and must not rest until the student has attained the level of an honourable member of the community. He should not become disheartened if his students sometimes fail to absorb his teachings, but he should praise them when they do make progress. He must never say or do anything to impair their morale.

TWO PRIME EXAMPLES
OF ISLAMIC EDUCATION

All contemporary social systems conceal secrets whose disclosure to people generally would impair their rulers' ability to govern and frustrate those rulers' private lusts. This is why they are always keeping truths hidden from people at large. The policies they set in motion prove contrary to reason and to the interests of society and people generally, so they fear that, if these matters were disclosed, they would be flooded with criticism and their interests would be endangered. This is why the Christian Church and other ecclesiastical bodies do not allow people freedom of thought but reserve to themselves the right to alter and interpret religious learning and to expound the scriptures. The people are supposed to accept whatever they say without question or independent exploration. This approach has blighted many religious systems, as the state of present-day Christianity illustrates.

This is not true of Islam, however, because it expresses confidence in its own worth and admits no points of obscurity and darkness within itself, by contrast with all other religious and non-religious systems. This fact has the following consequences: 1. Islam conceals no truth, nor does it permit its adherents to do so. The laws of this pure religion are aligned with the laws of nature and creation, and no reality can contradict them. In Islam, to conceal the truth is a major sin. God Most High expressly curses those who conceal the truth where He says, '*Those who hide the proofs and the guidance that We have revealed, after We had made it clear to the people in the scripture — Allah curses them, and those who curse will curse them*' (2:159). 2. Islam has commanded its adherents to subject its truths and concepts to independent thought. It tells them to stop wherever the least doubt occurs to them and proceed no further, but to strive freely to resolve their doubt with perfect fairness and open minds, so that their shining faith will never be shadowed by doubt and perplexity. God Most High says, '*Do not follow what you do not know*' (17:36).

REFRAINING FROM FREE THOUGHT
AND EXPRESSION OF THE TRUTH

To perceive truths through thought and reflection and to accept them are the most valuable product of the human organism, the sole distinction of man over other animals, and the basis of man's nobility and glory. Our fellow-feeling and instinctive realism never permit us to deprive people of their freedom of thought by imposing imitative beliefs or to lead them astray by concealing truths and so paralyze pious thoughts. One cannot, however, ignore the fact that someone may refuse to comprehend a truth or intransigently refuse to allow it to unfold. To express it to that person may place one's life or property in danger. Realism and regard for human welfare demand silence, and the needs to preserve the sanctity and veneration of sacred values, to keep humanity from being led astray, and to protect persons from other dangers to their lives, wealth, and possessions require concealment of truths.

In numerous traditions, the Imams (upon whom be peace) have strictly prohibited people from thinking about certain realities that are beyond the capacity of human individuals to understand. God Most High expressly allows concealment of the truth under conditions of *taqiyya* in two places in the Noble Qur'an: Al-i

163

'Imran:28 and an-Nahl:106.

CONCLUSION
In several situations, Islam holds that it is not merely permissible but mandatory that the truth remain hidden: 1. In the case of *taqiyya*, where there is no hope of the truth advancing, and expression of it leads to danger of life, wealth, or property. 2. Where the truth would make no sense to someone and to express it would lead him astray or provoke him to scorn and make fun of it. 3. Where free thought in the absence of intellectual capacity would distort the truth and lead one astray.

IJTIHAD AND TAQLID
The needs that the human species has in its environment and the actions it must undertake to relieve them are too numerous for the average person to recite. How then is he to acquire all the specialized knowledge they represent?

From another standpoint, since man carries out his activities through thought and volition and needs adequate information to decide upon a course of action, he must either inform himself about things he intends to carry out or ask informed people how to do them and act accordingly to their instructions, as we instinctively turn to a physician to cure our illnesses or rely on an architect to design a building, a mason to construct it, and a carpenter to fabricate the doors and windows. Therefore, except in minor instances, we consistently make use of this principle of relying on others' expertise, which is termed *taqlid*.

Someone who says, 'I will not allow myself to be governed by *taqlid*' either does not understand what he is saying or is mentally disturbed. Islam itself adopts this method in founding its law code on innate human nature. Islam commands its adherents to learn its principles and its decrees, and there is no source for its principles other than God's Book and the *sunna* (practice) of the Most Noble Messenger (peace and blessings be upon him and his family) and the Imams (upon whom be peace).

Plainly, it is not for everyone to learn all the principles of religion from the Book and the *sunna*; this is not feasible for some Muslims, or rather, it is only possible for a limited number.

It thus follows naturally that implementation of this religious injunction should be accomplished by Muslims who are in no position to reason through all these principles and decrees turning to others who are conversant with the reasoning behind religious commandments to carry out this task.

A scholar who has the expertise to reason through these decrees is called a *mujtahid*, and his act of reasoning is known as *ijtihad*. One who resorts to a *mujtahid* is called a *muqallid*, and his act of resort is known as *taqlid*.

It must certainly be realized that *taqlid* applies only to acts of worship, commercial transactions, and other concrete acts covered by religious law. The principles of religion are a question of belief, and one must never rely on others' views in questions of belief, because what is sought here is belief and faith, not action. One can never suppose that someone else's faith is one's own.

One can never say, 'God is One, because that is what my forbears have said or what our scholars say,' or else, 'There is indeed life after death, because all Muslims believe that'. Accordingly, it is incumbent upon each Muslim to understand the principles of his religion through independent reasoning, however rudimentary.

CHAPTER EIGHT

DUTIES TOWARD OTHERS

DUTIES TOWARD ONE'S MOTHER AND FATHER

It is by means of the mother and father that the child is created and receives its early upbringing. Accordingly, the holy faith of Islam greatly encourages us to obey and respect our parents, to the point that God Most High commends kindness to parents immediately after making reference to *tauhid*. He says, '*Your Lord has decreed that you worship none but Him and that you show kindness to your parents*' (17:23). In traditions that enumerate the major sins, misbehavior toward one's parents immediately follows *shirk*. The verse just mentioned continues, '*If one or both of them reach old age while with you, never scold them or repulse them, but speak to them kindly. And lower to them the wing of humility out of mercy, and say, "My Lord! Have mercy, for they cared for me when I was little"*' (17:23-24).

How well did Zal express it to her son
When she saw him strong as an elephant,
more than a match for a leopard,
'If you will recollect your tender years,
When you were helpless in my arms,
You have never shown me unkindness these days,
When you are a lion-man, and I, an old woman'[1]

In the holy religion of Islam, obedience to one's parents is mandatory except when they order one to refrain from a mandatory act or to commit a forbidden one. Experience teaches that those who vex their parents will not be successful in life and will not be delivered in the end.

DISOBEDIENCE TO PARENTS

Within the family, the mother and father stand to the children in the relation of a tree's roots to its branches: just as the propagation and life of the branches depend on the roots, so are the mother and father the foundation of the child's life. Considering the human society is composed of two strata, the parents and the offspring, the mother and father are the taproot of society.

To act badly toward one's mother and father and to vex them, beyond being ungrateful and mean-spirited in the extreme, erodes one's humanity and is destructive to society, since the mother and father will react to the child's disrespect with unkindness and neglect. From another standpoint, if members of the younger generation regard their parents with disrespect, they will expect no better from their own offspring; they will entertain no hopes of kindness and support from them in their own old age and infirmity, and so they will be discouraged from raising their own family. We see this to be the case with many young people today.

If this way of thinking were to become universal, procreation would cease, since an intelligent person would never devote his life to raising a sapling that would never yield fruit or shade and the sight of which would bring nothing but pain. We might suppose that the government could encourage people to form families through various incentives and thus solve the reproductive problem. It must be mentioned, however, that no social custom can long survive without support from nature (such as the kind feelings that exist between parents and children). Beyond that, in suppressing these natural instincts, people necessarily deny themselves the corresponding joys of the spirit completely.

RIGHTS OF CHILDREN

The things that we are obliged to do are termed 'rights' with respect to those who will benefit from them and 'duties' or responsibilities with respect to those who must carry them out. For instance, when someone performs a task for someone else for wages, to pay those wages is the duty of the employer, and to be paid them is the right of the worker. If the employer fails to pay these wages, the worker can demand them and assert his rights.

Since man is not created to live in this world forever, he must eventually depart. To preserve the human species from oblivion, God has arranged a method of reproduction. He has equipped people with the means to regenerate their kind and with the corresponding emotions.

In being so fully equipped, people naturally regard their offspring as part of themselves and see their offsprings' lives as the perpetuation of their own lives on earth. People will thus make every effort and endure hardships to comfort and please their children because, if their children were to fail or perish, it would be as if they themselves had failed or perished. In reality, they only act in obedience to what the order of the creation dictates, that the human species be preserved. Therefore, it is the duty of the mother and the father to carry out the decree of law and conscience alike with regard to their children, to bring them up well, so that they grow up to be worthwhile people. They must grant the child the humanity that they grant themselves. Let us turn to a part of what comes under this heading.

1. From the first day the child shows understanding of speech and gestures, parents must lay the foundations in his or her psyche of moral virtues and good qualities. Insofar as they can, they should avoid frightening him with superstitions and should prevent evil and indecent acts. They should also abstain from lying, backbiting, and indecent or abusive language in his presence. They should behave virtuously in front of him so that he will grow up to be chaste and of fine character. They should express industry, aspiration, and fairness so that he will assimilate their love of justice and their humanitarianism and have no part in intimidation, base intentions, and egotism.

2. Until the child is old enough to decide for himself, the parents must pay attention to his diet, sleep, and other needs. They must attend to his physical health, so that he has a sound mind and body and a strong constitution and is ready to be educated.

3. As soon as the child is ready for schooling (usually at age seven), the parents should entrust him to his teacher. They should expend every effort to find a competent teacher so that what he will hear will have a positive effect on him, refining his spirit, purifying his soul, and cultivating his morals.

4. When the child reaches an age that admits of participating in public gatherings or family get-togethers, the parents should take him with them to these meetings and acquaint him with the proper ways to associate with people so that he becomes familiar with social custom.

RESPECT FOR ELDERS
It is obligatory to extend respect of older people. As the Most Noble Messenger (peace and blessings be upon him and his family) has said. 'To honour and respect the old is to honour and respect God'.

DUTIES TOWARD RELATIONS
People to whom one is related through one's mother and father

are a natural source of social ties. Blood or genetic relationship makes one part of a larger family. In consideration of this natural unity, Islam commands its adherents to be kind to their relatives. The Noble Qur'an and traditions of the Most Noble Messenger (peace and blessings be upon him and his family) and the Imams (upon whom be peace) have strongly urged them to do so.

God Most High says, '*Heed Allah through Whom you hold one another responsible, as well as any ties of kinship. God is watching over you*' (4:1).

The Most Noble Messenger (peace and blessings be upon him and his family) has said, 'I urge my folk to be kind to relations; even if relations are separated by a year's journey, they must not sever their bonds of kinship'.

DUTIES TOWARD NEIGHBOURS

Since neighbours' proximity allows them to develop close ties and naturally makes them like a big family, a neighbour's friendliness or animosity has more effect than that of other people.

Someone who engages in nightlong revelry in his home is not going to bother someone living on the other side of town, but he will deny rest to his neighbour. A powerful man who spends his life carousing in his mansion will not upset poor people living far away, but he is fanning the flames of resentment in his indigent neighbour in his shack, and a day will come when he will pay for his behaviour. For reasons like these, the holy law of Islam has strongly urged us to look after our neighbours' interests.

The Most Noble Messenger (peace and blessings be upon him and his family) has said, 'Gabriel has so urged neighbours' rights upon me that I have supposed that God Most High would include one's neighbour among one's heirs'. He has also said, 'One who believes in God and the Resurrection will never vex his neighbour. If he borrows from him, he returns the loan. He

171

shares in the neighbour's joys and sorrows. He must not trouble his neighbour, even if that person is an unbeliever'. He has further said, 'If someone vexes his neighbour, the scent of Paradise will not reach his nostrils; if someone does not observe his neighbour's rights, he is not one of us; and, if someone is sated and, knowing that his neighbour is hungry, offers him nothing, he is not a Muslim'.

DUTIES TOWARD THE POOR AND NEEDY

Clearly, society is organized to provide for individuals needs. The most important task for the members of any society is to come to the aid of the needy and powerless and somehow to provide for the needs of those who cannot provide for their needs themselves.

It has grown evident today that indifference of the rich to the plight of the poor is the greatest danger threatening the survival of society, and that the rich themselves are the first casualties of this threat.

Fourteen centuries ago, Islam, noting this danger, commanded the rich to apportion a certain part of their wealth among the poor every year. Beyond alleviating their needs to this extent, it is commended to expend whatever one can to ease the lives of the poor, for the sake of God. As God Most High says, *'You will not attain to piety until you spend part of what you love'* (3:92). Innumerable traditions have reached us concerning service to the people. The Most Noble Messenger (peace and blessings be upon him and his family) has said, 'The best of people is the most useful to the people'. He has also said, 'On the Day of Resurrection, the one with the highest place in the regard of God Most High will be the one who most advanced the welfare of God's servants'.

> In disaster, be a helper to the helpers,
> So that divine grace will come to your aid.
> At all events, there will one day sprout,
> The seed of goodness that you plant now.

DUTIES TOWARDS SOCIETY

As we know, human individuals do engage in mutual aid and so benefit from each other's efforts in meeting their own needs. The societies that form from such people are like a greater human being of whom individuals are members or organs.

Each of the organs of the human body has a specialized task and contributes to its own well being while contributing to that of the other organs. Correspondingly, it benefits from their activities. If any of these organs were to become egotistical and not to serve the other organs (for instance, if the eyes refused to help with what the hands or feet were doing, or the mouth were to grow so engrossed in chewing that it would refuse to swallow), a person would soon die, along with these individual-istic, egotistical organs.

The individual members of a society have tasks analogous to those of the organs of a body. That is, a person must think of his own interests in the context of the interests of society and consider what would be profitable to society in his work, if he is himself to profit from his labours. He must benefit everyone if he is to realize a benefit. He must defend others' rights if his are to be preserved.

This is a truth that we comprehend through our God-given nature. The holy faith of Islam, too, in resting upon this nature and creation, decrees nothing less.

The Most Noble Messenger (peace and blessings be upon him and his family) has said, 'A Muslim is one from whose hand and tongue other Muslims are safe'. He has also said, 'Muslims are brothers to each other; they are one in the hand, heart, and purpose in the face of outsiders'. He further said, 'Whoever rises in the morning and gives no thought to the affairs of Muslims is not a Muslim'.

There was an incident that illustrates this point at the Battle of Tabuk, as the Most Noble Messenger (peace and blessings be upon him and his family) was advancing with the army of Islam toward the border of the Roman Empire. Three men did not participate in the battle, and, when the army returned and they went out to meet and greet him, he averted his face from them and made no reply. So did the other Muslims. No one in Medina would even speak to their wives, and they were finally compelled to take refuge in the surrounding hills and express their contrition and repentance. After several days, God accepted their repentance, and they returned to the city.

NOTES TO CHAPTER EIGHT

1. From the *Shahname*, the epic poem by Ferdousi. — Trans.

CHAPTER NINE

JUSTICE

The Noble Qur'an and the traditions of the Most Noble Messenger (peace and blessings be upon him and his family) and the Imams (upon whom be peace) speak of two kinds of justice: individual and social. The holy faith of Islam has given thorough consideration to both kinds.

INDIVIDUAL JUSTICE
Individual justice means that one abstain from lying, backbiting, and other major sins and not persist in committing other sins. One who is characterized by individual justice is called 'just', and, according to Islamic rules, if he has a scholarly bent, he can become a judge, a governor, a *mujtahid*, or holder of other responsible positions in society. But someone not characterized by individual justice cannot hold such positions, even if he is a great scholar.

SOCIAL JUSTICE

Social justice means that we not transgress against others' rights but that we regard everyone as equal under God's law. We must not exceed the due limits in enforcing religious rules and must not deviate from the true way under the sway of feelings and emotions. God Most High says, '*Allah enjoins justice*' (16:90). He also says, '*Allah commands...that , if you adjudicate among people, you adjudicate with justice*' (4:58). We are enjoined to speak and act justly in countless verses and traditions. God Most High expressly curses the unjust in several verses.

INJUSTICE, OPPRESSION

God Most High censures oppression in hundreds of verses as an ugly quality fit only for beasts of prey. (Oppression is treated in two-thirds of the Noble Qur'an's one hundred and fourteen *suras*.)

No one can be found who does not perceive the wrongness and evil of oppression with his natural conscience, or who does not more or less realize what agonizing misfortunes oppression has visited upon human society, what slaughter, how many broken homes.

Experience shows conclusively that, however solidly the palace of oppression may stand, it will not endure; sooner or later, it will collapse upon the oppressors. God Most High says, '*Certainly Allah will not guide the tyrants*' (6:114). The Imams have told us that a state may be guilty of unbelief and endure, but it cannot tyrannize and endure.

GOOD SOCIAL RELATIONS

We have no choice but to live in society and to associate with people. Beyond a doubt, social intercourse exists to keep our social natures alive and so to assure our ongoing material and spiritual progress and to help us to better solve our problems in life.

It follows that we should encounter people in a way that wins their affection and good will and that we should always grow more social and make more friends. If people's contacts with someone are onerous or acrimonious, they will come to dislike him, and a day will come when everyone will avoid him. Such a person will become a social outcast and will find himself alone in a crowd, a foreigner in his own country. Such a state is one of the most bitter misfortunes that can befall anyone. This is why the holy faith of Islam recommends that its adherents maintain good social relationships and helps them to do so with high norms for social behaviour and with traditional manners that are unexcelled expressions of grace and courtesy. For example, it has ordained that Muslims greet each other when they meet, and it is a virtue to be the first to extend a greeting, as the Most Noble Messenger (peace and blessings be upon him and his family) always was. He greeted women and children, and, if someone greeted him, he always replied with a finer greeting. God Most High says, '*When you are greeted, make a better greeting or return it*' (4:86). He has also ordered that we be humble when meeting others and offer respect to each according to his social station. God Most High says, '*The servants of the Merciful are those who walk upon the earth humbly and, when the ignorant address them, answer, "Peace"*' (25:63).

It must be noted that humility here does not mean regarding oneself as contemptible before people and denying one's own humanity. Rather, it means that one does not parade one's presumed virtues and privileges before others or treat them with contempt. Respect for others correspondingly does not mean deferring to them to the point of fawning servility but rather means that one must value each according to his religious and social merit, honouring great men and women according to their greatness and likewise honouring the common humanity of others.

To respect others also does not mean that one pass over anyone's unworthy act in silence, or participate in an assembly of legislators all of whom behave in a way contrary to human dignity or act contrary to religious law, or try to blend into society out of fear of notoriety. To respect others is really to respect their human dignity and religious and moral attainment, not to respect their external forms. When someone has cast off his human dignity and religious merit, there remains no reason to honour him. The Most Noble Messenger (peace and blessings upon him and his family) has said, 'One must not offend against God in order to obey others'.

ANNOYING OTHERS AND MISCHIEF

These are two similar vices, in that one annoys others by abusing them verbally and saying things that vex them or by abusing them physically by doing things that make them uncomfortable. Mischief, correspondingly, consists of doing things that cause people harm. At any rate, these two vices occupy a point diametrically opposite to what man has sought in forming society, an easier life and peace of mind.

Accordingly, because the holy law of Islam attaches the greatest importance to the well-being of society, it has forbidden these two vices. God Most High says, *'Those who annoy believing men and believing women without their having deserved it will assume [the guilt of] slander and [commit] a clear offense against themselves'* (33:58). The Most Noble Messenger (peace and blessings upon him and his family) has said, 'One who annoys Muslims has annoyed me, and to annoy me is to annoy God. Such people have been cursed in the Torah, the Gospel, and the Qur'an'. He also said, 'If someone glares at a Muslim to frighten him, God will frighten him on the Day of Resurrection'.

KEEPING GOOD COMPANY

Although we may associate with many people, life is such that we are bound to associate with some people more than others. These people are known as our friends.

Of course, this friendship and closeness is a kind of correspondence in morals, approaches to life, occupations, and the like between two people or more. Association results in one party gradually acquiring the habits and morals of the other, and so we should therefore choose to associate with good people, since we shall thus pick up their moral virtues, as well as benefiting from their unalloyed friendship and good will. We shall additionally enjoy their lasting friendship and good will and even rise in the estimation of people at large.

The Commander of the Faithful 'Ali has said, 'The best of friends is the one who guides you to good deeds'. He has also said, 'A man is judged by who his friend is'.

First say who you spend your time with,
So I may say who you are.
Whatever is the worth of your associates,
That is your soul's worth.

ASSOCIATING WITH EVIL PEOPLE

To associate with bad people and evildoers leads to all sorts of misfortune and bad ends. To demonstrate this point, it is enough to note that, if we ask criminals and malefactors like thieves and robbers how they went wrong, they will invariably respond, 'Associating with bad people has brought us to this state.' We will not find an antisocial person in a thousand who took up an evil course on his own initiative.

The Commander of the Faithful 'Ali has said, 'Shun the company of evil people, lest an evil associate turn you into someone like himself, since he will not accept you until he does this'. He has also said, 'Shun the friendship of the evildoer, since he will sell you out for a paltry sum'.

Associate little with bad people, or you'll get stuck,
The human psyche is very impressionable.

TRUTHFULNESS

Mutual relationships of human individuals, the basis of human society, are based upon speech. Accordingly, the truthful speech that discloses a hidden reality to someone else is an essential cornerstone of society, and society realizes important benefits from it that it could never do without.

179

We can sum up the benefits of truthfulness in a few sentences: 1. One who speaks truthfully enjoys the confidence of his fellows, who are relieved of the need to scrutinize everything he says. 2. Such a one has a clear conscience and is not tormented by his own lying. 3. Such a one is true to his word and does not betray a trust, since honest speech is conjoined with honest behaviour. 4. Truthfulness eliminates most dissension and conflict, most disputes arise from one or both parties denying the truth. 5. Many moral faults and offenses against laws and rules are automatically prevented, since the main reason people lie is to cover up such behaviour.

The Commander of the Faithful 'Ali has said, 'The real Muslim is one who prefers speaking the truth even when it is ruinous to him over lying even when it benefits him, and who finds inner peace in so doing'.

HARMFUL EFFECTS OF LIES

The previous discussion makes clear the harmful effects of lying. The liar is the enemy of human society and is labouring to ruin society with his lies, which are a gross treachery. Lies are like opiates that extinguish society's consciousness and capacity to understand by concealing reality, or they are like alcoholic drinks in making people drunk and denying their reason and power to distinguish good from evil. This is why Islam considers lying a major sin and holds that the liar has no religion. The Most Noble Messenger (peace and blessings upon him and his family) says, 'Three sorts of people are hypocrites, though they may pray and fast: liars, people who are not true to their word, and people who betray a trust'. The Commander of the Faithful 'Ali says, 'Anyone who tastes the pleasures of faith gives up lying, even in jest'. Not only is lying condemned as a sin in religious law, it is plainly unacceptable to reason. Obviously, an outbreak of lying in society will swiftly destroy the bonds of trust that are all that holds society together. As these bonds are eroded, people's extreme mutual suspicion will isolate them, although they may still have the appearance of a social body.

In our lives, we are continually involved with things external to ourselves. By acting upon and working with these things, we maintain our lives and attain our wants. Thus we as human beings use our intelligence and will to extend the reach of our lives on the basis of knowledge. We operate by thinking, and so our efforts depend directly upon the information available to us. We are continually organizing our mental conceptions and carrying out external activities according to them. For this reason, we find it absolutely essential to have correct information; insofar as we are denied it — not being told of the pitfalls before us or how far we must go, for instance — we shall certainly fail to accomplish anything. It thus grows clear that lies pose a grave danger to social life and that the liar is a degraded and dishonourable being who is society's enemy, discredited before the people and cursed by God.

BACKBITING AND SLANDER

To speak ill of others and censure them is called backbiting (*ghiba*) when true and slander (*iftira'* or *bihtan*) when false.

Of course, God Most High has created no one (except for the Prophets and the Imams) free of sin, and anyone, being imperfect, can slip or fall. People generally live behind the veil that God Most High has, through His far-reaching wisdom, drawn over their acts. If this divine veil were lifted to expose all our faults and errors, everyone would flee each other in loathing, and society would crumble to its foundations. This is why God Most High has forbidden backbiting, so that we should be protected from talk behind our backs, and so that our outward lives should appear beautiful, and this outward beauty should penetrate our inward ugliness. God Most High says, '*Do not backbite one another. Would any of you like to eat the flesh of your dead brother?*' (49:12).

Slander is ranked as more reprehensible than backbiting, and its vileness is patent to reason. God Most High presupposes its vile and unacceptable character where He says, '*Those who do not believe in Allah's signs are merely inventing a lie; such men are*

181

liars' (16:105).

TRANSGRESSIONS AGAINST PEOPLE'S HONOUR

According to Islam, it is a major sin to rend the veil of chastity and, depending on the circumstances, harsh penalties such as lashing, beheading, and stoning have been imposed for such acts.

Even if such ugly acts are committed by mutual consent, they undermine the foundations of the principle of heredity to which Islam has paid great attention and disrupt the functioning of the inheritance laws. Finally, they dissolve the natural bonds of affection between parents and children and so eliminate the natural effects of reproduction that in reality keep society intact.

SELF-RESPECT AND MORAL RECTITUDE

The order of the creation, which has made man social and obliged him to cooperate, has equipped him in a sense to lift himself up by his own bootstraps and to use the fruits of his labour to maintain his life in its own social environment.

A little consideration of this point leaves no room for doubt that self-respect consists in our employing our own God-given powers to reach our goals, not in depending on others' powers. This is one of the moral values innate in human nature. Self-respect is a dam that holds us back from a base existence and numerous evil and impermissible acts. One who has no self-respect and who depends upon others can readily hand over his will and individuality to others. He will do whatever they say, greedy for some morsel, sacrificing whatever they demand from him — his freedom, his dignity, his honour.

Most crimes, such as murder, banditry, theft, pickpocketing, perjury, sycophancy, treason, and selling out to foreigners, are the evil fruits of greed and parasitism. One who proudly wears the crown of self-respect, however, will not bow before any grandeur except the grandeur of God Most High and will kneel before no authority and pomp. Such a one will always rise to defend what he recognizes to be the truth. Self-respect is the best means for attaining and preserving one's moral rectitude.

CHARITY AND AID TO THE NEEDY

It is certain that the needy in any society have a right to help, and that it is the responsibility of the well-off to extend that help; they cannot shirk this duty. The holy law of Islam likewise urges that this right be observed, holding the well-off responsible for aiding the indigent.

In the Glorious Qur'an, God Most High refers to Himself as the Beneficent, the Bountiful, and the Forgiving and urges His servants to assimilate these qualities, to the point that He says, *'Allah is with the beneficent'* (2:194), *'Whatever they expend, it reverts to yourselves'* (2:272), and *'Those who...spend...from what He has provided for them may hope for a business that will never slacken'* (35:29).

When we carefully consider the social situation and the benefits of charity, the nobility these verses express becomes clear. In truth, all the productive forces of a society are meant to benefit everyone, but, in a society where some are too indigent to work, the production of wealth declines in direct proportion. The undesirable effects reach everyone; things may reach a point where the formerly well-off are worse off than anyone. If the well-off extend their beneficence and generosity to aid the indigent, however, they realize wonderful benefits, including: 1. others' affection, 2. a great deal of respect, for little capital outlay, 3. popular support (people will back those who do good), 4. freedom from the danger that the rage of the dispossessed will someday become a wildfire, engulfing everything, and 5. returns many times over their own small capital investment, as the economy begins functioning. There are innumerable Qur'anic verses and traditions urging charity and extolling its virtues.

COOPERATION

This generosity and beneficence constitute only one of the

many forms of cooperation, the basis of human society. The real nature of society is individuals' joining hands to do the work for everyone, put everyone's life on a secure footing, and take care of everyone's needs through mutual aid. One must not suppose that the holy faith of Islam asks our beneficience only through sacrifice of wealth. Rather, to come to the aid of the needy, even if money is not what they need, is what the holy faith of Islam, as well as the human conscience, is seeking.

To teach someone illiterate, to take the hand of someone blind, to guide someone lost, to aid one who has fallen — all are manifestations of generosity and beneficence, just as they all manifest the cooperation that we have assented to and relied upon since the time societies were first formed. It is obvious that, if people fail to carry out some aspects of the work of society, the basic operations will not get carried out and that, if people are unwilling to fulfill some minor functions, they will prove unwilling to carry out the task as a whole.

CHARITABLE WORKS AND DONATIONS
The value of an act of beneficence lies in its results. Of course, the more universal or enduring are these results, the more beneficial is the act. To cure a sick person is an act of beneficence and generosity, but it bears no comparison with building and operating a hospital that treats hundreds of patients a day. It is a virtue to teach a student, but this does not approach the value of establishing an institution that graduates hundreds of students every year. Thus, endowments and charitable works that have widespread and enduring effects represent an especially high degree of charity.

In the language of the holy law, such works are known as 'alms of lasting consequence' (as-sadaqa al-jariya). The Most Noble Messenger (peace and blessings upon him and his family) has said, 'Two things are a credit to a man: one is a pious offspring, and the other is alms of lasting consequence'. Traditions testify that God Most High grants blessings to one who engages in charity.

SELF-SACRIFICE

It is certain that, in the dictionary of the human conscience, life is synonymous with life with honour. A life that is not paired with honour and human happiness is no life at all. Rather, it is a death more bitter than natural death, and someone who does not value his own honour and happiness must flee such a base existence as a living death.

In whatever environment we inhabit, in whatever manner we choose to live, we understand through our God-given nature that death in the cause of what we hold sacred is a blessing. According to religious reasoning, nothing is more clearer or more logical than this, and has less to do with idle supposition or superstition. One who dies defending his own religious community by religious commandment knows that he has deprived himself of nothing but has given up his sweet yet ephemeral life in God's way to receive a sweeter, more precious, and eternal life whereby his happiness can never decline. As God Most High says, *'Do not think of those who are killed in Allah's way as dead. No, they are living, provided for by their Lord'* (3:169).

In secular systems, by contrast, human life is seen as confined to this ephemeral earthly life. They cannot say that we have a life or attain to happiness after death. They can only try to inculcate an irrational notion that one who is killed for his country or holy motherland will be remembered as a national hero whose name will be inscribed in gold in the book of history, to live on forever in this manner.

No pious act is as honored in Islam as laying down one's life in God's way. The Most Noble Messenger (peace and blessings upon him and his family) has said, 'For any virtuous act, there is an act of superior virtue, up to martyrdom, to which no act is superior'. The Muslims of the first generation sought divine forgiveness through the Most Noble Messenger (peace and blessings upon him and his family) and so attained the lofty state of martyrdom through his prayers. People did not cry for those who had departed the world through martyrdom, since they were alive and had not died.

GENEROSITY AND MUNIFICENCE

There is no need to explain the part property has in regulating life. It can assume such importance that many people regard it as the whole of life and can conceive of no other attainment for man than possession of wealth and devote all their energies to amassing money. Being so greedy and enamoured of wealth makes them stingy and unwilling to part with any of it for anyone. They may go a step farther and become misers who refuse to spend anything for their own benefit, so that neither do they eat nor do they feed anyone else. Making money becomes their only source of pleasure.

People who are given over to the vice of stinginess (and of course this is all the more true of misers) have become alienated from their human nature and are bankrupt in the marketplace of life, because:

1. They seek only their own happiness and prosperity in life; they are individualists, although human nature presents life to us as social, and individual life is doomed to perish in any event.

2. In displaying their wealth to others, they force the poor to be submissive and make them bow down like slaves without ever doing anything to help them. They thus perpetuate the spirit of idolatry and so corrode any sort of courage, loftiness of nature, or human dignity in society.

3. Besides crushing their own finer feelings of kindness, compassion, and fellow-feeling, they give rise to all sorts of criminality and baseness in society. Poverty is the biggest natural factor in such criminal or antisocial behaviour as villification, unchastity, theft, banditry, and murder, along with the rage, resentment, and vengefulness that the downtrodden feel toward the rich, which the stingy and miserly rich further inflame. Thus the stingy man is really Public Enemy Number One of society and will inevitably earn people's repugnance

along with God's anger and divine retribution.

The Noble Qur'an includes many verses condemning the vice of stinginess and conversely praising the virtue of generosity, charity in God's way, and aid to the needy. God Most High promises that wealth given in charity will be returned to the giver ten, seventy, or seven hundred times over. Experience likewise shows that those who open-handedly and nobly aid the poor or work for social progress steadily grow wealthier. If they should someday meet with hard times, they enjoy people's affection and the help they once extended to others all comes back to them.

Apart from the fact that they ease their consciences by acting well and nobly, the generous are responding to the divine summons both to fulfill incumbent duties and to carry out commendable actions. They have given expression to human feelings of kindness, sympathy, and humanitarianism and have gained the unalloyed affection and respect of the public. Finally, they have attained God's pleasure and eternal happiness at little cost.

JIHAD

Any creature will defend its life and interests and will arm itself in any way it can to combat its enemy. A human being has a natural conviction that he must defend himself and that he must destroy his enemy, who will stop at nothing to destroy him. Likewise, if someone interferes with his vital interests, he will rise to their defense and repel the aggressor by any means possible.

This innate tendency in a human individual is likewise innate in human societies. That is, an enemy who menaces the individuals of a society or the very independence of that society is effectively under a death sentence in that society. So long as man and human societies have existed, the idea has persisted that an individual or a society are free to resolve upon the most severe measures to confront their mortal enemies.

Islam as a religion concerned with society and founded upon *tauhid* regards those who refuse to submit to truth and justice as its mortal enemies and a disruptive force in society. It accords them no human dignity and worth. Since it presents itself as a universal religion and restricts its adherence to no nationalities or frontiers, it wars against anyone whose values are infected with *shirk* and who cannot be brought to acknowledge the truth and the holy law through plain reasoning and sage counsel, until he submits to the rule of truth and justice.

This is the essence of Islam's rules on *jihad*. They accord fully with the method that any human society naturally adopts in dealing with its mortal enemies.

Contrary to the assertions of its detractors, Islam is not the religion of the sword. Islam has never acted imperialistically, through the sword or political maneuvering. Rather, it is the religion God has created in conformity with people's created natures and to which He summons them by appeal to their native intelligence and reason, through His celestial speech.

A religion whose universal greeting is '*Salam*' ('Peace') and whose global program is, according to the Noble Qur'an, founded on the principle '*Peace is better*' (4:128), could never be the religion of the sword and force.

During the lifetime of the Most Noble Messenger (peace and blessings upon him and his family), as the light of Islam spread across the Arabian peninsula and the Muslims were engaged in major, fierce battles, no more than two hundred Muslims and less than a thousand unbelievers were killed, the latter figure including seven hundred members of the Qurayza tribe who were executed as a result of arbitration they had chosen. How unjust it is to call such a faith the religion of the sword!

CASES WHEN WAR IS CALLED FOR IN ISLAM
Islam is at war with four classes of people:

1. *Mushriks*, that is, those who disbelieve in *tauhid*, prophecy,

and the Resurrection. They must be first summoned to Islam, clearly enough that no point of doubt or other pretext remains. The precepts of the religion must be explained to them clearly. If they then embrace the religion, they are brothers of all other Muslims and share in their good times and bad. If they do not embrace it, and if they do not bow to it after these precepts have been made plain to them, Islam will make it a duty to wage *jihad* against them.

2. People of the Book (Jews, Christians and Zoroastrians), whom Islam holds are religious folk, possessing revealed scriptures and believing in *tauhid*, prophecy, and the Resurrection. Islam offers sanctuary to them on condition of payment of the poll-tax known as the *jizya*. This indicates their acceptance of Islamic rule, under which they retain their independence, are allowed to act according to their own religious rules, and are as secure in their lives and property as are any Muslims. In return, they pay the *jizya*, a token sum, to Muslim society. They may not, however, circulate anti-Islamic propaganda, aid the enemies of Islam, or do other things detrimental to Muslims.

3. Rebels, that is, Muslims who conduct armed uprisings against Islam and shed Muslims' blood. Islamic society wars against them until they surrender and cease from rebellion.

4. Enemies of the faith, who seek to undermine the foundations of the religion or to overthrow Islamic government. It is incumbent upon all Muslims to defend their faith against such persons as unbelieving belligerents.

If Islam and Muslim policy dictate, Islamic society can conclude temporary non-aggression pacts with the enemies of Islam. It does not have the right, however, to open friendly relations with them in a manner that would allow their words and actions to have a detrimental influence on Muslims' thoughts and actions.

FLIGHT FROM *JIHAD* AND DEFENSE
To turn one's back on the enemy and flee the battlefield means that one values one's own survival more highly than the survival

of society. It is, in truth, to abandon sacred values, along with the lives and property of one's fellows, to an enemy that threatens every aspect of that society's existence.

Thus, desertion for the cause of *jihad* and defense is accounted a major sin. God Most High expressly promises hellfire to the deserter, saying, '*Whoever turns his back on [the unbelievers], unless in a maneuver or turning to join a detachment, has incurred Allah's wrath, and his habitation will be hell*' (8:16).

DEFENDING ONE'S HOMELAND
For the reasons I have stated, defense of Islamic society and of Muslims' homes is one of the most important responsibilities Islam makes incumbent upon us. God Most High says, '*Do not claim those who are killed in the way of Allah "dead". No, they are living, only you do not perceive it*' (2:154).

The story of the men who took their lives in their hands and advanced into battle in the early days of Islam and of the martyrs who weltered in their own blood is astonishing as well as instructive. It was they who secured the foundations of this holy faith with their pure blood and their torn bodies.

COMBATING SOCIETY'S ENEMIES WITHIN
Just as we are obliged by nature to combat the external enemies of a society and preserve it from injury, so we must combat society's internal enemies. One is society's internal enemy whose opposition to extant law and custom creates disorder in public life. Organized societies must use their police power and punish their adversaries in various ways to maintain order and commerce.

Islam, in addition to providing various police powers and penalties, makes it incumbent upon all the members of society to enjoin good and forbid evil. Thus it broadens this struggle and makes it more effective. The main difference between Islam and other social systems lies in the fact that the others attempt only to reform people's actions, but Islam pays attention to both their actions and their moral values, combating corruption on both levels.

The sins and acts of disobedience that Islam has forbidden are acts that have unfortunate consequences for society. One must qualify this by noting that some acts directly corrupt the individual or individuals who commit them and so create a chink in society's armour. They are like localized wounds or symptoms of an organ of someone's body. Most sins against the bond of servanthood or in neglect of what is due God, such as failure to pray or to fast, are of this kind. Other actions directly threaten the life of the body. To lie or make false accusations are actions of this kind. According to Islam, disregard of one's duties toward one's parents, backbiting, and transgression against people's rights also have this status.

DEFENSE OF THE TRUTH
There is another sort of defense that is much more profound and sweeping than defense of one's homeland, and this is defense of the Truth, the sole object of the holy faith of Islam. This divine method exists to promulgate the Truth and reality; thus, our faith is known as the *Religion of Truth*, meaning a religion that belongs to the Truth, contains nothing but the Truth, and has no other object than the Truth.

In describing His book, which comprehends all realities, God Most High says, '[*It*] *guides people to the truth and to the straight way*' (46:30). Accordingly, it is necessary for every Muslim to accord with the truth, to speak the truth, and to defend the truth with all his power and in any way possible.

HOMICIDE
A form of evil that is reprehended in the holy law of Islam is homicide and killing of the innocent.

To kill someone is a major sin; God Most High equates killing one person with killing all people. This can only mean that to kill one person is a blow to the humanity that is the same in one person or a thousand.

EMBEZZLEMENT OF THE WEALTH OF ORPHANS

To the same extent that goodness toward the people is lauded by reason and by the holy law, evil conduct toward God's servants is reproved. In the holy law, however, there are some evils that are forbidden with particular vehemence. One of these is embezzlement of the wealth of orphans, which Islam regards as a major sin. The Noble Qur'an says explicitly that one who consumes the wealth of orphans is really consuming fire and will one day be consumed by the Fire. As the Imams have explained, the reason for all this emphasis is that, although an adult may be able to resist and to defend his rights when oppressed, a minor orphan has no such ability.

DESPAIR OF GOD'S MERCY

According to Islam, one of the most perilous sins is despair of God's mercy. God Most High says, '*Say, "My servants who have acted extravagantly against themselves — do not despair of God's mercy. God forgives all offenses; He is the Most Forgiving, the Merciful"*' (39:53). Elsewhere, one who despairs of God's mercy is considered an unbeliever, because such a one no longer has any motive in his life to do good or to abstain from minor and major sins or other reproved acts (the basic motive for these things being 'hope of God's mercy' or 'hope of deliverance from God's wrath'). Such a one has no such hope and is no different in his subjective state from one who has no religion.

ANGER

Anger is a state that arouses one to thought of revenge when it arises and that subsides when revenge has been taken. If one does not exercise the greatest self-control when under the influence of anger, one quickly becomes irrational and capable of justifying the most heinous acts to oneself. The process can reach a point at which one becomes more predatory than any natural predator.

Islam insists that this state be curbed and sharply reproves indulging it. God Most High, showing great favour to those who suppress their anger and show forbearance when they are angry, says, for instance, '[*Allah loves*] *those who control their anger*' (3:134). He also says that believers are '*those who forgive when they are provoked to anger*' (42:37).

BRIBERY

To accept money or gifts in return for a judgment or any other action that falls within the official responsibilities of the recipient is known as 'bribery'.

Bribery is a major sin in Islam, and one who commits it is denied the social benefits of religion (justice) and deserves God's torment. This is made clear in the Noble Qur'an and the *sunna*. The Most Noble Messenger (peace and blessings upon him and his family) has cursed anyone who gives or receives a bribe or acts as an intermediary in bribery. Also, Imam Ja'far has said, 'To accept a bribe in return for a judgment is tantamount to disbelief in God'. This degree of censure is for accepting a bribe to render justice; the sin of accepting a bribe to render injustice is much graver, and the punishment correspondingly harsher.

THEFT

Theft is an evil and illicit occupation that threatens the security of wealth in a society. Plainly, a person's prime asset in life is the wealth and property that he has spent his life acquiring, and he strives to protect it from any sort of encroachment. It provides backing for social life. Of course, to break through this wall of protection, disrupting this system, is to destroy the capital that someone has spent a life in acquiring. It means that the major portion of someone's efforts has gone to waste and been rendered ineffective.

Accordingly, Islam has established as a punishment for this vile act, against which the thief's own conscience recoils, that the thief's hand (four fingers of the right hand) be severed. God Most High says, '*As for thieves, male or female, cut off their hands as a requital for their acts*' (5:38).

GIVING SHORT WEIGHT
According to Islam, to give short weight is a major sin. God Most High censures and warns the perpetrators, saying: '*Woe unto those who defraud...Do they not consider that they will be raised again, to a terrible day?*' (83:4-5). One who gives short weight, besides oppressing the people and embezzling their wealth, loses their trust and denies himself their business and finally his capital.

PUNISHMENT FOR SINS
IN GENERAL IN ISLAM
Islam designates the sorts of behavior that I have described as major sins, and God Most High has explicitly promised that their perpetrators will be tormented.

Apart from the fact that severe punishments have been prescribed for some of them, those who commit them even once lose their honour, which is to say that the dignity accorded a member in good standing of human society is denied them.

One who commits a major sin gives up his honour and the privileges he enjoys as a member in good standing of society. He cannot occupy various posts in the Islamic government, cannot be a leader, and cannot lead communal prayers. His testimony is not accepted to anyone's advantage or detriment. His status will remain the same until he regains his honour through repentance and sustained piety.

THE NECESSITY OF WORK AND
THE IMPORTANCE OF TRADE AND INDUSTRY
Work is the foundation of the creation and the sole assurance that any created being will survive. God Most High has equipped each created being in accordance with its nature with the means to gain what is beneficial to it and to ward off harm.

Human beings, the most marvelous and complex forms in

creation, have greater needs than other creatures and must accordingly engage in more activities to secure these innumerable needs and to maintain the family structure that is natural to them. Islam, as a religion in accord with nature and society, has accordingly made it incumbent to have a legitimate occupation. The Most Noble Prophet (peace and blessings upon him and his family) has said, 'To pursue livelihood is incumbent upon every Muslim man and woman'. Islam accords no value to people who sit idle. When the Most Noble Prophet (peace and blessings upon him and his family) would see a physically powerful man, he would ask, 'Does he work?' If he was answered in the negative, he would comment, 'He has lowered himself in my eyes'. That is, to the Most Noble Prophet (peace and blessings upon him and his family), an unemployed person (and not elderly or disabled) was worthless.

In Islam, every person must, in accordance with his own aptitude and proclivity, choose one of the many occupations to which God Most High has guided human thought and so gain his livelihood. Thus he carries his part of the burden to provide for people's comfort. God Most High says, '*Man has nothing except what he struggles for*' (53:39). In brief, Islam urges work and earning one's livelihood in the strongest terms and has not neglected economic activity under the most difficult circumstances. Imam Sadiq (upon whom be peace) told one of his companions named Hisham, 'Even during battle, when the hostile forces are facing each other and the flames of war are lapping them, you must not neglect your economic role and the necessary activities to procure a livelihood; pursue your pecuniary efforts under these difficult conditions'. Thus, to be unemployed due to laziness is strictly forbidden in Islam.

IN REPROOF OF IDLENESS
The preceding discussion makes it clear that work and striving are the straight road that the creation has laid out before man. By following it, man attains his happiness. To deviate from this natural course even a little can only lead to ruin. To deviate

from something that is the basis for the system by which we live can only lead to misfortune in this life and the next. Thus, the seventh Imam (upon whom be peace) has said, 'Do not let weakness and fatigue show in your work; otherwise you will lose this world and the next'. The Most Noble Prophet (peace and blessings upon him and his family) cursed those who had grown used to idleness and so became a burden to others.

Today, psychological and sociological studies have made it clear that many social ills arise from unemployment. Unemployment stops the wheel of society's economic and cultural life from turning and contributes to every sort of moral decline and superstitious outlook.

THE VIRTUES OF FARMING
It is by farming that society is fed, and, because of its importance, farming is one of the best occupations for people, and Islam greatly encourages taking it up. The sixth Imam (upon whom be peace) has said, 'On the Day of Resurrection, farmers will occupy a higher station than any others'. The fifth Imam (upon whom be peace) has said, 'No work is better or of more general benefit than farming, since good and bad people, grazing animals, and birds all benefit from it and so wordlessly pray for the farmer'. The Most Noble Prophet (peace and blessings upon him and his family) has said, 'A Muslim who plants a tree or grows a crop of which people, birds and grazing animals eat receives the reward for almsgiving'.

Muslims are charged with making the most of their natural abilities, to the extent that one of the Holy Imams has said, 'If the hour should arrive for the world to be annihilated and the sun to collapse into chaos and one of you is holding a sapling, if you still can plant it, do plant it'. That is, do not let the thought of the annihilation of the world hold you back from a noble deed. The Commander of the Faithful 'Ali (peace and blessings upon him and his family) has said, 'God curse one who has water and earth and becomes destitute'.

SELF-RELIANCE

It was repeatedly mentioned in the section titled 'Beliefs' that the general program of Islam consists in our worshipping no one but the One God and bowing before no one but Him, the Fosterer of the Universe.

All beings whatever have been created and fostered by God and eat what He has provided. No one has precedence over anyone else except one who relies on God.

Every Muslim should rely on himself and use the gift of self-reliance that God Most High has given him. He should employ the means that have been provided him and go about his life; he should not pin his hopes on others and so partner a new idol with God every day. The servant must know that he is eating his own bread and not the master's bread. He must know that he is reaping the fruits of his own exertions and not getting free handouts from his employer. Any employee needs to feel sure that he is getting paid for his work and not getting a free ride from his chief or his office or the state or society. In sum, a free man must not pin his hopes on or bow to anyone but God, or he will inwardly suffer the same baseness and enslavement of *shirk* that idolaters manifest outwardly.

In conclusion, it must be noted that self-reliance means using one's innate self-worth in life and not sitting in expectation of others' help. It does not mean cutting oneself off from God Most High and imagining one can realize all one's aims alone.

HARM CAUSED BY A LIFE OF DEPENDENCY
To live as a parasite on others is really to give up one's honour as a human being and the dignity of independence. It is the source of every sort of crime and antisocial act arising from abjectness and degradation.

One who seeks to live off favours from others really has put his own intelligence and will on the auction block. He must flatter, he must do whatever they want and ask (constructive or pointless, good or evil). He submits to any shame and disgrace, he adulates foreigners, he consents to any form of injustice and oppression, and, finally, he is indifferent to all the rules and bounds of human life.

It is forbidden in Islam to beg except out of necessity, and the financial assistance to the poor that Islam ordains only applies to those poor whose earnings do not meet their needs or those who are unable to work.

CHAPTER TEN

ORDINANCES

As I noted at the beginning of this book, Islam's rules and teachings are of three kinds: credal, moral and juridical. This third kind covers Islamic ordinances. After we have acknowledged God, we must carry out such actions as prayers and fasting as signs of servanthood and compliance. Here I will explain the ordinances applying to prayer, and then those applying to fasting.

RITUAL PRAYER
God Most High says, '[*The inhabitants of Hell will be asked*], *"What has brought you to this fire?" They will answer, "We did not pray"*' (74:42-43). The Most Noble Prophet (peace and blessings upon him and his family) has said, 'Ritual prayer is a pillar of religion; if one's prayer is accepted by God, then one's other acts of worship are accepted, and, if it is not accepted, then they are not accepted'. Just as if someone bathes five times

daily, dirt does not collect on his body, so offering ritual prayers five times a day cleanses one of sin.

It must of course be realized that one who offers prayers without concentration is like one who does not pray at all. God Most High says in the Glorious Qur'an, '*Woe upon worshippers who are inattentive in prayer*' (107:4-5). Once the Most Noble Prophet (peace and blessings upon him and his family) entered a mosque and saw someone praying without fully bowing or prostrating; he said, 'If this man departs from this world in this condition, he will not depart this world as a Muslim'.

Accordingly, one must pray humbly and mindful to Whom one is speaking. One must carry out the bows, prostrations, and other actions correctly to gain the sublime benefits of prayer.

God says in the Noble Qur'an, '*Prayer restrains one from lewdness and iniquity*' (29:45). This is naturally true because prayer is surrounded by customs that, if observed, never allow evil actions. For example, one such custom is that the place of prayer and the worshipper's clothing must not have been illegally obtained; if so much as a thread of clothing was illegally obtained, the prayer is not valid. The worshipper in being compelled to abstain from what is forbidden to this extent is prevented from using property obtained by forbidden means or trampling on someone's rights. Furthermore, prayers are only accepted when one has set aside all greed, envy, and other vices and evil characteristics; certainly, these vicious characteristics are the origin of all misdeeds and the worshipper, in removing himself from these characteristics, will remove himself from evil and unseemly acts. If some people, despite the fact that they pray, commit evil acts, this is because they do not act according to Islam's regulations for prayer. Accordingly, their prayers will not be accepted, and they will not realize the sublime fruits of prayer.

The Holy Lawgiver of Islam has accorded so much importance to prayer as to require it of those who are dying. If they are unable to speak the *Sura Hamd* and other words of prayer aloud, they must say it to themselves, and if they are too weak to stand in prayer, they should pray sitting, and if they are too weak to sit, they must pray lying down. The point is that we are never exempted from prayer. If in the midst of battle, amidst the terror and confusion, one cannot find the *qibla*, one must nonetheless pray in any direction feasible.

OBLIGATORY PRAYERS

Six kinds of prayers are obligatory: 1. daily prayers, 2. *ayat* prayers, 3. funeral prayers, 4. prayers obligatory during circumambulation [of the Ka'aba], 5. prayers omitted by the parents, obligatory upon the oldest son, and 6. prayers one was hired to offer, or prayers one has vowed to offer.

PRELIMINARIES TO PRAYER

To pray, that is, to come before the Lord of the world and express servanthood and worship of His sacred essence, calls for necessary preliminaries without which the prayer is not valid. These preliminaries consist of: 1. cleanliness, 2. timeliness, 3. proper dress, 4. proper place, and 5. turning to the *qibla*. I will now discuss these in more detail.

CLEANLINESS

The worshipper must be ritually clean while praying; that is, he must precede his prayer with the ablution *wuzu* or the ritual bathings *ghusl* or *tayammum* as appropriate; his body and clothing must not be tainted with impurities.

IMPURITIES

Several things constitute impurities, including: 1. and 2. urine and feces[1] of an animal whose flesh is forbidden and which has spurting blood, that is, whose arteries spurt blood when severed, such as the wolf, fox, and rabbit, or of a bird or other animal whose flesh has become forbidden because it has eaten filth. 3. The carcass of an animal with spurting blood, whether its flesh is permissible or forbidden. Formerly lifeless parts of the carcass, however, such as the wool, hair, and nails, are considered pure. 4. The blood itself of an animal with spurting blood, whether its flesh is permissible or forbidden. 5. and 6. The dog and wild pig, all parts of which are impure, including the hair. 7. Alcoholic beverages and all essentially liquid intoxicants. 8. Beer.

PURIFYING AGENTS

Anything by which impurities can be removed is a purifying agent (*mutahhir*); these include: 1. Water, which purifies anything but only if it is itself pure, so that things like watermelon juice and rose water do not remove impurity, and ritual ablutions and bathing performed with them are not valid.[2] 2. Earth, which cleans the soles of the feet or the shoes. 3. Sunlight, which purifies the earth and tainted mats that are dried by its rays. 4. Transformation, by which an impure thing changes into a pure thing, as when a dog falls into a salt marsh and turns into salt. 5. Transfer, as when human blood or the blood of an animal having spurting blood is transferred to an animal not having spurting blood like a fly or a mosquito. 6. Removal of the impurity from outside an animal or inside a human being, as when an animal's back or the inside of a person's nose becomes bloody and then is cleansed with the removal of the blood, leaving no further need for cleansing with water. 7. By consequence, whereby, when one impure thing is cleansed, another becomes pure as a consequence, as when an unbeliever becomes a Muslim and his children also become pure as a consequence. 8. Reduction, which is when grape juice, which becomes impure by boiling, is reduced by two-thirds through evaporation, the remainder again becomes pure.

WUZU AND ORDINANCES PERTAINING TO IT

It is recommended that one brush one's teeth and rinse out one's mouth and one's nostrils before performing *wuzu*.

For *wuzu*, one must wash the face from the hairline to the chin and the hands and forearms from the elbow to the fingertips, and one must wipe the front part of the head and the tops of the feet. The following things must also be observed: 1. The relevant body parts must be pure. 2. The water used must be clean, pure, and lawfully acquired. 3. One must form the intention of carrying out *wuzu* to please God. Thus, if one carries it out to cool off or for some other reason, it is invalid. 4. One must observe the correct sequence of washing first the face, then the right hand, and then the left, and after that of wiping the head and then the feet. 5. The actions of *wuzu* must be done in unbroken succession, without allowing one member to dry while another is being washing or wiped. If, however, one performs them in unbroken succession but they dry quickly because of extreme heat and dry air, the *wuzu* is still valid.

Note that it is not necessary to wipe the skin of the head, but one may merely wipe the hair toward the front of the head. If, however, hair from elsewhere on the head is gathered to the front, it should be pushed back. Also, if the hair at the front is long enough to be combed, say, across the face, one must wipe the hair to its roots or part the hair and wipe the skin.

THINGS THAT INVALIDATE *WUZU*
Eight things invalidate *wuzu*: 1. urination, 2. defecation, 3. breaking wind, through the anus or some other opening created by surgery or a wound, 4. unconsciousness, 5. intoxication, 6. sleep through which both the eyes and the ears cease to function — if one ceases to see but continues hearing, *wuzu* remains valid, 7. lunacy, 8. sexual discharge, or other things that would require *ghusl*, ritual bathing, such as copious menstrual discharge.

GHUSL, RITUAL BATHING
Ghusl is two kinds, sequential and by immersion. Sequential *ghusl* consists of washing first the head and neck, then the right side of the body, and then the left side of the body. *Ghusl* by immersion consists of one immersing the entire body in water at once. *Ghusl* may be either incumbent or recommended; there are numerous occasions when bathing is recommended in

Islamic law, but only seven occasions when it is incumbent: 1. after sexual emissions, 2. bathing of the dead, 3. bathing oneself after contact with a corpse that was not bathed and has become cold, 4. having taken a vow to bathe, 5. at the cessation of menstruation, 6. after childbirth, and 7. after copius menstrual discharge. The first four forms apply to both men and women, and the last three only to women.

These things are forbidden to those who had had sexual emissions: 1. to touch the Noble Qur'an or the names of God, the Prophet, or the Imams, 2. to enter the Masjid al-Haram or the mosque of Medina, 3. to stop over in another mosque or to leave something there, and 4. to read one of the four *suras* that require prostration, that is, an-Najm, Iqra', Alif Lam Mim Tanzil, and Ha Mim Sajda. One should consult scholarly treatises for other rules applying to sexual emissions, menstruation, and childbirth.

Note that, as with *wuzu*, one must form the proper intention prior to performing *ghusl*, and the body must be clean, with nothing preventing water from reaching the skin.

TAYAMMUM
Tayammum is a ritual bath performed with earth or sand when one is unable to perform *wuzu* or *ghusl* for reasons such as lack of time, illness, or lack of water. Four things are required for *tayammum*: 1. intention, 2. to strike the palms of both hands at once on earth or other valid substances for *tayammum*, 3. to draw the palms of the two hands across the entire forehead from the hairline to the eyebrows, over the nose, and (preferably) rubbing the eyebrows, and 4. to draw the palm of the left hand across the right hand and forearm, and then to draw the palm of the right hand across the left hand and forearm. If the *tayammum* is in place of *wuzu*, this is sufficient, but if it is in place of *ghusl*, one should strike the hands on the ground and wipe the backs of the hands one more time.

RULES RELATING TO *TAYAMMUM*

1. In the absence of earth, one must perform *tayammum* with sand, and in the absence of sand, dirt clods, and, in the absence of dirt clods, stones, and in the absence of all these, dirt and dust that has been gathered. 2. *Tayammum* with plaster or other minerals is not valid. 3. If one can afford to purchase water, although it is expensive, one cannot perform *tayammum*. One must purchase water and perform *wuzu* or *ghusl*.

TIMELINESS

The *zuhr* (noontime) and *'asr* (afternoon) prayers have prescribed times that overlap.[3] The time for *zuhr* prayer extends from noon until no time remains to offer it. If someone mistakenly offers his *'asr* prayers during this time, his prayers are invalid.

The time for *'asr* prayer extends until no time remains to offer it before time for the *maghrib* (sunset) prayer. If one has not offered the *zuhr* prayer by this time, its time has lapsed, and one must offer the *'asr* prayer. The *zuhr* prayer and the *'asr* prayer have a shared time between the times exclusive to each, during which, if someone mistakenly offers the entire *'asr* before the *zuhr* prayer, his prayer is nonetheless valid, and he must later offer the *zuhr* prayer.

The *maghrib* and *'isha* (evening) prayers likewise have their specific times and a shared time. The time specific to the *maghrib* prayer extends from after sunset until no time remains to perform the three *rak'as* of the *maghrib* prayer.[4] The time specific to the *'isha* prayer extends until no time remains to offer it before midnight.[5] If one has not offered the *maghrib* prayer by this time, one must first offer the *'isha* prayer, and then the *maghrib* prayer. These two prayers have a time in common between the times specific to each, and if, during this time, someone mistakenly offers the *'isha* prayer before having offered the *maghrib* prayer, his prayer is valid, and he must afterwards offer the *maghrib* prayer.

PROPER DRESS

Several rules apply to the clothing of the worshipper: 1. It must be lawful; that is, it must either belong to him or be worn with the permission of its lawful owner. 2. It must not be ritually unclean. 3. It must not consist of animal skins, whether of animals whose flesh may be eaten or not. 4. It must not be made of the wool, hair, or down of an animal whose flesh may not be eaten, except one may offer prayers while wearing sable fur. 5. If the worshipper is male, his clothing may not include threads of silk or gold, nor may he wear gold ornaments. The same prohibition applies at all other times, not just during prayer.

PROPER PLACE

Several rules apply to the place where prayers are to be offered: 1. It must be lawful. 2. It must not be in motion, except that prayers may be offered in a moving vehicle such as an automobile or a ship in case of necessity; if the vehicle is moving away from the *qibla*, the worshipper should turn to it. 3. If the place is ritually unclean but not damp enough to dampen the body or clothing, it is acceptable, except that the prayer is invalidated if the place touched by the forehead in prostration is unclean, even if it is dry. 4. The place touched by the forehead may not be higher or lower than the places touched by the knees or the toes by more than the span across the four fingers.

TURNING TO THE *QIBLA*

The house of the Ka'aba, which stands resplendent in Mecca, is the *qibla*, and one must face it in prayer. However, if someone is far away, it is sufficient that he stand or sit to pray in a direction said to be the *qibla*. The same applies to other acts that must be performed while facing the *qibla*, such as slaughtering animals.

One unable to perform prayers even while sitting must perform them while lying on his right side, or, barring that, on his left side, with the front of his body facing the *qibla*. If this is impossible, he should lie on his back, with the soles of his feet facing the *qibla*.

If the worshippper is unable to learn from investigation which way is the *qibla*, he should try to get an idea from the *mihrabs* of mosques, graves in Muslim cemeteries, or other indications.

ESSENTIAL ELEMENTS OF PRAYER

There are eleven essential, or incumbent, elements of prayer: 1. intention, 2. the *takbir al-ahram* (pronouncing 'Allahu Akbar' at the beginning of prayer), 3. *qiyam* (standing), 4. *qara'at* (recitation of the *Sura Hamd* and another *sura*), 5. *ruku'* (bowing), 6. *sajda* (prostration), 7. *tashahhud* (testimony that Allah is the One God and Muhammad is His Prophet), 8. *salam* (greetings and blessings on the Most Noble Prophet and the pious), 9. proper sequence, 10. *tumanina*, offering one's prayers with dignity and calm, and 11. *muwalat*, offering all parts of the prayer in uninterrupted succession. Five of the eleven elements are pillars of prayer, or central elements, such that the prayer is invalid if they are omitted or added to intentionally or inadvertently. Omitting or adding to the others renders the prayer invalid only if done intentionally.

PILLARS OF PRAYERS

The pillars of prayer are: 1. intention, 2. the *takbir al-ahram*, 3. to stand (*qiyam*) while pronouncing the *takbir al-ahram* and standing in sequence with the *ruku'*, 4. the *ruku'*, and 5. the two prostrations (*sajda*).

INTENTION

Intention consists in one's offering prayer to carry out God's command. It is not necessary to express the intention verbally to oneself or aloud, as for instance by saying, 'I will offer the four *rak'as* of the *zuhr* prayer to carry out God's command.

THE *TAKBIR AL-AHRAM*

After the call to prayer (*azan*) and the *iqama* with intention, the prayer commences with saying 'Allahu Akbar'. Since saying this renders such acts as eating, drinking, laughing, and turning one's back to the *qibla* forbidden, this act of glorification is called the *takbir al-ahram*, the glorification that forbids. It is recommended that one raise one's hands while pronouncing the *takbir*; by this action, we call to mind the greatness of God and the smallness of all else, which we set aside.

QIYAM

It is a pillar to stand while pronouncing the *takbir* and to stand in sequence with the *ruku'*, but not a pillar to stand while reciting the *Sura Hamd* and the other *sura*, or to stand after *ruku'*. Accordingly, if one forgets the *ruku'* but recollects it before reaching the *sajda*, he must first stand in *qiyam* and then bow in *ruku'*.

RUKU'

After reciting the two *suras*, one must bow to the extent that the hands reach the knees. This action is called *ruku'*, during which one must say '*Subhana Rabbi l-'Azim wa bi hamdihi*' (Glory to my Lord, the Sublime, and praise to Him) once or else '*Subhanallah*' (Glory to God) three times. After *ruku'*, one must rise to a fully erect posture and then go on to the *sajda*.

SAJDA

Sajda, prostration, means placing one's forehead, hands, kneecaps, and tips of the big toes on the ground and saying either '*Subhana Rabbi l-'A'la wa bi hamdihi*' (Glory to my Lord the Highest, and praise to Him) once or else '*Subhanallah*' three times. One then sits. The *sajda* is then repeated twice, accompanied by the same utterance.

The site which the forehead touches must be earth or something that grows from it; foodstuffs, apparel, or mineral materials are not permissible.

THE *TASHAHHUD* AND THE *SALAM*

If the prayer consists of two *rak'as*, after one has risen from the two *sajdas*, one pronounces the *Sura Hamd* and the other *sura*. One then carries out the *qunut*,[6] and, after the *ruku'* and the two *sajdas*, one recites the *tashahhud*[7] and the *salam*[8]. If the prayer consists of three *rak'as*, one rises after the *tashahhud* and either recites the *Sura Hamd* alone or says '*Subhana 'llah wa l-hamdu lillahi wa la ilaha illa 'llah wa 'llahu akbar*' three times. Then one carries out the two *rukus*, the *tashahhud*, and the *salam*. If the prayer consists of four *rak'as*, one performs the fourth *rak'a* just like the third and utters the *salam* after the *tashahhud*.

THE PRAYER OF SIGNS
This prayer becomes incumbent in four circumstances: an eclipse of the sun, an eclipse of the moon (even if partial and no source of fear to anyone), an earthquake (even if no one is frightened), and weather conditions such as lightning and thunder or black or red winds (if most people are frightened).

The prayer of signs consists of two *rak'as*, each including five *ruku's*. It is prescribed that one first form one's intention, then say the *takbir*, recite the *Sura Hamd* and one other complete *sura*, bow in *ruku'*, rise, recite the two *suras* again, bow in *ruku'*, and so on for five cycles. After rising from the fifth *ruku'*, one performs two *sajdas*. One then rises and performs a second *rak'a* in the same way. One then recites the *tashahhud* and offers the *salam*.

In the prayer of the signs, one may divide a *sura* into five portions, first forming the intention, then reciting the *Sura Hamd*, then reciting at least one verse of the *sura*, then bowing in *ruku'*, then rising, and without reciting the *Sura Hamd* again, reciting the second portion of the previous *sura* and bowing in *ruku'* again, and continuing in this way until one has completed the *sura* before the fifth *ruku'* and final two *sajdas*. One performs the second *rak'a* according to the same rule and finishes the prayer.

THE TRAVELLER'S PRAYER
Someone who is travelling should shorten his prayers of four *rak'as* to two *rak'as* when six conditions are met: 1. His journey must be one of at least eight farsangs (about 48 kilometers), one

way or round trip. 2. He must have resolved to travel at least eight farsangs when he began. 3. He must not give up his intention *en route*. 4. His journey must not have a sinful purpose. 5. He must not be a traveller by profession. Accordingly, one who travels for a living (such as a truck driver) must offer his prayers in full unless he has remained at his home for ten days, after which he should perform the shorter prayers during his next three trips. 6. He must reach the limit of *tarakhkhus*, which means that he must have travelled too far from home to see the city wall or hear the call to prayer there.

CONGREGATIONAL PRAYERS

It is recommended that Muslims say their daily prayers in congregations; the spiritual reward of congregational prayers is thousands of times greater than that of solitary prayers.

There are several conditions of congregational prayers: 1. That the *Imam* (prayer leader) must be of age (fifteen), believing, just, and of legitimate birth. He must perform the prayers correctly. If the congregation is male, the leader must also be male. 2. There must be no curtain or other object obstructing the congregation's view of the *imam*, except that there is no objection to a curtain or some such thing if the *Imam* is a woman. 3. The *Imam's* position may not be elevated above that of the congregation, except that there is no objection to a slight elevation (equal to the span of four fingers or less). 4. The congregation must stand behind the *Imam* or in line with him.

Here are a few rules applying to congregational prayers: 1. Members of the congregation should themselves recite all parts of the prayer except for the *Sura Hamd* and the other *sura*. If, however, the worshipper's first or second *rak'a* is the *Imam's* third or fourth *rak'a*, he must himself recite the two *suras*, and if he fails to keep up with the *Imam* because he must recite the second *sura*, he should recite only the *Hamd* and catch up with the *Imam* during the *ruku'*. If he still cannot catch up, he should resolve to complete the prayer in private. 2. The congregation should perform the *ruku'*, the *sajda*, and the other acts of prayer together with the *Imam* or slightly after him. The congregation must certainly perform the *takbir* and the *salam* after the *Imam* has begun performing them, however. 3. If the worshipper joins the prayer while the *Imam* is in *ruku'* and joins in *ruku'*, his prayer is valid and counts as one *rak'a*.

FASTING
Fasting is an element of the holy faith of Islam. Everyone of majority must fast during the month of Ramazan, which means that, in obedience to God's command, one must abstain from anything that would invalidate one's fast from the call to prayer at dawn until dusk.

The holy act of observing the fast is heavily stressed and highly prized in Islam. The rewards and punishments associated with the fast are so important that, although God has prescribed them in advance, He says that He Himself will administer them. According to the Most Noble Prophet (peace and blessings upon him and his family), God has said, 'The fast is for My sake, and I will give the requital for it'. When we observe the special conditions attached to it, the fast is a powerful means to free us from bondage to psychic cravings, whims, and lust and to cleanse the spirit of the pollution of carnal sin. The Most Noble Prophet (peace and blessings upon him and his family) told one Jabir ibn 'Abdallah Ansari, 'Jabir, this is the month of Ramazan, when whoever fasts during the day and remains awake and mindful of God during the night, and preserves his stomach from what is forbidden and his lap from pollution, and holds his tongue, will emerge from sin just as he emerges from this month'. Jabir responded, 'Prophet of God! What good news this is!' The Most Noble Prophet (peace and blessings upon him and his family) continued, 'But Jabir, the conditions for this fast are very hard!' Imam Sadiq (upon whom be peace) has said, 'The fast is a firm shield against the fires of hell'.

RAMAZAN IS GOD'S MONTH
Islamic writings have applied many interesting and attractive

names to Ramazan, such as 'the blessed month' and the 'springtime of recital of the Qur'an'. The most sublime and beautiful phrase that has been given it, however, is 'God's month'. Although, of course, every month is God's month, this month nonetheless deserves this designation because of its special importance. The name itself conveys the month's special spiritual value. The greatest of the scriptures, the Glorious Qur'an, was revealed during Ramazan.

When the blessed month of Ramazan arrives, the gates of the mercy of the Fosterer are opened to His servants. A special purity and luminous quality are seen in the human spirit, and those who fast feel a special readiness to purify their souls and reform their morals. The Most Noble Prophet (peace and blessings upon him and his family) once said this regarding the glory and worth of 'God's month' on the last Friday of Sha'ban: 'People! God's month is brought to you with blessings, mercy, and forgiveness. It is a month that the Fosterer regards as the best of months. Its days are the best of days, its nights are the best of nights, and its hours are the best of hours. It is a month in which you are invited to be guests at God's table and are recipients of His kindness and generosity. In this month, your breath bears the spiritual reward for glorification and remembrance of God, and your sleep will have the requital for worship. In this month, whenever you turn to God's court, and rest at His threshold, He will answer your call, so ask God with sincerity and a pure heart to grant you success in carrying out the fast and reading the Qur'an, for one is unfortunate who is denied God's forgiveness and mercy in this bountiful and blessed month'.

FASTING CONDUCES TO PIETY
God Most High says in the Glorious Qur'an, '*Believers! Fasting is prescribed for you, as it was prescribed for those before, so that you may be virtuous*' (2:183). Islam commands its adherents to fast for one complete month (Ramazan) to allow time for the state of piety in its fullest sense to appear in them. Whenever

someone abstains from satisfying his natural physical wants, he can well manage to abstain from acting on his psychological impulses.

Of course, Islam does not hold it to be sufficient to abstain from food and drink to reach such a state of perfection through fasting. Rather, it commands the fasting person to abstain from anything that conduces to pollution and commission of sin and from anything that, through Satanic suggestion, encourages his rebellious psychological impulses.

THINGS THAT INVALIDATE A FAST

Several things void a fast, including: 1. eating or drinking, even things that are not normally consumed, such as dirt or tree sap, 2. sexual intercourse, 3. masturbation leading to ejaculation, 4. ascribing false statements to God, the Prophet, or his successors, 5. allowing thick dust to reach the throat, 6. immersing the head completely in water, 7. remaining in a state of impurity after sexual intercourse, menstruation, or parturition until the call to morning prayers, 8. using liquids for an enema, and 9. intentional vomiting. The reader is referred to scholarly studies for further explanation.

COMMERCE

Commerce means buying and selling or monetary transactions, such that the owner of the goods, the 'seller', transfers ownership of them in exchange for a sum of money, or, conversely, that the 'buyer' pays money to the seller in exchange for the goods. As may be seen, commerce is a contractual matter and needs two parties (the seller and the buyer) to take place. Accordingly, such general conditions on contracts as majority, sound mind, intention, and authority must be met.

Commercial actions are in the realm of binding contracts, which means neither of the contracting parties may revoke them after they have been agreed upon. The Lawgiver of Islam, however, considering that sometimes the buyer or seller may suffer considerable loss through negligence or error, and that this

213

would be contrary to social welfare, has established two safe-guards against such destructive outcomes: The first is known as 'rescission' (*iqala*), which holds that, if one party regrets the transaction and asks the other to rescind it, it is recommended that he do so. The second is called 'right of withdrawal' (*khiyar*), which is a special authority a party may exercise to revoke the transaction under certain circumstances. Here are some of the better known forms of this right: 1. when the meeting at which the transaction was made is still in progress, 2. when one of the parties to the transaction has suffered loss through being deceived, as for instance when goods were sold for less than, or purchased for greater than, their real value, in which case the deceived party may rescind the transaction at once, 3. when the buyer receives defective goods, in which case he may demand an exchange or rescind the transaction, 4. any transaction involving domestic animals, which the buyer may rescind any time up to three days after the time of purchase, and 5. conditional transactions, which either party may revoke if the condition is not met.

CASH, CREDIT, AND ADVANCE PAYMENT

Transactions fall into four categories in respect to how goods and money exchange hands: 1. cash transactions, in which both goods and payment are exchanged just when the transaction is concluded, 2. credit transactions, when the goods are transferred to the buyer at the time of the transaction, but payment is delayed, 3. advance payment transactions, when payment is made at once, but the goods are delivered later, and 4. 'unripe' transactions, when both payment and delivery of goods are delayed. Of these four categories, the first three are sound, and the fourth is invalid.

CONFESSION

The importance of confession for a society in reviving rights that are in danger of being crushed and lost goes without saying. A couple of words can reveal something that would otherwise involve the whole judicial apparatus of constructing a case, obtaining testimony, and inference. According to Islam, confession is also of great importance to the individual, in that it calls upon an instinctual tendency that Islam makes the greatest effort to keep alive and put to work. This is man's instinctive love of truth, the very contrary to his sensualism. God Most High addresses this speech to Islam's adherents: '*Believers! Stand up for justice as witnesses to Allah, even if it be detrimental to yourselves or your parents*' (4:135). The Most Noble Prophet (peace and blessings upon him and his family) has said, 'Speak the truth, even if it is detrimental to you'.

In legal terms, confession is speech that establishes the rights of another against the speaker, as for instance if one were to say, 'I owe so-and-so fifty dollars'. One making a confession must be of majority and sound mind, and he must make it of his own free will. Accordingly, the confession of a child, or of someone insane, drunk, talking in his sleep, or under coercion, is invalid.

FOOD AND DRINK
In the holy law of Islam, anything that is fit to be eaten or drunk is licit, with certain exceptions that have been described either in God's Book or in the *sunna* of the Most Noble Prophet (peace and blessings upon him and his family). These exceptions, consumption of which is forbidden, fall into two categories: living and lifeless.

The living things covered include creatures of the water, land, and air.

Of marine and fresh-water creatures, only water birds and fish with scales may be eaten; the rest, such as eels, sturgeons, turtles, seals, and porpoises, may not be eaten.

Land animals are of two kinds: domestic and wild. Among domestic animals, the sheep, goat, cow and camel are permitted. The flesh of horses, mules, and donkeys is permitted but disapproved. That of other animals such as dogs and cats is forbidden. Among wild animals, one may consume flesh of cattle, wild sheep, mountain goats, onagers, and gazelles. Of the rest, all flesh of predators and clawed animals, such as lions, leopards, wolves, foxes, jackals, and rabbits, is forbidden.

One may consume the flesh of birds that have crops and gizzards, that flap their wings frequently in flight, and that do not have claws, such as chickens, pigeons, doves, and partridges. The rest are forbidden. Certain forms of locusts are permitted, concerning which the reader should seek detailed discussions in scholarly treatises.

No flesh of any animal is permitted unless it has been properly slaughtered, as discussed in scholarly treatises.

The non-living things are either solid or liquid.

Of solids: 1. The carcass of any animal, whether its flesh is permitted or forbidden, is forbidden. The same holds for unclean things, such as the excrement of forbidden animals or foodstuffs that have become unclean through contact with unclean things. 2. Earth is forbidden. 3. Deadly poisons are forbidden. 4. Things which naturally arouse disgust in people are forbidden, such as the excrement of permitted animals, their nasal mucous, and the contents of their intestines. Likewise, fifteen parts of the bodies of permitted animals are forbidden. (Please refer to scholarly treatises for further discussion).

Of liquids: 1. Every sort of intoxicant is forbidden, even in small quantities. 2. The milk of animals whose flesh is forbidden, such as pigs, cats, and dogs, is forbidden. 3. The blood of animals with spurting blood is forbidden. 4. Unclean fluids such as the urine and semen of animals with spurting blood are forbidden. 5. Liquids into which something unclean has fallen are forbidden.

Forbidden things may be consumed in times of urgent necessity, to the extent needed to relieve the necessity. This would be true, for instance, if someone would face death from hunger, would fall ill or grow critically ill, or fall behind his companions from weakness on a journey and perhaps perish, unless he ate forbidden things. This exception does not hold for someone who is intent on theft, or who has left his country with the object of mounting a rebellion against the Islamic government.

A NOTE ON DIET

One of our foremost duties is to maintain our health, which anyone understands whose God-given intelligence is functioning at all. The effect various foods and beverages have on our health is transparent. Beyond that, they have an appreciable effect on our spiritual and moral well-being and social relationships. We can never doubt that the psychological state and social conduct of someone drunk are not the same as that of someone sober. Similarly, if someone grows accustomed to eating or drinking revolting things, the individual and social effects of this habit on him will be unbearable for his friends and acquaintances.

Here we understand through our God-given nature that we must accept some limitations on our diet. We must not eat or drink anything that can be consumed. God Most High, Who has expressly stated that He has created everything on the earth for man, Who has no need of man and what pertains to human life, and Who sees and knows best what is advantageous or detrimental to His creatures, has declared some foods and drinks licit and others forbidden.

Imam Riza (upon whom be peace) has said, 'God has made no food or drink licit unless it were beneficial to man, and He has forbidden none unless it would be harmful or fatal'. The wisdom of forbidding certain things is patent to any clear-sighted person, and the logic of forbidding other things emerges with study. There remain a few prohibitions whose rationale has not reached us, but it may someday grow clear to us, or, if not, it may still bear some wisdom and good sense. Considering that these rules stem from God's limitless knowledge, it must be said that they represent the best and most efficacious wisdom and sound policy available, even if we, with our brief lifetimes and limited scientific means, fail to perceive why.

USURPATION

One who seizes another's property by force and appropriates it without any grounds for ownership, or who forcibly seizes it and uses it even without claiming ownership, has committed the act known in law as 'usurpation' (*ghasab*). Usurpation is therefore taking possession of another's property without any such proper occasion as purchase, rental, or permission.

It grows clear from this that usurpation is an undesirable act that disrupts the principle of private possession and ownership. To the extent that this principle is necessary to maintain society, to that extent usurpation subverts society and prevents social progress.

If the influential members of society are allowed to lay their hands on the fruits of the labours of the poor without justification, the principle of private possession and ownership will be undermined. Everyone will adopt the same attitude toward what belongs to those weaker than themselves, and the poor will have to resort to any sort of self-abasement to enjoy the fruits of their own labours. In consequence, society will degenerate into a slave market, and law will fall into discredit and be replaced by the logic of force. Accordingly, Islam has set forth severe rules for punishing the usurper and holds that usurpation is a major sin. God's Book and the *sunna* teach us that God will forgive any sin except *shirk*, and that any sin, even *shirk*, can be forgiven upon repentance, but that one who usurps what belongs to others has no hope of escape from being called to account and punished by God unless he wins forgiveness from those whose rights he has abused.

Some ordinances on usurpation follow: 1. It is incumbent upon the usurper to return the usurped property to its rightful owner at once. If the rightful owner is not alive, the property must be returned to his heirs. Even if return of the propety would cause serious harm, as for instance if someone had usurped a stone or steel beam and used it along with hundreds of thousands of others to construct a building, he is obliged to demolish that structure, remove the usurped stone or beam, and return it to its owner unless the owner is willing to accept compensation for it. Similarly, if one usurps a few kilos of wheat and mixes them in a carload of barley, and the owner will not accept compensation, the usurper will have to remove every grain of wheat from the mix and return them all to their owner. 2. If usurped property is damaged, the usurper must pay for the damage as well as return the property. 3. If the usurped property is consumed, he must pay what it is worth. 4. If he deprives the rightful owner of the benefits from the usurped property, without having himself benefitted from it, he must make good on these benefits. An example would be if someone usurps a rental car and leaves it parked for several days.

Also, if someone adds value to usurped property, as if for instance he has usurped a sheep and fattened it on rich fodder, he has no right to the added value. If this value is separable, the property and any compensation such as fair rental value must be returned to the rightful owner, but the usurper may keep the added value. This holds, for instance, of usurped land that is cultivated, and the harvest that is realized.

PREEMPTION
If two persons jointly own a house or other property and one of them sells his part to a third party, the other partner has the right to acquire this part on the same terms and for the same price. This right is known as the right of preemption (*shuf'a*). Plainly, this right was established in Islam in order to regulate partnerships and prevent damages and other abuses that could result from actions of the partners. It often happens that an action of a new partner winds up working to the detriment of the partner possessing the right of preemption, or that their differing tastes lead to a succession of disagreements and conflicts, or that the possessor of the right of preemption gains benefits from free ownership of the property with no corresponding losses to the partner who sells. Preemption applies to land, houses, gardens, and other immovable property, not to movable

property.

PLACING BARREN LANDS UNDER CULTIVATION

To develop lands that have not been used (whether they have never been developed or where formerly developed and then abandoned by their inhabitants, becoming totally unused or turning into meadows or rushes) is always considered a good work in Islam. Besides entitling one to ownership, it leads to a spiritual reward. The Most Noble Prophet (peace and blessings upon him and his family) has said, 'Whoever places barren land under cultivation, that land belongs to him'. Imam Sadiq (upon whom be peace) has said, 'Whatever community develops land has prior right to it; the land belongs to them'. In Islam, barren lands belong to God, the Prophet, and the Imam (that is, they belong to the Islamic government); they are spoils.

One may place barren lands under cultivation and assume ownership of them under the following conditions (if several persons seek ownership, the one who acts first has priority): 1. permission of the Imam or his deputy, 2. that no one else has marked its boundaries with stones or the like, 3. that it not fall within someone else's property limits by virtue of being a river bank, adjoining a well, bounding cultivated land, or the like, and 4. that it not be exempted land such as the site of a deserted mosque, land held in trust, or public property of Muslims such as streets or roadways. (A word of explanation: To develop land has a customary meaning, according to which to say 'So-and-so developed some land' establishes his ownership of it. Of course, development means different things in different contexts; in agriculture it is accomplished by plowing, whereas in construction it is accomplished by erecting a wall.) 5. Minerals that are exposed and which anyone can remove without excavation and extraction are free for everyone to avail themselves of to the extent of their needs. However, if removal of minerals requires excavation, extraction, and other forms of skilled labour, as is the case with gold or copper mining, the one who extends the effort to extract them becomes their owner. 6. Large streams

220

and rivers are the common property of Muslims, along with floods of rain and snow melt that pour from the mountains. Whoever is nearer to them or more upstream has precedence over others.

LOST PROPERTY

Any property that is found and whose owner is unknown is called 'lost property' (*luqta*): 1. If such an object has a value of no more than a *mithqal* (about five grams) of silver, the finder may pick it up and use it, but if it has a greater value, he should not pick it up, and, if he does, he must seek for its owner by usual means for one year and surrender the object upon finding him. If he does not find the owner, he should give it as alms to the poor on his behalf. 2. If such an object is found in a ruin whose inhabitants have become extinct, or in a cave or on barren lands with no owner, then it belongs to the finder. If it is found on lands under ownership, the finder should ask its previous owners about it. If they lost or hid it and can identify it, he must return it to them. Otherwise, it is his. 3. If an animal with no known owner is found, the rules for lost property apply to it. 4. If a lost child is found on the road, it is incumbent upon every Muslim to take it along and take care of it. 5. If stolen property is entrusted to someone, the rules for lost property apply to it. He must surrender it to its original owner; he may not return it to the thief.

NOTES TO CHAPTER TEN

1. The site contaminated by urine must be cleaned with pure water, but the site contaminated by feces may be cleaned by water or by three stones or similar things if the feces have not spread beyond the immediate area. Otherwise, it must be cleaned with water. It must also be noted that if the feces cannot be removed with three stones, more

must be used to clean the area completely.

2. A volume of water having a weight of at least about 384 kilograms is called a *kur* and is considered not to become impure when tainted with impurity, whereas a lesser volume, called *qalil*, does become impure. *Qalil* water can be made pure by addition of enough pure water (including rain) to make a *kur* volume.

3. If a stick or some such thing is plunged straight into the ground, it will cast a shadow to the west in the morning, when the sun is out, and, as the sun rises, the shadow will shorten. It will reach its shortest length at noon, after which it will extend to the east, lengthening as the sun progresses west. Accordingly, when the shadow has reached its shortest length and begins to lengthen, noon has clearly passed. It must be noted that, in some cities, such as Mecca, the shadow will totally disappear at noon, and it will be clear that noon has passed when the shadow reappears.

4. The time of *maghrib* begins about fifteen minutes after the setting of the sun. It is marked by the disappearance of the redness of the sky to the west that appears after the sun sets.

5. Midnight in Islamic law is eleven and one-quarter hours after noon.

6. After reciting the *suras*, one raises the hands towards the face and recites any desired supplication, such as '*Rabbana atina fi'd-dunya hasanatan wa fil'l-akhirati hasanatan wa qina azab an-nar*' ('Our Lord, give us a benefaction in this world and a benefaction in the next world, and spare us the torment of fire').

7. The *tashahhud* consists in saying this sentence: '*Ashhadu an la ilaha illa 'llahu wahduhu la sharika lahu wa ashhadu an Muhammadan 'abduhu wa rasuluhu. Allahuma salla 'ala Muhammadin wa ali Muhammad*' ('I bear witness that there is no god but Allah in His oneness, Who has no partner, and I bear witness that Muhammad is His servant and Prophet. God bless Muhammad and his progeny').

8. The *salam* consists in saying: '*As-salamu 'alayka ayyuha 'n-nabiyu wa rahmatu 'llahi wa barakatuhu. As-salamu 'alayna wa 'ala 'ibadi 'illahi 's-salihin. As-salamu 'alaykum wa rahmatu 'llahi wa barakatuh*' ('Peace upon you, O Prophet, and God's mercy and blessing. Peace upon ourselves and upon God's righteous servants. Peace upon you all and God's mercy and blessing').

Index

A

225

colonialism, 40
Copts, 64, 65
Creator *see* Allah

D

Damascus, 72, 130, 133
dar an-Nadwa, 76
Day of Requital *see* Resurrection

E

Egypt, 65, 83, 128
Ethiopia, 75
Euphrates, 125
Europe, 40, 45

F

Fadak, 78, 127
Fatima, 90, 108-110, 116, 118, 127, 128, 136, 137

G

Gabriel, 156, 171
Ghadir Khumm, 85, 115, 119
ghasab, 218
ghaybat al-kubra, al-, 139
ghaybat al-sughra, al-, 139
ghiba, 181
ghusl, 155, 201, 203-205
God *see* Allah
God's Sanctuary *see* Masjid al-Haram
Gospel, 25, 66, 73, 91, 178

H

Hadi, 136
hadith (pl. *ahadith*), 108
Hajj, 64, 85, 114
Hamza, 80
Harun, 136
Hasan 'Askari, Imam, 117, 138, 139
Hasan Mujtaba, Imam, 108-110, 116-118, 128-133
Hatim Ta'i, 105

227

Hawazan, 83
Hijaz, the, 64, 68, 72, 82, 84
Hijra, 68, 77-79, 81-85, 91, 92, 109, 118, 124, 127
Hisham, 195
Holy Spirit, 66
Hud, Prophet, 63
Hudayba, Treaty of, 83
Hunayn, Battle of, 83
Husayn, Imam, 47, 108-110, 116-118, 128-133
    martyrdom of, 130

I

Ibn Ziyad, 130
Ibrahim (son of the Prophet), 108
Ibrahim, Prophet, *see* Abraham
iftira, 181
ijtihad, 164, 165
'ilm, 158
Imam, 210, 211
Imamate, the, 111-113, 133, 134, 137, 140
Imams (of the Prophet's household), 63, 108, 111, 113, 115-141, 153-
    155, 160, 163, 164, 171, 175, 176, 181, 192, 196, 204, 220
'Imran, 64
Injil see Gospel
iqala, 214
iqama, 207
Iran, 138, 139
Iraq, 128, 129, 136, 139
'isha, 205
Islam, 22, 36-42, 45, 64, 67, 72, 74-76, 78-85, 91, 92, 97, 99, 100, 104,
    108, 110-114, 118-121, 124, 126, 128-130, 132, 134, 143, 146, 147,
    188-200, 211-213, 215, 218-220
    schools of thought in, 107, 113, 134, 137
Islamic State, 120, 220
Isma'il, Prophet, 64
Israel, 64
Israelites, 65
Issac, Prophet, 64

J

Jabir ibn 'Abdullah Ansari, 115, 211

Jacob, Prophet, 64
Ja'far ibn Abu Talib, 75, 84
Ja'far as-Sadiq, Imam, 117, 134, 135, 156, 157, 193, 195, 211, 220
jahiliyya, 100
Jesus, son of Mary, 25, 27, 61, 64, 109
  the Messiah, 66
jihad, 160, 187-191
jizya, 189
John, Gospel of, 66
Ju'da, 129
Judaism, 25, 45, 64

K

Ka'aba, 64, 68, 69, 75, 83, 85, 101, 103, 133, 154, 201, 206
Karbala, 129, 130, 133-135
Khadija, 69, 72, 74, 76, 108, 127
Khandaq (Trench), 81
Khaybar, 78, 82, 124, 127
Khazraj, 78
khiyar, 214
Kufa, 129, 130, 133

L

Last Day, the. 27
Lat, 70
Lord *see* Allah
Luke, Gospel of, 66
luqta, 221

M

Madyan, 65
magrib, 205
Mahdi, 136
Mahdi, Imam (Muhammad ibn Hasan), 117, 139, 140
Ma'mun, 137, 138
Mani, 105
Manichaen sect, 105
Mansur, 136
Marhab Khaybari, 82
Mark, the Gospel of, 66
Marv, 138

N

Najran, 109
Nesturius, 72
New Testament, 25
Nile, the, 64
Noah (Nuh), Prophet, 59, 61, 62, 111

P

Palestine, 64
Pharaoh, 64, 65
prophecy, 35, 36, 58, 59, 114, 124, 140, 188, 189
Prophet's Mosque *see* Masjid an-Nabi

Q

qara'at, 207
qibla, 201, 206, 207
qiyam, 207, 208
qunut, 208
Qur'an, the, 22, 24, 36, 42, 46-50, 52, 54, 61-64, 66-68, 74, 92, 94, 95,
      97-106 108, 119, 120, 122, 126, 128, 145, 151, 154, 161, 163-165, 171,
      175, 176, 178, 183, 187, 188, 191-193, 200, 201, 204, 212, 215, 218
      eloquence of, 104-106
Quraysh, the, 72, 81, 91, 115
Qurayza, 188

R

Rajab, 86
rak'as, 205, 208-211
Ramazan, 86, 211, 212
Rawzat al-Wisal, 86
Red Sea, 65
Resurrection, the Day of, 24, 27, 35, 62, 143-147, 151, 171, 172, 178,
      189
Riza, Imam, 117, 122, 137, 138, 217
Roman Emperor, the, 83, 84
ruku, 207-211

S

Sabeans, 27

A Glance
at the Life of the

Holy
Prophet

of Islam

Dar Rah Haqq's Board of Writers
Translated by N. Tawheedi

A Glance
at the Life of t[

Holy
Prophe
of Isla

Dar Rah Haqq's Board of Wri[
Translated by N. Tawheedi

A Glance
at the Life of the

Holy
Prophet

of Islam

A Glance
at the Life of the

Holy
Prophet

of Islam

Dar Rah Haqq's Board of Writers
Translated by N. Tawheedi

A Glance at the Life of the

Holy Prophet

of Islam

Dar Rah Haqq's Board of Writers
Translated by N. Tawheedi

Design by: F. Farhang

January 2002

Library of Congress Catalog Card Number: 88-62666
ISBN 0-922817-01-4

January 2002

A glance at the life of the holy prophet of
Islam/ Dar Rah Haqq's Board of writers;
translated by N. Tawheedi.-- [s. l: s. n],
2002.
151 p.
Cataloging based on CIP information.
Bibliography: p.: 131 - 139.

I.Mohammad. Prophet, d. 632. I.Mo'assese-ye
Dar Rah-e Haqq. Hey'at-e Tahririyeh.
II.Towhidi, N.

BP22.9.G530493   297.93
2002
                M78-21069

Contents

*In the Name of God
the Merciful, the Compassionate*

Chapter 1

The Pre-Islamic World

Before the advent of Islam, people all over the world were sadly impoverished in thought, opinions, and individual and social attitudes. Although such conditions were not the same in all parts of the world, generally speaking, all the people of the world shared superstitious beliefs, intellectual deviations, inhumane social traditions, myths and social and moral conflicts.

Before Islam emerged, the Jews had changed the religion of Moses into hidebound dogma and its principles into hollow, lifeless rules and precepts. The spirit of materialism had penetrated into people's lives. Unfortunately, Christianity, which had been presented for the moral rectification and spiritual refinement of the people, was changed in nature by the Christian clergy and became a vehicle for the passionate ambitions of most of them. Since it lacked complete, comprehensive laws and regulations for social systems, it proved unable to provide the people with deliverance and comprehensive guidance.

It was due to such conditions that people all over the world

13

shared superstitious ideas, inhuman social traditions, myths, social and moral conflicts.

The fire of corruption and perdition was raging. Superstitions and false views ruled people in the name of religion! Paganism and the concept of the Trinity had been imposed upon them. Many worshipped idols, fire, cows and stars. Most shameful of all was the widespread worship of the sexual organs of men and women.[1] This same moral and spiritual corruption and regression, which had spread everywhere, caused dishonesty, darkness and deviations in human societies. Bloodshed, murder, tyranny, and oppression prevailed all over the world. In fact, humanity had been put on the verge of the abyss of total destruction!

ARABIA DURING THE DARK PRE-ISLAMIC TIMES

Arabia, which has been called 'the burnt land', was then a strange place. A collection of red-hot deserts, valleys, and sand hills was called 'Arabia'. There was hardly any water or plant life in it.

It would have been a mistake to name the people's dwellings 'houses'. They were rather catacombs in which living beings named 'human beings' fidgeted and lived miserably on dates and stinking water! Tribal fights and disputes formed the basic principle of the Arabian social system. Makkah was no more than an idol-temple. Its inhabitants included traders and usurers who even exchanged human life for money.

The people of the Arabian Peninsula suffered from their tribal and pastoral life in the deserts, coupled with blood-thirsty feudalism. The economic crisis resulting from the exploitation of the people by the ruling class and by bands of usurers had robbed human life of its meaning and darkened the horizon of social well-being.

The wealthy usurers who engaged in trade in Makkah had amassed enormous amounts of wealth by illegitimate means and exploited the weak and poor classes of society. In fact, they increasingly exacerbated anti-human social class differences through usury and oppressive exploitation.

Due to their ignorance, the Arab tribes in those days generally engaged in worshipping natural phenomena and in idolatry. The House of God, the Ka'aba, was used as the idol-temple of the Arabs.[2]

Any one of the indecent, degrading social and moral customs in Arabia at that time was enough to destroy the honour of a whole nation. Before Islam, the anti-human deviations of the Arabs had created a situation whereby the fruit was crime and corruption, the nourishment was corpses, the motto was fear and dread, and the logic was the sword.

The Arabs wrongly believed that only those were superior who descended from the Arab race and had Arab blood! As a matter of fact, the twentieth-century form of nationalism and racism was quite prevalent among the Arabs during the first pagan period.[3]

In addition, the Arabs vainly gloried in their wealth and the number of their children. Each tribe having wealth and a large number of offspring prided itself on them and considered them to be among its crowning achievements.

Plunder, robbery, savagery, aggression, and treachery were their obvious characteristics, and genocide was considered a sign of bravery and courage. As the Arabs before the time of Muhammad (peace and the mercy of God be upon him and his descendants) believed the birth of a daughter to be harmful or were either afraid of poverty and destitution, they either killed their innocent daughters or buried them alive. If a man was given the news that his wife had borne a baby daughter, his face would become red with rage. He would then seclude himself plotting what to do with his newborn daughter! Should he bear the shame and disdain and take care of her or should he bury her alive and banish the disgrace and disdain from himself

15

because in some cases even the existence of one daughter in a family was considered shameful.

'And they ascribe daughters to God, glory be to Him, and for themselves (they would have) what they desire. And when a daughter is announced to one of them, his face becomes black and he is full of wrath. He hides himself from the people because of the evil of that which is announced to him. Shall he keep it with disgrace or bury it (alive) in the dust? Now surely evil is what they judge' (16:58-59).

'And do not kill your children for fear of poverty; We give them sustenance and yourselves (too); surely to kill them is a great wrong' (17:31).

In the *Nahj ul-Balaghah*, Imam 'Ali has described the social conditions of the Arabs in the following way, '...And you Arabs were at that time followers of the worst beliefs and lived in a land of burning deserts. You lived on the stony ground amidst poisonous snakes that fled no voice or sounds. You drank polluted water, ate rough, unwholesome foods, shed each other's blood, and removed yourselves from your relatives. Idols had been set all around you and you did not avoid sins...'.[4]

Thus the Arabs lived in a filthy, depraved environment and as a result of misdirection and immaturity, had turned into brutal, plundering, and seditious people. Like most people of that time, they had adopted superstitious, illusive myths, and false notions as 'religion'.[5]

It goes without saying that for a basic reformation of such a society, a fundamental, comprehensive, and all-embracing revolution was quite necessary. However, the leader of such a vital movement and revolution had to be a divine man sent down by God so he would be and would remain devoid of tyranny, and any aggressive, selfish tendencies, and would not destroy his enemies for his own selfish interests, under the pretext of purification, but would try to reform and rectify them, working solely for God's sake, for the people's welfare,

16

and for the improvement of human societies.

There is no doubt that a leader who is himself immoral, unscrupulous, and without praise-worthy human characteristics is unable to rectify human societies and save the people. It is only divine leaders who, inspired by Almighty God, are able to make profound basic transformations in all phases of the people's individual and social life.

Now we must try to understand what kind of person such a leader of the worldwide revolution was and what changes he made in the world.

Chapter 2

The Prophet's Birth and Childhood

Makkah was covered by a heavy blanket of darkness. No signs of life and activity could be observed in it. Only the moon slowly emerged from behind the darkened surrounding mountains and cast its pale, delicate rays upon the simple, austere houses and upon the sandy regions outside the city.

Little by little, midnight gave way to dawn. A gentle breeze rustled through the burning land of the Hijaz and prepared it for a short rest. Now the stars, too, added to the beauty of this pure banquet of nature and smiled at the residents of Makkah.

It was now early dawn and the early rising, vigilant night birds were singing beautifully in that heavenly weather. They seemed to be speaking in a romantic language to their Beloved! The horizon was on the verge of the brightness of dawn but still a mysterious silence prevailed over the city. All were asleep. Only Amina was awake, feeling the contractions she had been expecting.

Gradually the contractions became stronger. Suddenly Amina saw several unknown women in her room. The room was filled with light and there was fragrance in the air. She wondered who they were and how they had entered her room through the closed door.[6]

Soon her baby was born, and thus, after several months of waiting, Amina had the pleasure of seeing her child in the early dawn of the 17th of Rabi ul-Awwal.[7]

All were overjoyed with the child's birth. But when Muhammad (peace and the mercy of God be upon him and his descendants) illuminated Amina's dark and silent room of prayer, her young Abdullah, was not present. He had passed away in Medina while returning from Damascus and had been buried there, leaving Amina alone.[8]

THE WONDERFUL BABY

The Prophet was born and his blessed birth gave rise to numerous wonderful incidents in the sky and on the earth, especially in the East, the cradle of civilization.

News of these events spread quickly and informed the people of an imminent, very significant incident. Since this newborn child was predestined to destroy the people's old superstitious beliefs and customs and to lay new foundations for human progress and prosperity, from the very beginning he sounded the reveille.

On that blessed night, the Persian monarch Anushiravan's magnificent palace, which incarnated a false fantasy of power and eternal monarchy and upon which people looked with fear and awe, trembled.[9] Fourteen of its turrets collapsed, and the fire in the fire-temple of Persia, which had been flaming for 1,000 years, was suddenly extinguished.[10]

So the humiliated worshippers of that false, destructive object of worship, whose minds had been blocked by the obstacles of prejudice and false imitation and who thus could not reflect upon nature took notice of the truth and were attracted toward a totally different direction. The drying out of the Savah Lake awakened the people of another great region.[11]

HALIMA, THE PROPHET'S NURSE

For many centuries it had been customary among the Arabs to give their newborn children to women from the tribes around the city to be wet-nursed. This was done so that their children would grow up in the fresh air and the natural environment of the desert and also learn the eloquent Arabic dialect whose purest form was to be found at that time in the desert.[12]

For this reason and since Amina had no milk to feed her child, Abdul Muttalib, his grandfather and guardian, felt it necessary to employ an honorable, trustworthy lady to look after the child of his dear son, Abdullah. After making appropriate inquiries, he selected Halima, who was from the Bani Sa'd tribe (a tribe famous for bravery and eloquence) and who was rated among the most chaste, noble women.

Halima took the infant to her own tribe and looked after him as though he were her own child. The Bani Sa'd tribe had long been suffering from famine in the desert. The dry desert and lack of rains had added much to their poverty and misery.

But from the very day he entered Halima's house, good fortune and blessings entered with him. Her life, which had been filled with poverty and destitution, suddenly changed into a happy and prosperous one. The pale faces of Halima and her children became rosy and full of life. Her dry breasts swelled with milk, and the pasture of the sheep and camels of that region turned fresh and green, whereas before he came to their tribe, people lived in poverty and faced many difficulties.

He grew up more rapidly than other children, ran more nimbly, and did not stammer like them. Good fortune and auspiciousness so accompanied him that all the people around him easily realized this fact and admitted it. Halima's husband, Harith, told her, 'Do you know what a blessed baby we have been given?'[13]

IN THE STORM OF EVENTS

The Prophet was just six years old[14] when his mother, Amina, left Makkah for Medina to visit her relatives and probably to pay a respectful visit to her husband's grave. He accompanied his mother on that trip. But after visiting her relatives and expressing love and loyalty to her husband at Abdullah's graveside, on her way back to Makkah, Amina passed away at a place named Abwa'.[15] Thus, the Prophet had lost both his mother and father by that tender age when every child needs a father's affections and a mother's loving embrace.

A GLIMPSE INTO THE PROPHET'S CHARACTER

Just as the Prophet's birth and the events that followed his blessed birth were extraordinary and suggestive of his majesty and supreme character, so his behaviour and manner of speaking in childhood also made him different from other children. Abdul Muttalib realized this fact and respected his majesty greatly.[16]

Abu Talib, the Prophet's uncle, used to say, 'We have never heard any lies from Muhammad, nor have we seen him misconduct himself or make mischief. He never laughs unduly nor speaks idly and he is mostly alone'.[17]

The Prophet was seven years old when the Jews remarked, 'In our Books we have read that the Prophet of Islam refrains from eating any food which is religiously prohibited or doubtful. Let's try him'.

So they stole a hen and sent it to Abu Talib. Not knowing that the hen had been stolen, all ate from the cooked hen but Muhammad, who avoided even tasting it. When they asked the reason for this avoidance of the food, he answered, 'This food is forbidden by God, and God protects me against anything that He has forbidden...'.

Then the Jews took a hen from a neighbour, intending to pay for it later on, and sent it to Abu Talib's house. Again he avoided eating the hen, saying, 'This food is doubtful and...'.

Then the Jews said, 'This child has an extraordinary character and a supreme position'.[18]

Abdul Muttalib, the chief of the Quraysh tribe, did not treat his grandson like other children, but held him in great respect and reverence.

When a special place was arranged for Abdul Muttalib at the Ka'aba, his offspring surrounded that special place, inhibited by Abdul Muttalib's dignity and glory from stepping into his abode. But the Prophet was by no means impressed by so much grandeur and honour and would always directly go to that particular seat. Abdul Muttalib's sons tried to hinder him, but he protested and said, 'Let my son go. I swear by God that he has a glorified, majestic position'.

Then Muhammad sat beside the chief of the Quraysh, Abdul Muttalib, and spoke with him.[19]

Chapter 3

Some scenes from the Prophet's childhood and youth

A FEW SCENES

Muhammad went through the difficulties of orphanhood in his childhood with the support of his high-spirited grandfather, Abdul Muttalib, and his affectionate uncle, Abu Talib. It seems that the heart-rendering pains of orphanhood must have severely tormented his pure delicate soul. It is logical to believe that these sufferings were necessary for the foundation of his supreme character and that such difficulties taught him how to resist the hardships of life and to bear the heavy responsibility later to be put on his blessed shoulders.

As time went on, Muhammad grew up and his childhood gave place to youth, when instincts and potentials bloom. Although he was deprived of a mother's care and a father's affection, he received affectionate care and attention from Abu Talib, who, due to his moral attitudes and in obedience to his father's emphatic order, protected and supported him. In fact, Muhammad represented three things to Abu Talib: a son, a reminder of his brother, Abdullah, and of his father, Abdul Muttalib. So the Prophet became a beloved member of Abu Talib's family, lived in his house, and was treated as his own son. To the Prophet, Abu Talib was an affectionate father, a loyal uncle, and a compassionate preceptor. These two — uncle and nephew — were so fond of each other that their lives seemed to be intertwined. This very intense affection had caused Abu Talib to refuse to ever part from him. He would take his hand in his own and go with him to the famous Arab markets of 'Akaz, Majnah, and Zil-Majaz. Even when he was to accompany the caravan on travelling on business from Makkah to Damascus, he could not bring himself to part with his nephew. So Abu Talib took him along to Damascus. Riding on a camel, the Prophet started the long journey to Yathrib and Damascus.[20]

BAHIRA'S INTERVIEW
WITH THE PROPHET

On the day the Quraysh caravan was nearing Basra,[21] Bahira, a devout monk, caught sight of it through his monastry's window. He observed the caravan shaded by a little cloud that kept pace with it.

Bahira came out of his monastry, stood in a corner and instructed his servant, 'Go and tell them that today they are all my guests'.

All came to him but the Prophet, who was standing beside the property and equipment of the caravan. Seeing that the cloud had ceased to move, Bahira asked his guests, 'Are all the members of the caravan present here?' They answered, 'All but a youth who is the youngest'. Bahira said, 'Tell him to come as well'. So he was asked to come to the monk's room. The keen eyes of Bahira noticed that the cloud over his head moved with him. Taken by surprise, Bahira kept staring at the young boy. When the meal was over, the pious monk told him, 'I have a question to ask you and you must swear by Lat and 'Uzza[22] to answer my question'.

Muhammad said, 'These two you have asked me to swear by are the most detestable things to me'. Bahira said, 'Swear by Allah to answer my question'.

He said, 'Ask your question'.

After a short interview with him, Bahira knelt down before him and started kissing his hands and feet, saying, 'If I live till you start your divine mission, I will most faithfully aid you and fight your enemies. You are superior to all of Adam's offspring...'.

Then he asked, 'Whose son is this youth?' The caravan members pointed to Abu Talib, saying, 'His son'. Bahira said, 'No. His father must be dead!'

Abu Talib said, 'You are right. He is my nephew'. Bahira then said, 'This youth will have a brilliant, extraordinary future. If the Jews find out what I have realized about him, they will destroy him. Take great care lest the Jews should hurt him'.

Abu Talib said, 'What is he destined to do? What have the Jews to do with him?' Bahira said, 'He is predestined to become a Prophet, and the angel of inspiration will come down and make divine revelations to him'. Abu Talib said, 'God will not leave him alone and will Himself protect him against the Jews and his malevolent enemies'.

THE PROPHET AS A SHEPHERD AND A CONTEMPLATIVE MAN

Although Abu Talib was rated as a man of status among the Quraysh, his income was not sufficient to support his family. Now that Muhammad was of mature age, he was naturally inclined to find a job to ease the heavy burden upon his uncle's shoulders. But what kind of job should he engage in to suit his supreme character?

Since he was destined to become a great Prophet and a sublime leader, to face unrestrained obstinate people, to fight against the superstitious beliefs and wrong customs of the period of ignorance, and to lay the foundations of the magnificent palace of justice and proper laws and regulations, he found it expedient to become a herdsman.

Our Holy Prophet would take the sheep and cattle of his relatives and those of the people of Makkah to the surrounding deserts to graze. He gave his uncle the wages he received in return.[24]

This engagement outside the noisy, agitated environment of the city and away from people's disputes and conflicts gave him an invaluable opportunity to acquire much experience, of which the sweet fruits appeared during his prophethood and time of leadership.

Indeed, during this period, he acquired many superior human characteristics such as generosity, good temper, magnanimity, good behaviour towards neighbours, tolerance, truthfulness, trustworthiness, and avoidance of vices. He became known as 'Muhammad, the Trustworthy'.[25]

THE PROPHET'S CHASTITY

When childhood gives its place to maturity and human instincts and potentialities bloom, youngsters suddenly find themselves in the stormy stage of maturity — much more exciting and agitating than childhood. During this critical period of life, various kinds of deviations, seditions, moral deteriorations, and forms of heedlessness threaten the young and their future life. Unless they are properly directed and carefully looked after, or themselves endeavour to control and restrain their overflowing instincts, they will so fall into the terrible abyss of misery and immorality that they can hardly attain happiness and prosperity for the rest of their lives.

The Prophet lived in a severely polluted environment, the atmosphere of which was darkened with all kinds of moral deteriorations and sins. In the Hijaz, not only the youth, but also the aged had become most shamefully involved in sexual deviations and unchasity. In every alley and neighbourhood, black flags had been hung over some houses as a sign of corruption, inviting unvirtuous people inside.

The Prophet grew up in such a foul society, but though he remained unmarried until the age of 25, the sordid environment could not affect him the least bit, nor did anybody observe any immoral action springing from him. Both his friends and his enemies regarded him as the best model of chastity and virtue.

The poems commemorating his blessed marriage with Khadija — the great lady of the Quraysh — remind us of his modesty. Addressing Khadija, the poet says, '...O Khadija, among all the people of the world, you have attained a sublime position, the most honourable position. You have been granted the honour of being wife to Muhammad, the great man whose peer has not been born by any woman in the whole world. All praiseworthy virtues and majestic qualities plus modesty are to be found in him and will be so forever'.[26]

Another poet had said, 'If Ahmad is weighed against all other creatures, he will outweigh them, and truly his virtues are obvious to the Quraysh'.[27]

Chapter 4

The Prophet's
First Marriage

Youth is the period of the blooming of instincts and the emergence of one's sexual potencies. When youngsters, both male and female, are of mature age, they are drawn to the opposite sex, and a fire of passion starts flaming in their hearts that will not be extinguished unless they form a union of marriage. It is only in this way that they will find peace of mind.

Therefore, to make the proper use of such potentials and to prevent the various deviations that overflowing sexual instincts may create in human societies, Islam has emphatically ordered that the youth should marry as soon as possible and not shun the command of marriage on the pretext that they may be unable to support their family later on.

'And marry those among you who are single and those who are fit among your male slaves and your female slaves; if they are needy, God will make them free from want out of His grace; and God is

31

*Most Generous, Knowing. And let those who do not find the means
to marry keep chaste until God makes them free from want out of
His grace'* (4:31-32).

But there may be times when financial conditions do not permit
one to undertake the responsibilities of married life. No doubt,
under such circumstances, marriage must be postponed until
conditions are favourable, and, all through this period of
celibacy, the youth must necessarily acquire virtue and chastity.

Muhammad suffered just such hard conditions. Due to financial
problems, he was unable to take a wife until he was 25.[28] So he
found it advisable to temporarily refrain from marriage and to
wait for a suitable occasion when life's conditions would allow
the formation of a family.[29]

KHADIJA'S BUSINESS PROPOSAL

Khadija, who was an honourable wealthy woman, used to put
her wealth at the disposal of others who traded for her and
received wages in return for their services.

As Muhammad's fame for honesty, virtue and trustworthiness
spread throughout Arabia and reached Khadija, she started
seeking his cooperation. Then she made this proposal to him: 'I
will put at your disposal some property plus a servant, Masara,
and pay you more than others'.

Being well aware of his uncle's financial problems due to his old
age, low income, and large family, Muhammad accepted
Khadija's offer.[30]

KHADIJA

Khadija, the daughter of Khuwalid, was a lady of supreme
character. She had been twice married, to Abu Halah and Atigh
Makhzumi, and twice widowed. Though she was forty years
old, her enormous wealth, popularity, and prestige had led
many wealthy and powerful Quraysh to court her.

But she did not accept any of them as her husband and avoided
marriage, for she knew well that they either were interested in

her wealth or were men whose character she detested.[31]

PROPHET'S JOURNEY TO DAMASCUS

When the commercial caravan of the Quraysh was ready to start moving towards Damascus and the Prophet, too, had made provisions for the trip and was about to join the caravan, Khadija ordered her servant, Masara, to accompany him to Damascus and be always ready to serve him.

Obviously, it is not possible to explain in detail this historical journey, and we content ourselves with mentioning the following points: This journey brought about many blessings and much good fortune, such as enormous profits in commerce, the manifestation of the Prophet's wonderful personality to the people in the caravan, the meeting with the Christian monk, the prediction of his prophecy,[32] and the preliminary causes of an auspicious matrimonial union. When the trading was over, the caravan returned from Damascus.

Masara explained the trip to Khadija in detail, reporting the huge, unprecedented profits they had gained. She also spoke about the Prophet's excellent character and his generosity, as well as his many other virtues manifested during this journey.[33]

Upon hearing this and hearing about the predictions of a learned Jewish man about his divine character and his marriage with the most honorable woman of the Quraysh, Khadija not only started to cherish his love in her pure heart, but also came to realize that he was her ideal husband.[34]

Also, her uncle, Warqa ibn Nawfal, had talked to her about the predictions of the last prophets, and about the good news of his marriage with Khadija.[35] These words, too, added to her love and enthusiasm.

But how was she to talk to him about her desire and heavenly affection? This was not so easy for Khadija, who was herself the most respected woman of the Quraysh.

33

KHADIJA'S PROPOSAL OF MARRIAGE

Khadija asked Nafisa, who was her close friend and whom she always trusted with her secrets, to speak to the Prophet about marriage. Nafisa went to him and asked, 'Why do you not get married?' He answered, 'My living conditions and financial situation do not allow me to get married'. Nafisa said, 'Will you agree to get married if this problem is solved and a rich, beautiful, and honorable woman from a well-known family asks you to marry her?'

He asked, 'Who is this woman you are talking about?' Nafisa answered, 'Khadija'.

He said, 'How is it possible? She has rejected the proposals of many of the Quraysh aristocrats and rich men. Would she marry me?' Nafisa said, 'This union is possible and I will arrange it'.

When he became quite sure of Khadija's inclination towards marriage with him, the Prophet talked to his uncles about the matter. They were very pleased with this good news, and they attempted to arrange the marriage for their blessed nephew. And finally this auspicious marriage was celebrated with special ceremonies.[37]

The Prophet spent 25 years of his life with Khadija, who was not only a loving wife for him, but also his best and most helpful mate.[38] This period is considered to be the best period of his married life.

Khadija, peace be upon her, was the first woman who believed in the Prophet's divine prophecy. She put all her wealth at his disposal to propagate and promote Islam.[39] Six children were born of his marriage: two sons named Qasim and Tahir who passed away as infants in Makkah and four daughers named Ruqiyah, Zaynab, Umm Kulsum, and Fatima, who was the most prominent and honoured of them all.[40]

Khadija was so devoted to her husband and showed such great

sympathy and self-sacrifice for him and for the promotion of his religion that not only did he love her dearly and respect her highly during her lifetime, but even after her death. Each time he remembered her, his blessed heart filled with sorrow[41] and he wept at her loss. Khadija's brilliant sun of life set at the age of 65, ten years after the actualization of the prophetic mission of the Prophet.[42] In this way, the house of our Holy Prophet became deprived of the light of Khadija's existence forever.

Chapter 5

The Philosophy of the Marriages of the Holy Prophet of Islam

SOME EXAMPLES OF THE ACCUSATIONS BROUGHT AGAINST HIM BY CHRISTIANS

At the beginning of the 18th century, Christian writers began a new crusade against Islam. Through writing and circulating books over-flowing with insults and false accusations, they intended to distract the people of the world from the divine religion of Islam and to turn them against the great leader of Islam, Prophet Muhammad (peace and the mercy of God be upon him and his descendants).[43]

These myths, false writings, and prejudiced works of the Christian bigots originated in the Middle Ages, especially in the 15th century, when one John Andre Maure wrote a book against the Prophet's religion that was used by the later anti-Islamic writers. And since other writers did not know the Arabic language, they contented themselves with copying out of his books on Islam.[44]

Thus, the writers whose so-called sacred books openly accuse prophets[45] of adultery have written about our great leader, 'He followed passions and sensual desires and though he ordered his followers not to take more than four permanent wives, he himself had more wives'.[46]

With this insult, they have tried to introduce our Holy Prophet as a sensual man to the unaware Christian readers, thus to stain his supreme character and to hinder the spread and propagation of Islam.

But this fantasy turned out to be vain. Before long, the honest Christian writers began to defend the Holy Prophet of Islam and to apologize for the accusations brought against the Qur'an and the Prophet of Islam.

It is clear to those of us who believe in the perfect innocence of prophets, that such insults are quite unbelievable and far from the truth, but it is necessary to make the facts clear to those who do not agree with us in this matter.

THE JUDGMENT OF HISTORY

It has been written by impartial truth-seeking historians, both Muslims and Christians, that the numerous marriages of the Holy Prophet of Islam, were by no means due to sensuality and sexual passions, for if this were so, he would never have married Khadija who was 40 years old and who had lost most of her beauty and vivacity in the houses of her two former husbands, when he himself was only 25, the age of the sexual passions of youth and when young men are preoccupied with choosing young wives.

The Prophet lived most sincerely and faithfully for 25 years with Khadija[47], and, though many beautiful Arab maidens and women were eagerly longing to marry him, not once did he take another wife during his married life with Khadija. No doubt if our Holy Prophet were interested in following sexual passions,

38

he could not have refrained from mating with young women during this long period.

GROUNDLESS VIEWS OF BIGOTED CRITICS

What if such unjust people were asked, 'Why did the Prophet spend his youth with an aged widow and not marry other women? Why did he take several women as wives in the last ten years of his life, which was the period of old age and when he was having to handle many problems regarding both the internal and external policies of Islam, it was not convenient for him to undertake the responsibilities of marital life?'

And what if they were asked, 'Was it not extremely troublesome and difficult to take care of helpless women each having several orphans? Is it consistent with the pleasure-seeking nature of a man to bear the companionship of women with varied moods and manners?'

Surely they have no choice but to admit that the Prophet was never sensual and pleasure-seeking and that they have accused him out of hostility and bigotry.

John Davenport says, 'How is it possible for a sensual man to content himself with just one wife for 25 years in such a place where polygyny was common and prevalent.[28]

THE NUMBER OF WIVES OF THE HOLY PROPHET

After Khadija passed away, when the Holy Prophet was 53 years old, he took other wives including 'Aisha, Hafsa, Zaynab bint Khuzayma, Umm Salma, Sauda bint Zama, Zaynab bint Jahash, Juwayriya, Safia, Maymuna, Umm Habiba and Marya.[49]

The conditions and circumstances that necessitated the several marriages of the Prophet should be studied. The main reasons for his marriages are the following:

1. To take care of the orphans and the destitute

The Prophet took some of his wives in order to maintain the prestige and reputation they had when they previously had been living in comfort and honour but whose faith and honour were endangered due to the loss of their guardians — husbands, fathers, sons and their tribes — forcing them to abandon Islam and select polytheism and atheism. Sauda was like this. Her husband passed away in Ethiopia, where they had migrated, leaving her alone and without support. The Prophet, who had lost Khadija and had no other wife, married Sauda.[50]

Zaynab the daughter of Khuzayma was a widow who had, after her husband's death, fallen into poverty. She had always been a generous and benevolent woman, known as 'the mother of the poor'. To guard her honour and reputation, the Prophet took Zaynab as his wife. She passed away in the lifetime of God's Messenger.[51] Umm Salma, too, was faithful and aged and had helpless orphans. She was another wife of our Prophet.[52]

2. To establish proper laws and customs

Another reason was to establish proper laws and customs and to nullify wrong customs and beliefs of the period of ignorance and idol-worship. At the Holy Prophet's order, Zaynab, the daughter of Jahash and the Prophet's cousin, married Zayd ibn Harith. This was an example of annuling class differences which Islam forbids. Zaynab was a granddaugher of the Quraysh chieftain Abdul Muttalib and Zayd's family were slaves. The Holy Prophet had bought his freedom. For these reasons, Zaynab considered herself superior to her husband, Zayd, thus making her marital life bitter and unbearable. No matter how much the Holy Prophet advised them, she did not change her manners, so finally Zayd, feeling no love for her any longer, divorced her.[53]

At God's command, the great Prophet of Islam married Zaynab after her husband, Zayd, had divorced her in order to wipe out the custom of not marrying the former wives of adopted sons (for they regarded their adopted sons as their real sons), which custom was unduly prevalent among the people in the dark periods of paganism.[54]

False Accusations

Some Christian writers have, in their dishonest judgments and accusatory remarks, gone so far as to claim that the Holy Prophet of Islam had fallen in love with Zaynab's beauty. This claim is so far from the truth that it is clearly rejected by all authentic histories and logical indictions because if the Prophet of Islam were a slave to his passions and entangled in such sensual thoughts, or if Zaynab were so attractive as to fascinate him, he would have fallen in love with her when she was still a maiden, when he himself was young and more vivacious, especially considering the fact that Zaynab was a close relative of his and usually relatives know about each other's beauty or lack of it.

3. To set free the slaves like Juwayriya

Juwayriya was from the famous tribe called the Bani Mustalaq who were defeated and taken captive in their fight with the Islamic forces. The Prophet married Jawayriya the daughter of Harith, who was their chief. When the Muslims observed that the captives had thus become relatives of the Prophet, they freed many of them. According to Ibn Hisham, this blessed marriage resulted in freedom for one hundred families from that tribe.[55]

4. To form friendly relations

Some marriages occurred to form friendly relations with great Arab tribes, to hinder their obstruction, and to maintain internal policy. For these reasons, the Holy Prophet of Islam married 'Aisha, Hafsa, Safia, Maymuna, and Umm Habiba.

Umm Habiba was the daughter of Abu Sufyan, whose family members were bigoted enemies of the family of the Holy Prophet of Islam and especially of our Prophet himself. Umm Habiba's husband gave up Islam in Ethiopia, became a Christian, and died there. She was then extremely troubled and worried for she was herself a Muslim while her father, Abu

41

Sufyan, was rated among the greatest enemies of Islam. Thus she could not take refuge with him and was alone and helpless. Therefore, to help and support this poor woman and to make friends with the Bani Ummayad, the Prophet married her.[56]

Safia was the daughter of Hayy ibn Akhtab, the head of the Bani Nazir tribe. To guard her prestige, the Prophet took her as his wife after the Jewish captives were scattered among the Muslims, thus establishing family relationships with one of the greatest Bani Israel tribes.[57]

Maymuna, whom God's Messenger married in the year 7 AH, was from the tribe of Bani Makhzum.[58] With the exception of 'Aisha, most of the wives of the Holy Prophet were either widows or divorcees at the time they were married to the Prophet and most of them had lost their beauty and youth, proving that the marriages of the Holy Prophet had been out of sacred motives and for benevolent reasons, so that no one can bring such accusations as sensuality and seeking of false pleasure against him.

Chapter 6

The Character of the Holy Prophet before the actualization of the prophetic mission

THE PRINCIPLE OF HARMONY

Psychologists believe that the environment lays the foundations of people's character and their way of thinking and that the principle of harmony causes the people to follow the society's dominant patterns of thought and behaviour.[59]

Although some of these psychologists have gone to extremes in this matter and have regarded this theory as a general and all-embracing principle, according to which all social phenomena without exception may be analyzed, the principle of the effect of the society on people's morale is undeniable.

Therefore, an environment of virtue and health produces pious and normal offspring, and a corrupt, deviated society will naturally lead people into the pit of corruption and deviation.

Thus, those who remain untouched by the society's deviating factors, must be exceptional people.

THE ENVIRONMENT OF ARABIA BEFORE THE ADVENT OF ISLAM

At that time, the whole world, especially Arabia, was steeped in ignorance, corruption, and turmoil. The Arabs were suffering immensely from superstitions and unchasteness. Ignorance had darkened the lives of the Arabs, who were leading tormented lives. Plunder and murder were quite prevalent — plunder of the people's meager properties and unjust killing!

Most shameful of all was their worship of lifeless statues — idols.[60] False beliefs and class differences were strong. What was lacking was law and justice. The apathetic, wealthy people amassed wealth by exploiting the weak and by overcharging the orphan and the widow. They lorded over the poor class and exploited them.

Their manners in business were so illogical and unjust that they would hold women responsible for their husbands' debts and would detain the husbands for the indebtedness of their poor wives.[61]

Instead of acquiring knowledge and virtue, they prided themselves in their ancestors and in the large numbers of their relatives; sometimes they even went to cemeteries[62] and counted the number of their dead relatives to prove there were more people in their tribe than in other tribes.

Murder, bloodshed, drinking, and illegitimate sexual intercourse were quite ordinary and commonplace.[63] Amr ul-Qays, the famous Arab poet, discussed his satanic sexual relationships with his cousin 'Anizah. Curiously, such poems were ranked among the greatest works of literature and were hung in the Ka'aba.[64]

Such was the situation and moral conditions of a miserable society out of whose dark horizon came the light of Islam.

It is crystal clear that a person who not only is not affected by such a corrosive society, but also grieves over it and attempts to combat it, possesses a great divine character and is competent to lead people and guide them onto the path of salvation.

PROPHETS WERE NOT PRODUCTS OF THEIR ENVIRONMENTS: THEY CREATED THEM

All went to the idol-temples except the Prophet who, without being taught by anybody, made his way to Mount Hira, the mountain where he devotedly worshipped the Creator of the universe and praised His glory and power.[65]

'And you did not recite before it any book, nor did you transcribe one with your right hand, for then could those who say untrue things have doubted' (29:48).

Favoured by Almighty God, he distinguished his path from the very beginning, denounced the wrong manners of his people without any hesitation or fear, and proceeded against those wrong deeds and beliefs.[66]

Not only was not one single moment of his blessed life spent in idolatry, but, as we have already mentioned, he hated to hear the names of idols.[67]

His chasteness and purity were known to all. His extreme honesty led the people to give him the title of 'the Trustworthy', and this great virtue led Khadija to trust him with her commercial property.

The behaviour of the Prophet toward the people and his manners were so pleasant and excellent that they attracted all people. 'Ammar said, 'The Prophet and I were engaged as shepherds before the advent of the prophetic mission. One day I suggested to him, 'Let's go to the Fakh pasturage'. He agreed.

'The next day I went there and saw that he had preceded me but prevented his sheep from grazing there. I asked him the reason. He replied, 'I did not wish my sheep to graze here before your sheep because we had taken this decision together'.[68]

Thus the Prophet took a different direction than his people and was by no means infatuated with tribal customs and moods. In reality, under the control of the divine power, he advanced on his path of evolution and perfection.

For all these reasons, people had great respect for him and relied heavily on his views in solving their problems.

THE INSTALLATION OF THE BLACK STONE
When the Holy Prophet was 30 years old, the Quraysh decided to repair the House of God, the Ka'aba, and since all the tribes of the Quraysh wished to have the honour of this great task, each took on the task of repairing one part of the House of God.

First Walid started to demolish the House and then the others helped him until the pillars that the Prophet Abraham (peace be upon him) had laid down, appeared. Now it was the time for the reconstruction of the Holy House, and each tribe undertook one part of it. When the process of construction reached the point where the Black Stone was to be installed, severe disputes arose among the Quraysh tribes. All of them wanted to have the honour of completing the task.

Little by little, the dispute turned into harsh enmity, and the various tribes got ready for a bloody war. The sons of Abdul Dar filled a large jar with blood and put their hands into it, thereby giving each other a pledge of death at the battlefield.

This terrible discord went on for four or five days until Abu Amayah, who was the oldest of the Quraysh, said, 'My proposal is that we select the first person who enters the mosque as an arbiter and that all of us accept his view on the problem so it will be solved'.

The Quraysh accepted his proposal and waited to see who would enter the mosque first. Suddenly the Holy Prophet of Islam came in. As soon as the people caught sight of him, they said, 'This is the Trustworthy one. This is Muhammad. We will accept his decision'.

The Prophet did not know about the matter. When they explained their problem to him, he said, 'Bring me a piece of cloth'. Although the Quraysh did not know what he meant by that order, they brought the cloth immediately. The Holy Prophet spread the cloth, put the Black Stone in the middle of it, and said, 'Each tribe should take hold of one side of the cloth so all can share in the honour'. The Quraysh did as he had told them and lifted the Black Stone to the point where it was to be installed. Then the Holy Prophet, who observed that if he let any of them install it, conflict and disputes would arise, himself lifted the Black Stone and installed it in its place. Through this excellent device, he put an end to the terrible enmity and conflicts.[69]

This incident clearly demonstrates the supreme character of the Holy Prophet of Islam and his excellent thought and intelligence, which ended a serious dispute without any bloodshed.

Chapter 7

The Beginning of the Revelation

We have so far taken a glance at the earlier part of the blessed life of the Holy Prophet of Islam. Now we must talk about some of the most momentous phases of his life. By the age of 40 he was still living among an extremely backward people who were devoid of any traces of civilization and humanity. These hard conditions severely tormented his pure soul. He observed nothing in that society but the darkness of ignorance. He would go to the Ka'aba, but instead of witnessing the worship of God, he witnessed idolatry. He would then leave the Ka'aba and go among the people. But there, too, he was troubled by what he saw. He was pained by the ugly customs and false thoughts of his people. The pitiable condition of the poor and the destitute caused him great anguish. The deplorable situation of women, who were treated worse than animals, as well as the prevalence of gambling, wine drinking and murder tortured his blessed heart.

When he dealt with people as a merchant, their immoral

behaviour gave so severe an emotional shock to him that he had to go to a lonely place where he would not be tormented by people's inhuman behaviour. For these reasons and to find peace of mind, he would go to Mount Hira and there think deeply about the amazing phenomena of nature and the vestiges of God's All-Embracing Compassion.[70]

THE PROPHET AT THE AGE OF FORTY

By the time the Holy Prophet of Islam reached the age of 40, he was ready for his divine mission.[71] One day suddenly, while he sat in a cave at Mount Hira, Gabriel, the Angel of Revelation, appeared to him and said, 'Recite!' He said in surprise, 'What shall I recite?' Again the divine voice very clearly and openly called out, 'Recite, O Muhammad!'

And a third time Gabriel repeated,[72] *'Recite in the Name of Your Lord Who created. He created the human being from a clot. Recite and your Lord is Most Honourable, Who taught (to write) with the pen, taught the human being what he knew not'* (95:1-5).

An indescribable excitement and eagerness overcame the Holy Prophet, for he had come into contact with a supreme supernatural world. His high spirit had now found a sacred support and an eternal refuge. He saw in himself the power of prophecy. No longer was any worry or agitation to be found in his blessed being. There was now just peace and confidence within him.

Was the Prophet really going through the learning process in that cave on Mount Hira? Some orientalists and foreign authors have answered this question in the affirmative. They have remarked, 'On Mount Hira, the Prophet thought deeply about the concepts of the Bible as well as the instructions of the prophets. There he spent his time in meditation and enjoyed this intellectual meditation'.[73]

This remark is meant to imply that he was a self-made man who invented the religion of Islam by studying and carefully thinking about the Old and New Testaments! But there are certain documents that attest to the contrary, some of which are:

1. If the Holy Prophet of Islam had derived the Qur'an from the Bible and from the teachings of the prophets before him, the conceptions and contents of the Qur'an would have had to perfectly resemble those in the Old and New Testaments, whereas the purport of the Qur'an is quite different from that of the Old and New Testaments.

2. The magnificent and extremely beautiful wording and style of the Qur'an have brought the greatest literary men of the ages to their knees, proving that the Holy Prophet of Islam has been in direct contact with the Creator of the world. The Holy Prophet could have derived such a style from no other book.

3. No credible authentic source has ever mentioned such false accusations. Rather, these bigoted rumours are made by the Christian clergy and by the western orientalists who have selfish, hostile motives.

4. If the Qur'an had been brought into existence through study of the Old and New Testaments, those intending to fight against the Qur'an through tampering with some of its verses could have more easily made reference to the Old and New Testaments and would have achieved their purpose with a great deal less trouble.

5. All agree that the Prophet was unlettered.[74] Is it logical to believe that an uneducated, unlettered person, brought up in an ignorant, backward society that was devoid of any knowledge, learning or scholarly books could offer such an amazing book, full of startling facts and extremely advanced learning? Such bigoted persons have to be asked, 'How was the Holy Prophet of Islam able to study the Old and New Testaments? How is it possible for an unlettered man who has not been taught by any teacher nor gone to any school, to make predictions of the future and relate events of the past?'

WHAT IS REVELATION?

What is certain is that there have been relations between prophets and the Creator of the universe, that they have received the facts from the original source of creation, and that these relations have had to do with their purified selves and fortified spirits.

It is obvious that if these relations with the divine source were taken away from the prophets, they would have no such supreme position. All the honour and value of the prophets lie in their having relations with the divine source. So there has been no ambiguity in their sayings, and they were all quite sure of what they said and knew very well the Source, Support, and Cause of their words and teachings, unlike those who claim a 'discovery' that might be made as a result of undergoing some ascetic practices. Such people often have no realization of what they have discovered. In fact, their claims are often mingled with fantasy and mere imagination and are sometimes untrue.

The superiority of prophets to such people is so obvious as to need no explanation. Divine prophets have seen and said nothing but the truth, and not even one single unclear, ambiguous point has ever been found in their speeches and teachings. Thus, divine revelation has resulted from a relation between God and His prophets. This relation has sometimes been made through the medium of Gabriel and sometimes directly, without any medium.

IS REVELATION A KIND OF HYSTERIA?

Some western writers who are no doubt prejudiced have been dubious about the descent of revelation upon our Holy Prophet[75] and have considered it a sort of disease called hysteria.

Fortunately, this false accusation is so vain and baseless that it calls for no arguments to prove its falsehood. It is well-known that hysteria has certain moods and indispositions, none of which has been observed in the Holy Prophet of Islam. As John Davenport has said, 'This remark that Muhammad has suffered the attacks of epilepsy is one of the false, awkward sayings of the Greeks by which they meant to stain the prestige of the propagator of a new religion, and turn the world of Christianity against his moral behaviour and qualities.'[76] Even in the deepest moments of revelation, none of the piercing cries of severe agitation common in hysteria have been observed in the Holy Prophet of Islam.

Another reason is that when the person suffering from hysteria recovers from such indispositions, and comes to an ordinary state, that person does not remember anything from what he has seen or heard in his state of hysteria, while the contrary was the case with the Holy Prophet of Islam. He did not speak to anybody during the time revelations came upon him and after each revelation was over, he started talking to the people about the meaning of the revelation and announced everything he had heard or seen. Moreover, the expressions of a hysteric are usually related to the delusions brought about by his suffering and exhausted nerves.

For example, some hysteric people imagine terrible faces that threaten them with death, and their cries are all about such things. And so far nobody has observed a hysteric say something that turns out to be law, knowledge or guidance, like the Islamic rules and teachings that, after 14 centuries, nobody has been able logically to find a single fault with.

REVELATION AND TODAY'S SCIENCE

Unlike what some people might imagine, the advent and advance of scientific discoveries not only have not reduced or damaged the importance or high position of the orthodox religion of Islam, but they have confirmed and supported them.

The inventions of radar, radio, and teletypes have proved the fact that revelation is by no means inconsistent with the laws of nature or incompatible with the secrets of creation. The same God who has provided so many facilities, abilities, and mysterious ways of communication is able to set up special relations and communications with His prophets, though these two sorts of communications are not comparable.

In addition, the advance of the sciences of extra-sensory perception, hypnotism, telepathy and the like have made it clear that the facts of our world are not limited to the framework of our material senses.

Thus both history and science bear testimony to the fact that the Holy Prophet of Islam has been selected by God for the divine mission of leading mankind into the path of virtue and salvation and saving it from the deadly pit of corruption and deviation and that all those excellent ideas and advanced programs were inspired through divine revelation.

The world of Islam is proud of its great leader, the Prophet, whose divine religion not only brought life and prosperity to the world of his own time, but today, after the passing of 14 centuries, is truly the best guide of civilized societies. Each day more and more educated people come to realize the magnificence and value of his profound precepts and teachings.

Chapter 8

The Prophet's Method
of Propagating Islam

When the Holy Prophet began descending Mount Hira to go home, he found that he was in a different mood; in a strange mood; in fact in another world; in a divine atmosphere. He was not a prophet before going to the mountain, but now he was related to the Source of Creation, had communicated with the Divine Origin, with the Divine Authority. He was now witnessing what Bahira, the Christian monk, and others had predicted about him, and he well knew that a momentous task had been laid upon his shoulders. He was deeply absorbed by the task. If he had any worries, it was not because he was unsure of his prophethood. He had heard the tidings from such learned people as Bahira, and he had witnessed Gabriel bringing the good news, 'You are God's Messenger'.[77] These were enough to assure him of his divine mission and prophethood.

In addition, God has always, through clear proofs and

55

compelling confirmations assured any prophet He has selected for guiding mankind of his prophethood, so he would endeavour to rectify, purify, and educate human beings with the strongest determination.

Therefore, it becomes clear that it is most baseless and wrong to say that Muhammad did not know that he had become a prophet until Khadija talked to him and assured him of his prophecy.[78]

KHADIJA WAITING FOR THE PROPHET

What happened on the day of the beginning of the Prophet's prophetic mission caused him to return home later than usual. Khadija, who had never observed her affectionate husband to be late, was worried. Suddenly she saw him enter the house but with quite a new expression and in a new mood. He was now excited and moved. Khadija asked him, 'Why are you so late today?'

He explained the whole event to her. Khadija had long been expecting such a blessed day, for she had heard her servant, Masara, quote from the Christian monk they had met on their journey to Damascus that he, Muhammad, is the Prophet of God to the people.[79]

The Jewish and Christian priests had formerly given her the good tidings that Muhammad was to be a prophet and that he had a supreme status. So she got up and after making the necessary inquiries, contacted Warqa ibn Nawfal, who was a learned Christian person, and told him about the event. Warqa said, 'I swear by God that the same great angel Gabriel who descended to Moses, peace be upon him, has descended unto him, and no doubt he is the prophet of these people, of this *Ummah*'.[80]

Then, to help Khadija realize the extreme significance of the matter, Warqa told her about the signs of the descent of the Angel of Revelation.[81] Khadija then returned home and after brief consideration, accepted the prophecy of Muhammad (peace and the mercy of God be upon him and his descendants), thus attaining the honour of taking the lead in adopting the supreme faith of Islam among all the women of the world.

'ALI, THE FIRST MALE WHO CAME TO BELIEVE IN THE PROPHET'S FAITH

At a time when a severe famine had broken out in Arabia, Abu Talib's financial condition was difficult; indeed unbearable. To reduce his uncle's financial problems, the Prophet took his son, 'Ali, to his own house and took care of him and raised him like an affectionate father.[82] He had great talent and peerless intelligence. He obeyed the Prophet most sincerely. He soon became quite aware of the Prophet's truthfulness, and, so when he was but ten years old, he accepted the Prophet's faith with perfect awareness, thus becoming the first male to adopt Islam and to believe in the divine faith of the Prophet.[83]

THE PRESENTATION OF RITUAL PRAYERS AS A RELIGIOUS DUTY

After monotheism, worshipping the One God, the first duty that became incumbent upon the Holy Prophet and his followers was the ritual prayer, which in fact demonstrates the significance of ritual prayer as the basis of man's relation to God and as a way of giving thanks for God's endless blessings. So the great leaders of Islam, especially the Holy Prophet of Islam, have laid great emphasis on ritual prayer, saying, 'Ritual prayer is the pillar of faith'[84] and 'Anybody who disregards the ritual prayer will not enjoy our intercession with God on the Day of Judgment'.[85]

Almighty God described the nature of ritual prayers and the way to perform them through Gabriel to the Prophet, who taught it to 'Ali and Khadija and also ordered congregational ritual prayers.[86]

THREE YEARS OF PROPAGATION IN PRACTICE

For three whole years after the actualization of the prophetic mission of the Prophet, he propagated his faith in secret because the corrupt environment of Arabia, which had been polluted with idolatry and paganism for centuries, was by no means ready for the open propagation of Islam, which is perfect monotheism and opposed to any kind of polytheism.

In the beginning, the Prophet was faced with extremely difficult problems and obstacles that seemed to prevent him from achieving his divine goal — the propagation of Islam. Thus the Holy Prophet of Islam praised the One God before the eyes of the idolaters who worshipped numerous gods and whose worshipping assumed the form of whistling and clapping. He performed the ritual prayers, which included spiritual discourse and praise of Almighty God, Who has no partner nor any peer. The Prophet, accompanied by 'Ali and Khadija, went to the crowded places like the Masjid ul-Haram and Mana and performed the congregational ritual prayers before the eyes of the enemies of Islam and thus, through his practice, fought polytheistic faiths.[87]

'Atif, a merchant of that time, has said, 'I had gone to 'Abbas, the son of Abdul Muttalib, on business, when suddenly I observed that a man entered the Masjid ul-Haram, looked up at the sky and the sun and stood praying in front of the Ka'aba. A little later, a woman and a boy came in and accompanied him in his prayer. I asked 'Abbas about that religion of which I had not yet heard! 'Abbas said, "This man is Muhammad (peace and the mercy of God be upon him and his descendants), the son of Abdullah. He believes that his God is the Creator of heaven and earth and that God has assigned him to guide people. For the time being his faith has no believers other than these three people. This woman you see is Khadija, the daughter of Khuwalid, and this boy is 'Ali, the son of Abu Talib, who have accepted his faith"'.[88]

In this way the Holy Prophet of Islam went on with his divine task until gradually the number of Muslims increased and, contrary to the ill-wishes of the opponents of Islam, this faith prevailed. When the atmosphere became suitable for the open propagation of Islam, the Prophet was divinely ordered to act accordingly.

THE INVITATION TO HIS RELATIVES AND THE FIRST MIRACLE

The propagation through practice of Islam by the Holy Prophet and the increase in the number of his followers paved the way for the open invitation of the people to Islam. God commanded the Holy Prophet of Islam to invite his close relatives. *'And warn your nearest relatives'* (26:214).

In this way, backbiters could not say, 'Why do you not call your own relatives to worship the One God and warn them of God's severe punishment?' Moreover, the support of the relatives of the Prophet would help the promotion of Islam. So the Holy Prophet told 'Ali to prepare a meal and invite their relatives, who numbered about 40. After preparing the meal, 'Ali invited them. All the relatives of the Holy Prophet accepted the invitation and ate the meal prepared by the blessed hands of 'Ali. Although the food was not sufficient for even one person, all 40 people were full after eating that blessed food and, strangely enough, the food had not diminished at all. This amazed all of them but the obstinate Abu Lahab, who said without thinking, 'This is magic and charms'. The foolish man disregarded the fact that magic and charms cannot feed people!

On that day the Prophet said nothing about the matter. Perhaps his silence was due to the fact that he wanted them to realize the difference between a 'miracle' and 'magic' because if magic were the cause the guests would feel hungry after leaving the house of the Holy Prophet.

Since this gathering did not give any favourable result, the Holy Prophet invited them for the next day. Again the same reception was repeated and all were filled. Yet the food was not reduced even after the meal was over.

Then the Prophet said, 'O sons of Abdul Muttalib. God has

assigned me to warn you of the painful torments of the wrongdoers and give you the good news of His reward to the pious believers. Become Muslims and follow me to achieve salvation. I swear by Almighty God that among all Arabs I do not know anyone who has brought his people anything better than what I have brought you. I have brought you prosperity and salvation both in this world and in the hereafter. The Gracious God has commanded me to call you all to worship Him. Now which one of you is willing to help me with the task? Anybody who announces his readiness to help me will be my brother, my successor, and the executor of my will'.

Nobody answered but 'Ali, who was the youngest. He stood up and said, 'O Prophet of God. I am your assistant. I am your supporter'.

The Prophet asked him to sit down. He repeated the same saying three times but no one except 'Ali replied to him. Then the Prophet pointed to 'Ali and said, 'He is my brother, my successor and the executor of my will among you. Listen to him and obey him'.[89]

It was on this very day that a number of people came to believe in the faith of the Holy Prophet of Islam,[90] but ignorance and bigotry hindered some of his relatives from believing in his message. However, this gathering was effective in gaining support for the Holy Prophet.

In addition to the fact of the extraordinary event — 40 people being fed with a small amount of food — there is another remarkable point in this event — the remarks the Holy Prophet made about his cousin 'Ali on that day. They clearly prove the fact that 'Ali was the Prophet's righteous successor and Caliph, and thus we must regard 'Ali as the successor of the Holy Prophet of Islam.

Thus the way was paved for the public invitation of the people to Islam and open propagation of this divine faith. The Prophet demonstrated indefatigable perseverance in fulfilling this divine duty and did not stop his invaluable teachings, outreach and struggles for a single hour. It was then that the magnificent banner of Islam was hoisted and truth began to be promoted.

Chapter 9

The Public Mission
of the Prophet of Islam

Three years had passed from the time when the Holy Prophet of Islam was divinely assigned to be a prophet, during which time he did his best to secretly guide those who were capable of being guided onto the path of piety and virtue. Whenever he observed a person who had gone astray, being drowned in the pit of idol worship and moral decay, he tried hard to save him. He entered the scene through the gate of affection and benevolence and with his logical, eloquent speeches urged the people to adopt the monotheistic faith of Islam.[91]

But since his faith had to prevail all over the world and be communicated to all human beings, he attempted to make his mission public and open and to declare his aims and plans to all.

THE PROPHET'S SPEECH ON MOUNT SAFA
To promulgate the holy religion of Islam to all Arab tribes and all over the world, God commanded the Holy Prophet to openly

declare his prophetic mission and explain to the masses the truth of his faith.

So he made his way to Mount Safa, stood on a high place, and exclaimed, '*Ya sabaha-hu*'.[92] His voice resounded on the mountain and attracted the attention of the people. Large crowds from various tribes hurried toward him to hear what he was going to say. The Holy Prophet turned to them and said, 'O people! Will you believe me if I tell you that your enemies intend to ambush you at dawn or at night?'

They all answered, 'We have not heard a lie from you throughout your life'.

The Holy Prophet said, 'O people of the Quraysh! I warn you to fear God's punishment. Save yourself from the fire.[93] My position is the same as that of the sentry who sees the enemy from afar and warns his people of the danger of their enemies. Does such a person ever lie to his people?'[94]

Abu Lahab, who feared lest the Prophet's words should impress the people, broke the silence and addressing him said, 'Give our oath to you? Have you gathered us here to tell us such words?'

Abu Lahab interrupted the Prophet so rudely and did not let him continue his speech. In return for so much insolence, denial of the truth, and cooperation with the idol worshippers and polytheists, God revealed the verse that severely reproves Abu Lahab.[95]

'*In the Name of God, the Merciful, the Compassionate. Perdition overtake both hands of Abu Lahab and he will perish. His wealth and what he earns will not avail him. He shall soon burn in fire that flames and his wife, the bearer of fuel, upon her neck a halter of strongly twisted rope*' (111).

THE EFFECT OF THE SPEECH OF THE HOLY PROPHET

The Prophet's logical, eloquent speeches greatly impressed many of the people who heard his words. In most gatherings and public places, people talked about the new faith more than anything else. To those who had suffered from the extortion of the cruel oppressors and were tired of the injustices and inhuman conditions prevailing in Makkah, the celestial words of the Holy Prophet opened a door to the world of hope and prosperity and gave new life to their half-dead bodies. But the selfish malevolent Quraysh chiefs refused to submit to Islam, and, since the Holy Prophet mentioned their deviations and faults at every opportunity, they decided to hinder this spiritual and intellectual revolution by any means possible.

Obviously, the idol worshippers and the oppressive Quraysh chiefs well realized that if idolatry were abolished and all the people worshipped the One God and adopted the gainful religion of Islam, no room would be left for their extortion and oppressive rule.

Therefore, they held a council and started talks on the day's issue, trying to find ways to extinguish the Prophet's revolution.

They reached the conclusion from their talks and exchange of views that they should all go to the house of Abu Talib — a Quraysh chief who was like a father to the Prophet — and ask him to prevent the Prophet from further activities toward propagating his faith by any means he found expedient. For this purpose, they went to Abu Talib, who calmed them down.

THE QURAYSH COMPLAIN TO ABU TALIB
Again the chiefs of the Quraysh went to Abu Talib's house. Their speaker said to him, 'You possess a high status among us and the Quraysh tribe. You are our chief, our master, and our lord. We all have great respect for your honour and high position. We have already asked you to hinder your nephew. We have told you to stop him from offending the faith of our forefathers, denouncing our idols, thoughts and beliefs. But you have not paid any attention to our demands and have not attempted to stop him. We swear by God that we will not tolerate disrespect toward our gods and denunciation of the

faith and beliefs of our fathers. You must prevent him from doing these things or we will fight both he and you who support him until either you or we are killed'.

Abu Talib tried to solve the problem peacefully, and after they had left the house, he talked to the Prophet about the matter. Addressing Abu Talib, the Holy Prophet of Islam remarked, 'I swear by Almighty God that even if they put the sun in my right hand and the moon in my left, and in return, demand of me to quit the propagation of Islam and pursuance of my divine aim, I will never do what they want me to. I am determined to carry on my duty toward God to the last moment of my life, even if it means losing my life. I am strongly determined to attain my goal'.

He left his uncle's house sadly. Abu Talib called him and said, 'I swear by God that I will not quit supporting you and will not let them hurt you'.[96]

Once again, the Quraysh attempted to achieve their objectives through Abu Talib. This time they took 'Ammarat ibn Walid to him and said, 'This youth is strong and handsome. We will give him to you to adopt as your own son and in return you must stop supporting your nephew'.

This severely annoyed Abu Talib who gave this answer to their ridiculous request, 'What an unjust proposal! You ask me to take care of your son and give my own son to you to kill him! I swear by God that such a thing will never take place'.[97]

THE QURAYSH TRY TO BRIBE THE HOLY PROPHET

The infidel Quraysh imagined that the Prophet had material or sensual ambitions and that through such ambitions they would be able to induce him to stop his propagation of Islam. With such an intention, they went to him and said, 'If you demand money and wealth, we will make you the wealthiest man among all Arabs. If you are interested in lordship and position, we will make you our absolute chief. If you like sovereignty, we will make you our own sovereign. If you are not able to get over the indisposition you yourself call revelation, we will have the best physican treat you — provided that you quit the propagation of your faith, not create dissension among the people any longer, and not denounce our gods, our thoughts, and the beliefs of our ancestors'.

In answer to those ignorant people, the Holy Prophet said, 'I am neither interested in wealth, nor in lordship nor sovereignty. The One God has assigned me as a Prophet and granted me a Book. I am a Messenger of God and my mission is to warn you of God's severe punishment and give you the tidings of God's reward for the faithful. I have performed my duty. If you follow my instructions, you will achieve prosperity and salvation, and if you refuse to believe in my faith, I will be persistent and resistant until God passes a judgment between me and you'.[98]

Finally, the Quraysh chiefs decided that it would be to their advantage if the Prophet would agree to stop denouncing their gods and idols and, in return, they, too, would stop disturbing him. So again they went to Abu Talib and asked him to talk to the Prophet about their request. The Holy Prophet of Islam answered, 'Shall I not ask them to utter a phrase that is best for them and that brings them prosperity, honour and eternal salvation?'

Abu Jahl said, 'We are ready to utter ten phrases, let alone one single phrase'.

Then they asked the Holy Prophet of Islam what that phrase was. He said, 'There is no god but God'.

This divine strategy severely upset and disappointed the Quraysh chiefs. The obstinate Abu Jahl said, 'Ask for something other than this statement'.

The Holy Prophet of Islam answered with the utmost decisiveness and the strongest determination, 'I will demand nothing other than this, even if you put the sun in my hand'.[99]

Realizing that neither blandishments nor threats would work with him and that they could by no means prevent him from pursuing his goal, the infidel Quraysh chiefs decided to treat him most severely.

Chapter 10

The Obstacles on the Way and the Tortures Inflicted by the Quraysh

From the very day the Holy Prophet of Islam started his public propagation of Islam, the Quraysh chiefs resorted to any means to silence him.

As usual, they first began with attempts to lure him and tried hard to get him interested in wealth, status, and other material benefits that they promised to give him if he submitted to their ungodly will, and, after realizing that this method was of no use in their dealing with him, they attempted to threaten and then to torment and torture him.

Thus a new stage — an exceedingly troublesome phase — started in the blessed life of the Holy Prophet of Islam. The enemies of Islam, who had well understood that the triumph and rule of Islam would surely put an end to their law of the sword, tyrannies, and exploitation of the deprived people, launched their combat against the Holy Prophet of Islam most brutally and ruthlessly, discarding all moral and humane principles — if they had any — and taking up the arms of rancour and cruelty so that they could hamper the spread of Islam and guard the interests of the Quraysh chiefs and men of power.

Of course it cannot be denied that one of the reasons for the opposition of the people of that age to the perfect faith of the Holy Prophet of Islam was their intellectual immaturity. But from the very day the Quraysh tribe heard that the Holy Prophet of Islam called the idols and wooden and stone statues they worshipped valueless and useless, they exhibited the utmost enmity and opposition toward Islam. The Prophet asked the people, 'What do you want with these lifeless objects?.' They were even more enraged when the Prophet denounced the wooden and stone idols of the Quraysh left to them by their ancestors, which they regarded among their ancient glories.

On the other hand, the divine teachings of the Holy Prophet of Islam were inconsistent with the interests of the oppressive class of the chiefs of the Quraysh who wanted to continue exploiting the poor people and possessing innumerable slaves, as well as with the interests and inhumane desires of the usurers who wished to amass wealth at the expense of the deprived class of their society.

It goes without saying that in an environment where no divine law is obeyed and no human right is respected, the strong will forcibly violate the honour, property, and chastity of the defenceless people, and so the new faith — Islam — which severely opposed and fought this wrong social system, enraged those whose interests and selfish considerations were endangered.

Such notorious people as Abu Jahl, Abu Sufyan, Abu Lahab, Aswad ibn Abd Yaghwan, 'As ibn Wa'il, 'Utbah and Shaybah, Walid ibn Maghirah, and 'Aqibah ibn Abi Ma'ayyat were among the leaders of the opponents of Islam.

Cruel, false accusations, physical torment, foul language, economic and financial pressure and boycotts were among the inhumane methods used by the Quraysh chiefs against the Prophet and his faithful companions.

Here some examples of the offences and torments which the enemies of Islam inflicted upon the Holy Prophet are mentioned:

1. One day a number of Quraysh gave the uterus of a sheep to their servants to throw at the blessed face and head of the Prophet. They obeyed their brutal master, thus making the Prophet rather sad.[100]

2. Tariq Maharibi has narrated, 'I saw the Holy Prophet saying in a loud voice to the people, "O people! Say there is no god but God so you would find salvation".

'He urged the people to submit to Islam and become monotheists while Abu Lahab followed him step by step and threw stones at him injuring him so that his feet were covered with blood, but the Holy Prophet continued to guide the people and show them the path of eternal salvation and prosperity. Abu Lahab cried out, "People! This man is a liar. Do not listen to him".'[101]

3. In addition, the Holy Prophet of Islam, as well as his loyal friends and those who had newly adopted Islam, were most severely tortured and tormented by the infidels.

One day, the Holy Prophet of Islam observed 'Ammar Yasir and his family being tortured by the enemies of Islam. Addressing 'Ammar and his faithful family, he said, 'I give you, 'Ammar's family, the good tidings that Paradise will be your eternal abode'.[102]

Ibn Athir has written, 'Ammar and his parents suffered severe tortures from the idol worshippers. The idol worshippers forced them out of their house in the hot burning weather and tortured them under the burning rays of the sun, inflicting the most unbearable tortures upon them so that they would leave the faith.'

71

Sumayyah, 'Ammar's mother, was the first woman martyr of Islam, killed by a blow from Abu Jahl's weapon. Yasir, 'Ammar's father, too, died under the torture of the infidels. 'Ammar himself was most cruelly tortured by the enemies of Islam but resorted to dissimulation and thus saved his own life.[103]

4. Bilal, an Ethiopian slave, was among the Prophet's most faithful followers, and, because of his faith in Islam, his ruthless master brutally tortured him. At midday when it is scorching hot, his master would make Bilal lie down on the burning hot desert pebbles and sand and put a large and heavy stone on his chest to force him to stop obeying the Holy Prophet of Islam and to worship their idols instead of worshipping the One God.

Bilal resisted all his threats and tortures most bravely and admirably and responded just by repeating the word 'Ahad' (One), meaning 'God is One and Peerless and I will never become an idol worshipper'.[104]

Unfortunately, there is no room in such a relatively small book to narrate in detail all the sad stories of the Muslims of early Islam. Thus we content ourselves with observing that the enemies of Islam resorted to any means at their disposal in their fight against Islam and the Muslims, some of which were:

Economic struggle: The Quraysh had started a fierce economic struggle against the Prophet and his followers. One of the inhumane weapons they used against the Muslims was economic pressure and boycott of any sort of transactions with the Muslims.

Psychological warfare: Prohibiting of marriage with Muslims, cutting off all relations with them from the Quraysh, and accusing the Holy Prophet of Islam of witchcraft, telling lies, and the like were psychological tactics meant to break down the resistance and perserverance of the first Muslims.

Physical torment and torture: Another anti-human method of fighting the new movement and its adherents used by the Quraysh was physical torture of the Muslims, which resulted in the martyrdom of a number of faithful Muslims at the beginning of Islam.

In spite of all the brutal methods that the infidel Quraysh utilized in their struggles against Islam, the Holy Prophet and the Muslims, Islam advanced and the Prophet continued to urge the people to go the right way. Islam and the Muslims continued their efforts and struggles.

To maintain their faith in Islam, the Muslims underwent extremely severe torture, sufferings, and hardships and showed admirable resistance in following this honorable path.

A careful and just survey of the conditions of the Muslims at the beginning of Islam reveals the significant fact that, unlike the picture the enemies of Islam have always tried to present, Islam, this holiest of faith, has not been promoted at the point of the bayonet or by the sword, but for 13 years, the Holy Prophet of Islam and the faithful Muslims tolerated the tortures, torments, and swords of the infidels and the idol worshippers to promote this divine religion revealed by God for their salvation.

Chapter 11

The Migration of the Prophet: the Source of Historical Transformation

GOING INTO EXILE TO ACHIEVE THE DIVINE GOAL

The Holy Prophet of Islam was well aware of the fact that people who were plunged in prejudice, superstition, and ignorance would not abandon their beliefs and ways easily and that it would take extensive struggle, severe hardships, and sincere self-sacrifice to save them from the pit of corruption and guide them onto the path of virtue and monotheism. He could easily read in the faces of the people of Makkah, the opposition to Islam and their bigoted determination to fight the Muslims.

The divine foresight of the Holy Prophet of Islam had given him a dark image of the future. With such an insight and divine knowledge, he held high the banner of prophecy and adopted patience and tolerance. The Prophet struggled with the enemies of Islam in Makkah for 13 years and resisted all their torments and obstructions, but the opponents of Islam did not give up their devilish beliefs and manner and utilized all their power to destroy Islam.[105] Under such circumstances, the universal mission of the Holy Prophet of Islam necessitated his migration to a calm, suitable place and to find a new arena for his work and mission.

YATHRIB — READY TO SUBMIT TO ISLAM

At the time of the pilgrimage to the Ka'aba, some of the men of importance of the Khazraj tribe came to Makkah and met with the Holy Prophet in the Masjid al-Haram. He explained the divine faith of Islam to them and encouraged them to believe in this religion, which is the faith of peace and fraternity. The Khazraj chiefs, who were tired of their deep-rooted disputes and conflicts with the Aws tribe, felt that Islam was exactly what they needed, and so they most willingly submitted to Islam.

When the Khazrajis, who had become Muslim, were about to return to Yathrib, they asked the Holy Prophet of Islam for a missionary, and he assigned Mas'ab ibn 'Umir to accompany them. Thus, the people of Yathrib were informed of the rising sun of Islam and hurried to gain information about the new faith.

The most effective factor in making the people ready and eager to adopt Islam was listening to the luminous verses of the Holy Qur'an. Mas'ab reported the conversion to Islam of the chiefs and leaders of both the Khazraj and Aws tribes to the Holy Prophet. Later on, a large number of the people of Yathrib who had come to Makkah to take part in the Hajj pilgrimage held a secret meeting with the Prophet at midnight and swore allegiance to support him just as they supported and protected their own families.[106]

THE PLOT TO MURDER
THE HOLY PROPHET OF ISLAM

Dawn had hardly broken when the infidel Quraysh were informed of the allegiance of the Yathribi Muslims. They

76

hurriedly attempted to frustrate it and hinder the advance of Islam. For this purpose, they held a council in the place where the Quraysh gathered to pass judgment and to consult each other. After a great deal of talk and consultation, it was resolved that they select one man from each tribe to rush into the house of the Prophet at night and murder him so that the basis of the propagation of Islam would be destroyed.[107]

But Almighty God made the Holy Prophet aware of the intrigue of his enemies and commanded him to leave Makkah by night.[108] The Prophet, upon receiving this revelation, decided to leave his homeland and migrate to Yathrib.

'ALI'S SELF-SACRIFICE

When the Holy Prophet of Islam was divinely commanded to migrate to Yathrib, he called 'Ali, disclosed his secret to him, gave him the people's trusts to be returned to their owners and then said, 'I have to migrate, but you must lie in my bed'. 'Ali sincerely obeyed the Holy Prophet and lay in his bed, thus devotedly exposing himself to the dangers that threatened the Holy Prophet of Islam.[109]

'Ali's self-sacrifice was so sincere and significant that God praised it in the Holy Qur'an.[110]

THE HOLY PROPHET OF ISLAM
GOES TO THE THAWR CAVE

At midnight the enemies of Islam surrounded the house of the Holy Prophet to carry out their satanic plot. But since God was the supporter and protector of the Prophet, He saved him from harm at the hands of the murderous infidels.

While reading verses from Sura Yasin, the Holy Prophet of Islam came out of his house and through a by-way, went to the Thawr cave, which was situated outside Makkah. Abu Bakr was informed of the matter and accompanied the Holy Prophet.[111]

The infidels rushed towards the Prophet's bed with drawn swords in their hands, but to their surprise, they found 'Ali in his place. Upset and enraged, they asked, 'Where has Muhammad gone?' 'Ali answered, 'Had you assigned me to watch him? Well, you intended to expel him and he has left the city'.[112]

Realizing that all their plots were frustrated, the idol worshipping Quraysh took serious measures but all in vain.

ON THE WAY TO YATHRIB

After staying in the Thawr cave for three days, the Holy Prophet of Islam proceeded towards Yathrib.[113] One of the Makkans, Saraqa ibn Malik, attempted to pursue him, but his horse's hoof sank into the ground three times and threw him down, so he repented and returned to Makkah.[114]

On the 12th of Rabi al-Awwal, the Holy Prophet of Islam reached a place called Quba,[115] where he stayed for a few days.[116] Abu Bakr insistently asked the Prophet to begin travelling towards Yathrib, but the Holy Prophet refused to go without 'Ali. He said to Abu Bakr, 'Ali has endangered his own life to save mine. He is my cousin, my brother, and the dearest among the family to me. I will not leave here until he joins me'.[117]

After fulfilling the mission assigned to him, 'Ali joined the Holy Prophet in Quba, but his legs were so bruised that he could hardly walk. The Holy Prophet embraced him most affectionately, blessed his hurt legs with the saliva from his own mouth which healed 'Ali's swollen legs. Thus together they started towards Yathrib.[118]

YATHRIB EAGERLY AWAITING THE HOLY PROPHET

Yathrib had taken on an extraordinary air and intense excitement and eagerness had overtaken the whole city. In every alley and neighbourhood people impatiently awaited the Holy Prophet of Islam.

He entered Yathrib on Friday.[119] People were overjoyed and could not stop looking at the resplendent countenance of the Prophet.

The Holy Prophet of Islam settled in Yathrib and there laid the foundations of Islam and a magnificent culture based on justice and faith.

After the blessful entrance of the Holy Prophet of Islam into Yathrib, its name was changed into Medinat ul-Nabi, meaning 'the City of the Prophet'.[120] That year, the year the Holy Prophet of Islam migrated from Makkah to Yathrib, was recognized as the origin of history, due to this significant historical event, the triumph of righteousness and justice. The illuminating sun of Islam gave new life to the people. They discarded all the old superstitious beliefs and thoughts and all the wrong deeds and manners of the past, replacing them with the perfect life-giving culture of Islam.

A LESSON FROM THE HIJRA

14 centuries have now passed since the momentous historical event of the Hijra — the migration of the Holy Prophet from Makkah to Medina. A careful study of history reveals the sincere and indefatigable efforts of the Muslims in the cause of the migration and laying the foundation of Islam.

After migration to Yathrib, the migrant Muslims had obviously rid themselves of the torment and torture of the infidel Quraysh and found a peaceful, agreeable environment. Nevertheless, they showed no tendency towards self-indulgence and pleasure-seeking. Rather they ceaselessly endeavoured to establish an Islamic civilization and to spread the divine faith of Islam.

It was these very sacrificial efforts and hard work of the Muslims that rescued them from slavery and so many miseries and brought them honour, prosperity, and glory.

It is indeed necessary for the Muslims all over the world to be constantly reminded of the devotion and incessant efforts of the Muslims in the early days of Islam, who relied on their faith in

God and, through obeying the instructions of the Holy Prophet, managed to make a holy revolution and attained great achievements. It is of vital significance to Muslims in all places and at all times to take a lesson from the lives and sacrificial endeavours of those truly devoted Muslims. Each year, on the occasion of the anniversary of the migration, sincere reflection on the lives of these godly men and women will effectively serve this purpose.

It is also incumbent upon us to teach posterity the fact that the Muslims of the beginning of Islam owed their glory and greatness to their faith and their sincere efforts and that we must try to adopt their manners if we want to regain the honour and greatness that devoted Muslims really deserve.

Chapter 12

Laying the Foundation for an Islamic Fraternity in Medina

The existence of sympathy, sincerity, and harmony among the people of a society makes that society a living one — one that is fit for human life and evolution, in which all can find salvation and progress and can enjoy each other's sympathy and sincerity.

In the process of establishing such an ideal human society, Islam does not pay the least bit of attention to such considerations as race, language, skin colour, and geographical location. Rather, this holy religion regards all Muslims as equal.[121] It looks only at the people's faith in God, which is the root of all unity.

'Islamic brotherhood' is the phrase best revealing this all-embracing unity. This meaningful, clear expression in the Holy Qur'an describes this Islamic precept: *'Truly the faithful are brothers'* (49:10).

THE PROPHET'S INITIATIVE
IN CREATING ISLAMIC BROTHERHOOD

After having settled in Medina and after building a mosque that was indeed the military and constitutional base of the Muslims, the Holy Prophet of Islam took an excellent initiative. He laid the foundation of Islamic brotherhood, so that great unity and sincerity would be engendered in Muslim society and so that the emigrant Muslims would know that, though they had lost a number of their friends and relatives and had been forced to leave their homes, in return, they had gained brothers who were much more loyal and sympathetic from every point of view.

Therefore, besides the general fraternity and brotherhood that exists among all Muslims, the Prophet concluded contracts of brotherhood among his followers. He announced each two Muslims to be brothers. He himself selected 'Ali as his own brother and said, "Ali is my brother".[122]

In the Holy Qur'an, Islamic brotherhood has been elevated and held in reverence: *'And hold fast to the covenant of God, all together, and remember the favour of God upon you when you were enemies, then He united your hearts so by His favour you became brethren, and you were on the brink of a pit of fire, then He saved you from it; thus does God make clear to you His communications that you may follow the right way'* (3:3).

ISLAMIC BROTHERHOOD:
BYWORD OF UNITY AND FRATERNITY

Islamic brotherhood is not a honorific expression but a reality mingled with the spirit of faith whose fruits emerge one after the other.

Our Holy Leader Imam Sadiq has explained some of the fruits of Islamic brotherhood in the following way: 'A believer is the brother and guide of another believer. He does not betray or oppress him, nor does he ever cheat his brother. A believer never breaks his promise'.[123]

One of the requirements of Islamic brotherhood is that whatever a Muslim desires for himself, he should desire for his brother in Islam, and he should help his Muslim brothers by any means possible, whether by his wealth or by his speech or by any other means. It is far from Islamic brotherhood if you have enough food, water, and clothing while another Muslim is hungry, thirsty and naked.

Imam Sadiq, peace be upon him, has said, 'If you have a servant and your brother in Islam does not have any, you must send your servant to help your brother prepare food, clean clothes, and perform any other needed work'.[124]

Islamic fraternity has overshadowed all relationships, even family relationships. The Qur'an openly says, '*You shall not find a people who believe in God and the latter day befriending those who act in opposition to God and His Apostle, even though they were their own fathers or their sons or their brothers or their kinsfolk*' (58:22).

It was the principle of Islamic brotherhood that made the Ethiopian Bilal and the Persian Salman brothers and two of the best companions of the Holy Prophet of Islam. In the light of Islamic brotherhood, many deep-rooted enmities were reconciled and divided groups were united. This unity requires that all Muslims share each other's sorrows and joys like members of a large family. Muslims should be sincere and affectionate toward each other, and their watchword should be unity and brotherhood.

Islamic brotherhood firmly holds all Muslims responsible toward each other and establishes an all-embracing responsibility so that Muslims cannot be heedless of each other's troubles and problems but every Muslim must, within his own abilities, endeavour to solve the problems of Muslims and to create possibilities for the advancement and promotion of Islam.

This responsibility is divided into two parts:

Economic Cooperation: This responsibility is related to meeting people's economic needs, such as hygiene, education, shelter, employment, and the like, and part of the precepts of the Holy Qur'an and the instructions of religious leaders deal with this as well as with fundamental precepts and programs such as *zakat* (the poor-due prescribed by Islam), almsgiving, charity, and the like.

Scientific and Educational Cooperation: This part includes propagation, guidance, and teaching. That is to say, all Muslims are duty-bound to communicate to others whatever they have learned and not to neglect each other's guidance. Also, there are two basic principles among the practical precepts of Islam that urge Muslims to call upon each other to perform their religious duties and to refrain from committing sins. These precepts, which are indeed most beneficial to Muslims, are rated among the most significant requirements of Islamic brotherhood. But unfortunately, Muslims seem to have forgotten this great precept due either to imaginary fears or to selfish interests, and perhaps due to both.

As we clearly observe, in most Muslim societies, prohibition from committing sins and mutual encouragement to obey religious instructions have long been neglected. This deplorable situation has resulted in the ruin of the ethical spirit of Islamic brotherhood, and following this ruin, other superiorities and advantages of this living society are lost.

ISLAMIC BROTHERHOOD IN THE PRESENT AGE
In our age, Muslims need real unity more than ever. God has endowed Islamic countries with invaluable resources which others intensely covet. Thus, they try every means possible to divide Muslims and distract them from their critical situation. It goes without saying that dispersion, lack of unity, and negligence are extemely effective causes of ruin and slavery, and obviously the world-devouring enemies of Muslims are quite aware of this fact.

Therefore, we Muslims must be alert and vigilant in order to overcome those who clearly intend to exploit us, devour our natural resources, and bring us humiliation and misery.

The solution to our problems concerning our brutal enemies lies in Islamic brotherhood of which the foundation has been laid by the blessed hands of the Holy Prophet of Islam, and in following Islamic precepts.

No matter how powerful the Muslims are, still they greatly need unity. So the lesson of unity and Islamic brotherhood should be effectively taught to primary school students, and later on, as youngsters grow older and are promoted to higher grades, practical training programs treating Islamic brotherhood and other precepts of Islam must be added to their education, to strengthen their Islamic spirit. Moreover, it is one of the greatest duties of Muslim parents to bring up children who are real Muslims and sympathetic to other Muslims.

It is crystal clear that if the Muslims had observed the principles of Islamic brotherhood and had been united and sympathetic, they would never have suffered so much tyranny, humiliation, and exploitation from the non-Muslims. But it is a pity that the Muslims' negligence has given the covetous exploiters an opportunity to enslave, humiliate, degrade, and plunder millions of Muslims in Africa, Asia, and all over the world, Muslims who really deserve lordship and superiority if they follow Islamic precepts.

Chapter 13

Jihad: Religious and Spiritual Struggle in the Way of God

More than 1,000 million Muslims in different parts of the world unitedly celebrated the beginning of the 15th century of the actualization of the prophetic mission of the Holy Prophet of Islam.

This celebration was held to glorify the great day when the Prophet hoisted the flag of peace and brotherhood and laid the foundations of universal peace and peaceful co-existence; just as Almighty God has said to the Prophet, '...*And We have not sent you but as a blessing to the worlds'* (21:107).

Islam has best resolved the racial and class differences that are the causes of most wars, conflicts, and disastrous events, whereas the so-called civilized world of today is deeply involved in bloody wars and ruinous conflicts and each day the world's murderous statesmen and supercriminals find a new pretext under which to fan the flames of war.

87

Islam's care for peace and justice is so great that in the Qur'an, the followers of the Book, the Jews and the Christians, have been explicitly urged to adopt unity and harmony in the moving expression, *'Say: O followers of the Book! Come to an equitable proposition between us and you that we shall not serve any but God and (that) we shall not associate aught with Him...'* (3:74).

When the Muslims migrated to Medina and the flag of victory was hoisted over their heads, numerous peace proposals were offered to the Prophet by his opponents and he welcomed them. An undeniable testimony to this fact was his peace agreements with several Jewish tribes that were concluded in the first year of the Hijra.[125]

THE PURPOSE OF JIHAD

Islam is a dynamic, comprehensive school that aims at the rectification of the social and economic systems of the world in a special manner.

Unlike the beliefs of the ancient Romans, the Jews, and the Nazis, Islam is not restricted to a certain community or a certain race, but is for all human beings and aims at human prosperity and salvation. This divine faith requires all Muslims, guided by the holy precepts and instructions of Islam, to endeavour to rescue the oppressed masses, to establish peace and justice, and to acquaint the unaware people of the whole world with Islam and Islamic rules and regulations.

The combatants of Islam do not intend to gain control of a land or overthrow an oppressive rule to replace it with a similar rule through jihad. Rather, jihad is a pure humanitarian struggle fulfilled in God's way and for human evolution and the rescue of the oppressed people. This struggle culminates in the elimination of all sedition and in the establishment of peace and prosperity.

This great undertaking and the dynamic precepts of Islam put an end to the negligence and degradation of large groups of people, just as they end the oppressive rule and tyrannical lordship of those who live in luxury at the expense of the poor and the defenseless.

Human nature urges that the corrupt members of society be destroyed like weeds so the way may be paved for human salvation and prosperity and so the oppressed may be released from the tyranny of the oppressor. Humanitarian, justice-loving, and noble people adhere to this holy struggle and embark upon it.

GOD'S WORDS
'And were it not for God's repelling some men with others, the earth would certainly be in a state of disorder, but God is gracious to the creatures' (2:251).

In the theory of Islamic law, war is not an end in itself, but it is regarded as the final means of hindering tyranny and aggression and paving the way towards salvation for mankind.

Once the spokesman for the Arab Muslims said to Rustam Farrokhzad, the Iranian military commander, 'God has assigned us to lead the people who worship other people into worship of the unique, peerless, One God, to urge them to leave a degrading life for a noble one and to rescue them from the torments of false religions through Islamic justice. We will let go of the land of any people who accept our invitation to Islam and will go back to our own land."[126]

DID ISLAM PREVAIL BY
THE FORCE OF THE SWORD?
As a matter of fact, through jihad, the Muslims have mainly meant to establish connections with the people who are under the oppressive rule of tyrants, so the oppressed masses would become acquainted with Islamic rules and precepts and so they would comprehend the glory and genuineness of independence and salvation. The Muslims are well aware of the fact that the oppressed masses will most willingly accept Islam as the best divine faith if Islam is correctly explained to them.

In fighting the infidels, the Muslims did not force people to become Muslims but gave them the choice to retain their own faith provided they submitted to the conditions of peace. In return, the Islamic government would protect them.

In the peace agreement of Hudaybiyah, the Holy Prophet of Islam undertook that no Muslim would shelter any of the infidel Makkans[127] even if they became Muslims before or at the time of seeking refuge with the Muslims in Medina and would return them to Makkah, and he stood by his promise.[128] If the Holy Prophet had wished, he could have taken the same promise from his enemies that if a person left Islam and sought refuge with the infidels of Makkah, he would be returned to Medina.

When Makkah was conquered by the Prophet and his followers, he gave the Quraysh freedom of choice. He did not force anybody to adopt Islam. He wanted them to become Muslims as a result of their true understanding of Islam and of their own free will, not by force. He ordered the Muslims not to kill anybody in Makkah except for a few who were constantly causing trouble for the Muslims.[129]

When the infidels asked him for refuge, he would give them refuge and the opportunity to study Islam and then to submit to it freely. For instance, Safwan ibn Umayyah fled to Jeddah when Makkah was conquered by the Muslims. When some people asked the Holy Prophet for refuge on his behalf, he sent his turban for him as a sign of refuge to give him immunity on returning to Makkah. Safwan returned from Jeddah and asked the Prophet to give him a respite of two months. He agreed to his request and gave him a respite of four months. And Safwan accompanied the Holy Prophet of Islam to Hunayn and Ta'if and finally discarded infidelity and submitted to Islam of his own free will.[130]

CONCLUSION

We conclude that in Islam, the sword is resorted to only in dealing with those who have realized the truth and yet fight it and thus try to hinder others from achieving salvation, and that force is applied to banish tyranny, to release the oppressed, and to create favourable conditions for human progress and evolution.

The sincere and loyal faith of the Muslims at the beginning of Islam and their resistance to all torture and hardship are themselves the best testimonies to the fact that Islam was not promoted by force. History bears witness to this reality: that the Muslims at the beginning of Islam were so devoted to their faith that they persevered in it through their struggles no matter what torture and torment the infidels inflicted upon them. Many of them even left their homeland and migrated to other places.

The Ethiopian Bilal was among those who took the lead in accepting Islam. Abu Jahl made him lie on the burning hot pebbles, placed a heavy stone on him, the torture of which is, needless to say, beyond endurance. When the faithful Bilal was being tormented, Abu Jahl shouted at him, 'Disbelieve in Muhammad's God. Discard Islam.' But Bilal just repeated, 'The One. The One',[131] meaning God is the One, and 'I worship the One God'. In fact Bilal, as well as many other faithful Muslims at the beginning of Islam, suffered a great deal from the enemies of Islam who had aimed most obstinately at the destruction of Islam.

All of them tolerated all the pains and torture and did not leave their faith even for a single moment. We see therefore very clearly how the accusation that Islam prevailed by force and by the law of the sword is false and far from the truth.

Having found no weak point in Islam, the opponents of this divine religion obviously resorted to such accusations to stain Islam, unaware of the fact that Islam prevails because it is the most supreme divine faith, perfectly compatible with human nature. It gives shelter to the oppressed, deprived masses and presents solutions to all problems facing human beings, whether they be in the material, spiritual, emotional, educational, or political realms.

A Frenchman has written, 'Islam easily prevailed, and this should be rated as one of the special characteristics of Islam. Islam persists forever wherever Muslims step'.[132]

Another Christian writer has written: 'The commercial and cultural contacts beyond the borders of Islam have by far been more effective in the expansion and promotion of the Islamic world than have been military conquests'.[133]

Chapter 14

The Motives of the Wars of the Prophet

Unlike the self-centered rulers and kings all over the world who embark on wars for expansionist purposes, for the exploitation of human powers, and for the plunder of other people's wealth and natural resources, the Prophet of Islam refused to resort to the sword and fighting unless it was necessary and unavoidable. Instead, he advanced carrying the torch of the Holy Book and the divine laws and would get involved in war only to remove the stumbling blocks — the thorns in the way of salvation — to hinder oppression and tyranny, and to hoist the flag of justice and truth.

The battles of the Prophet of Islam against the infidels were, needless to say, meant to remove those brutal selfish pagans from the scene who for the sake of their own satanic passions and desires inflicted all kinds of oppression against God's pure creatures and prevented the promulgation of Islamic precepts and beliefs. He only fought to bring about conditions of justice and equity under which human beings could materialize the ideology of world peace and mutual understanding.

Can such a war be considered illegitimate and unjust? It goes without saying that such struggles are necessary and that no Prophet could avoid combating those who intend to bring ruin on human societies and cause corruption and social decay. No doubt any wise, humanitarian person accepts such combat and admires it because there is no other way to achieve the sacred ends of the Prophets.

Jesus Christ, peace be upon him, had a short prophetic life and lived under conditions that did not permit war, so he did not attempt any wars. Otherwise, he too would have destroyed the weeds and troublemakers of human society.

Christian propaganda purposely misinterprets the holy wars of the Prophet of Islam and ascribes large numbers of casualties to them to weaken the morale of Islamic nations, to hinder the ever-increasing expansion and prevalence of Islam, and to make the murder of millions of innocent people by the masters of churches and in the crusades appear trivial and negligible to the people of the world.

Here we will first point out the motives of the Prophet of Islam in the wars he undertook, and then we will briefly cite the casualties of all the wars at the time of the Prophet, so the truth may be made clear. In this way, readers can realize the philosophy of Islamic wars for themselves and can also see that the casualties of these holy wars were trivial in comparison with those of other wars.

THE WAR OF BADR

For 13 years after the advent of the prophetic mission of the Prophet of Islam, he and his followers were tormented and tortured by the infidel Quraysh in Makkah. Finally, the Prophet of Islam left Makkah and migrated to Medina. Yet the infidel Makkans did not stop tormenting the Muslims who had remained in Makkah and also did not let them leave Makkah and migrate somewhere else.[134]

At the same time, the Makkan enemies of Islam had decided to put Medina under a severe economic siege. They had forbidden all caravans from carrying provisions and foodstuffs to Medina. This siege lasted such a long time that the people of Medina were faced with many troubles and hardships and had to go as far as the coasts of the Red Sea to buy foodstuff.[135]

Abu Jahl, too, wrote an extremely harsh and rude letter to the Prophet of Islam and in that letter warned him to expect the attack of the Quraysh.[136]

It was on this occasion that God said, *'Those who have been expelled from their homes without a just cause except that they say, "Our Lord is God." Had there not been God's repelling some people by others, certainly there would have been pulled down cloisters and churches and synagogues and mosques in which God's name is much remembered; and surely God will help him who helps His cause; most surely God is strong, mighty'* (22:39-40).

In the second year of the Hijra, the Holy Prophet of Islam arose to guard Islam, to defend the basic rights of the Muslims, and to frustrate the satanic conspiracies of the Quraysh. In the war of Badr, they confronted the Quraysh troops. Though the number of Muslim combatants was one-third that of the infidel forces, the Muslims defeated the infidels by their power of faith and by God's help.[137]

THE WAR OF UHUD

Since a considerable number of the infidel troops had been killed in the Badr war, the next year, the third year after the Hijra, the Quraysh prepared for war to take revenge for their defeat in the Badr war. They proceeded to Medina. They faced the army of Islam in a place called Uhud. Since a number of the Muslims in the war did not fully obey the instructions of the Holy Prophet, the Muslims did not become victorious in the Uhud war.[138]

THE AHZAB (TRENCH) WAR

In the fifth year of the Hijra, a Jewish tribe called Bani Nazir went to Makkah and incited the Quraysh against Islam and the Muslims. The Quraysh took advantage of the opportunity, gathered a huge army from different anti-Islamic groups, and started toward Medina.

To guard Medina, the headquarters of Islam, the Muslims dug moats all around the city and lined up in front of the enemy army, whose number amounted to 10,000. 'Ali, peace be upon him, overcame and defeated their commander, and finally the war ended to the advantage and victory of the Muslims.[139]

THE BANI QURAYZAH WAR

The Bani Qurayzah[140] had concluded a peace agreement with the Holy Prophet of Islam, but they violated that agreement in the war of Ahzab and rendered help to the Quraysh.[141] Since the Prophet had recognized them as a 'dangerous' people, the Muslims had no choice but to kill them.

After the war of Ahzab, the Prophet ordered his army to proceed against the Bani Qurayzah. For 25 days, the Bani Qurayzah were besieged by the Muslim army, and they finally surrendered.

The Aws tribe asked the Holy Prophet of Islam to forgive them and spare them the punishment of death. He asked them, 'Are you ready to select Sa'ad Ma'az, who is one of the men of status among you, as the arbiter and accept his arbitration?' They all agreed, hoping that Sa'ad would take their side. But Sa'ad Ma'az's verdict was to kill their fighters, to take their possessions as booty, and to take their women captive.

The Holy Prophet said, 'The arbitration of Sa'ad Ma'az is the same arbitration God has passed upon such people'. Then all their fighters were killed.[142]

THE BANI MUSTALAQ WAR

The Bani Mustalaq were a group of the Khaza'ah tribe who

took measures against the Muslims. The Holy Prophet of Islam came to know their plots and proceeded against them with his combatants to repel their brutal assault, fought them in a place called Maris'a, and defeated them. This war occurred in 6 A.H.[143]

THE KHAYBAR WAR

Large numbers of Jews lived in the Khaybar forts and had military and economic relations with the infidels. Since the security of the Muslims was constantly threatened by those anti-Islamic Jews, in 7 A.H. the Muslims started towards Khaybar, which was the headquarters of the enemy, surrounded the fort, and, after a triumphant war, made the Jews submit to the Islamic government.[144]

THE MUTAH WAR

In 8 A.H., the Holy Prophet of Islam sent Harith ibn Umar with a letter to the king of Basra, but his messenger was killed in a place called Mutah.[145] At the command of the Prophet, the army of Islam marched towards the enemy, and in Mutah they confronted the army of Marqal, the king of Rome. His army comprised 100,000 Roman and non-Roman fighters. A war broke out between the two armies in which Zayd ibn Harith, Ja'far ibn Abi Talib, and Abdullah ibn Rawahah, the three famous commanders of the army of Islam, were martyred, and the Muslims could not overcome the infidels, so they returned to Medina.[146]

THE CONQUEST OF MAKKAH

In the Hudaybiyah peace agreement, the Quraysh had promised the Holy Prophet of Islam not to transgress against or oppress the Muslims and their confederates, but they violated the agreement and helped the Bani Bakr tribe to destroy the Khaza'ah tribe, which was one of the confederates of the Muslims. To hamper their aggression, the Prophet approached Makkah in secrecy, entered it through an elaborate device, and conquered the city. Then he made a pilgrimage to God's House

— the Ka'aba — and delivered a historic speech in which he declared, 'You should beware that you have been bad neighbours for God's Prophet. You refuted us, tormented us, expelled us from our homeland, and yet did not content yourselves with so much torture and troublemaking; you even did not let us have peace in Medina and attempted to fight us. But in spite of all this, I set you all free and let you go unpunished'.[147]

This great tolerance and forgiveness brought about the submission of the people of Makkah to Islam. In this triumphant battle, the Prophet ordered the Muslims not to fight for any reason other than defense and against the violations of the infidels. However, he passed a death sentence upon eight men and four women, and conflict arose between the army of Khalid and a number of infidels who had fought under the leadership of Akramah ibn Abu Jahl in which a number were killed.[148]

HUNAYN AND TA'IF

The Havazin tribe had gathered an army against Islam. The Holy Prophet was informed of their satanic intentions and mobilized 12,000 Muslim soldiers to confront them. The two opposing armies fought each other in the valley of Hunayn, and finally the Islamic army defeated the army of the infidels and subdued them.[149]

After this victorious war, the Prophet attempted to fight the Saghif tribe, who had conspired with the Havazin against Islam, but after having besieged it for a while, he dispensed with its conquest and returned to Makkah.[150]

Some other less severe wars also took place between the army of the Holy Prophet of Islam and the infidels, and also several journeys for the propagation of Islam were made during these blessed times.

Now the data on casualties, from both the Muslim army and the infidel's army, of all the wars that took place between the Muslims and the infidels are presented, having been gathered from credible documents.

The Names of the Wars	Tarikh Khumays	Sirat ibn Hisham	Tarikh Yaqubi	Tabaqat	Bahar al-Anwar	Tarikh Tabari
Badr	84	84	86	84	84	84
Uhud	93	92	90	109	109	70
Ahzab	9	9	14	11	9	9
Bani Qurayzah	800	850	750	700	900	850
Bani Mustalaq	12	—	—	10	10	—
Khaybar	32	23	—	98	—	3
Mutah	21	13	—	13	—	3
Makkah	39	20	—	33	—	21
Hunayn and Ta'if	96	101	—	87	112	85
Other wars	250	122	—	119	333	210

Notes:
1. This data has been presented, observing, in the case of differences, the maximum numbers, and we have left blank any place for which we have not found any data.

2. *Tarikh al-Khumays* is one of our sources of acquiring data and is a collection of tens of books on commentary, *ahadith* (traditions of the Prophet of Islam), and history.

It goes without saying that, in comparison with the casualties in the crusades of the Christians, those of the Islamic wars against the infidels are trivial, and also there is no doubt, therefore, that none of the wars of the Holy Prophet of Islam were launched out of motives of expansion, revenge, or aggression. Rather, they were aimed at the replusion of the aggressors, defense of the honour of the Muslims, and independence and the exaltation and prevalence of right, truth, and justice.

A Frenchman relates, 'While Islam has made it incumbent upon Muslims to make jihad, it has ordered Muslims to treat the followers of other faiths with tolerance, justice, and remission and has given them freedom of religion'.[151]

Chapter 15

The Universal Mission
of the Prophet of Islam:
A Faith for both East and West

Islam emerged like a limpid fountain and increased in depth and expanse as time went by. It finally became a great river passing through various human societies, irrigating fields in which seeds of humanity were to be planted, satisfying the thirst of human beings for salvation and justice. It is going on and will surely continue to do so as long as there are human beings on earth because human nature is thirsty for this heavenly faith and would perish if it were denied it. Islam is truly the only power that is able to wipe out all wrong manners, all corruption, and all corrosive attitudes in all places and at all times and to lead human beings onto the path God has determined for them.

Obviously, Islam does not please those who oppress, the colonialists, the arrogant, and their like. So they have always tried hard to hinder it, but in spite of so many wicked policies and plots of the world-exploiters and despite the serious attempts of the enemies of Islam to misrepresent this holy faith, Islam has prevailed.

Islam contains the secret of victory as well as of prosperity. The fact that Islam is a divine faith, not a man-made one, is testimony to the rightful claim that all the laws, rules, instructions, and precepts necessary for human happiness and salvation are to be sought in it.

Is it not the case that God has created human beings as well as all other beings? Is it not the case that the Creator knows all about His creatures? Is it not true that the same gracious God who has created so many wonderful natural resources to meet human material needs has also endowed human beings with divine resources to satisfy their spiritual wants?

Thus being presented by God, it is totally compatible with human nature and consistent with all human wants and needs: material, spiritual, and emotional. Most important of all, it provides all the necessary means for human evolution towards salvation so that when man leaves this world for the eternal one, he will be deserving of Paradise there and not hell, just as God wants man to be. It goes without saying that all laws and precepts in the holy faith of Islam have been made on the basis of human nature, which is the same in all human societies and at all times. So those who say, 'East is east and west is west' and 'An eastern Prophet cannot be a good leader for western people', are absolutely wrong. For human beings, whether of the east or the west, have their nature, their natural character-istics, and their wants in common. There is no difference between people in this respect, no matter how different their race, colour, traditions, geographical conditions, and the like may be. And just as eastern people need an innate faith — a faith compatible with their nature and capable of satisfying their various human needs — western people are in need of such a divine faith, exactly to the same extent. A simple comparison can serve to clarify the matter. Human beings all over the world and at all times need food, water, and oxygen to survive, and there is no human being found without a need of them for his survival. Just so, all of them need spiritual nourishment for their souls, their emotional health, their spiritual survival, and, most significant of all, their finding salvation.

There are, of course, many proofs to this righteous claim that Islam ensures human happiness and salvation in all parts of the world, and at all times. Those who oppose this divine faith and try to misrepresent it are in fact the greatest enemies of human beings.

MAKKAH: THE STARTING PLACE FOR THE PROPHET'S PROPAGATION OF ISLAM

It is crystal clear that when the Holy Prophet of Islam illuminated the dark atmosphere of Makkah with the call of monotheism, he did not mean to lead just the people of the Hijaz or the Arabs, but his divine mission was to communicate God's message to the whole world and to start this momentous task from Arabia.

One proof of this true belief is that at the beginning of his mission, he said to his own relatives, 'Truly, I am God's Messenger to you, in particular, and to all people, in general...'.[152]

There are also some verses in the Qur'an that confirm this claim. Consider the following three verses: *'Say, O people, "Surely I am God's Messenger to you all"'* (7:158). *'And We have not sent you but as a mercy to the worlds'* (21:107). *'And this Qur'an has been revealed to me that with it I may warn you and whomsoever it reaches'* (6:19).

Such verses reveal the fact that the divine mission of the Prophet was not revised to become universal after his migration to Medina and the prevalence of Islam. From the very beginning, his holy mission was meant for all people, for all parts of the world, and for all times.

In answer to the question asked of Imam Sadiq, 'Why is the

Qur'an always new and fascinating no matter how many times it is read or taught?', he said, 'God has not sent the Qur'an for a special time or for a particular group. The Qur'an is for all and forever, so till doomsday it will be new and enchanting at all times and to all groups of people'.[153]

ANOTHER TESTIMONY TO ISLAM'S UNIVERSALITY

In 6 A.H., the Holy Prophet of Islam dispatched several representatives to rulers and kings of different parts of the world, each with a letter in which he invited them to become Muslims and submit to God's faith. All these letters had the same purport, that is, the invitation to monotheism and Islamic fraternity.

Since the Holy Prophet's mission was divine, in obedience to God's command, consistent with human nature, and meant to lead people to God's path, it highly impressed such just, truth-seeking people as Najashi, Muquqs, and others, so they submitted to Islam.[154]

Research made on the collection of the Prophet's letters indicates that he sent 62 letters to kings, chiefs of tribes and clans, and heads of convents. The texts of 29 of these letters are available.[155]

Now we will take a glance at parts of the letters of the Holy Prophet of Islam.

A LETTER TO KHUSROW, THE KING OF IRAN

In the Name of God
the Merciful, the Compassionate

From Muhammad, God's Messenger, to Khusrow, the King of Persia. Greetings to the followers of the right path, to those obedient to God and His Prophet, to those who bear witness to God's Oneness, who worship the One God, and who bear witness to the prophecy of God's servant, Muhammad.

Truly I call upon you to obey God's command and convert to

Islam. I am God's Messenger to all the people so that living hearts will be awakened and illuminated and so that infidels will have no excuses. Submit to Islam so you will be safe and immune, and if you disobey me and turn down my invitation, you will be blamed for the sins of the magi.[156]

A LETTER TO HARQAL, THE KING OF ROME

In the Name of God
the Merciful, the Compassionate

...I call upon you to submit to Islam. If you become a Muslim, you will share the Muslims' gains and their losses, and if you do not want to become a Muslim yourself, then let your people freely convert to Islam or pay the poll tax, paid in lieu of conversion to Islam, and do not restrict them in choosing their faith.[157]

The letters of the Holy Prophet of Islam were not exclusively written to kings. Rather, he sent letters to various nations and to the followers of other faiths so all would be informed of the rising of the sun of Islam.

A LETTER TO THE RULER OF YAMAMAH

In the Name of God
the Merciful, the Compassionate

This is a letter from God's Messenger, Muhammad to Hawzah. Greetings to the one who follows the path of salvation and the instructions of the divine guides.

You, the ruler of Yamamah, note that my faith will advance to the farthest place where man can go, so submit to Islam to be immune.[158]

A LETTER TO THE JEWS

In the Name of God
the Merciful, the Compassionate

This is a letter from Muhammad, God's Messenger, Musa ibn 'Imran's brother and co-missionary. God has assigned to Muhammad the same mission He had assigned to Moses. I swear to you by God and by the sacred commands descended upon Moses on Mount Sinai that: Have you found in your Holy Book predictions of my prophetic mission to the Jewish community as well as to all other peoples? If you have found this, then fear God and convert to Islam, and if you have not found such a divine prediction, then you will be excused.[159]

A LETTER TO BISHOP NAJRAN

In the Name of God
the Merciful, the Compassionate

This is a letter from God's prophet Muhammad to Bishop Najran: Truly I call on you to worship the real adored God instead of worshipping God's creatures.[160]

OUR DUTY IS TO CONVEY
THE MESSAGE OF ISLAM

The speedy advance and promulgation of Islam were due to the sincere, indefatigable endeavours of our Holy Prophet more than anything else.

In the propagation of Islam, the Holy Prophet utilized two powerful, effective forces: one, proficient speakers who had realized the truth and righteousness of Islam and who deeply loved and admired the Holy Prophet of Islam, and, two, the amazingly impressive letters, which revealed the vivifying precepts of Islam and which, in reality, were crystal clear reflections of Islam. He sent his messengers to different parts of the world although there were many hardships in their way and the needed means and facilities were scarce or unavailable.

Now the holy soul of our Prophet is worried about Muslim societies, and no doubt he watches them to see how they attempt to promote Islam, to communicate the precepts of Islam to people all over the world, and also to see if they make use of modern technologies and media to propagate the holy teachings of Islam.

So it is incumbent upon us to mobilize all our forces and powers to promote the cause of Islam and to spare no effort or self-sacrifice in the propagation of this holy faith, so our eastern and western brothers and sisters in Islam may be led to this vivifying fountain of truth. It will be a great achievement for us to have the honour of such an invaluable service to Islam and to humanity in general. Just as our Holy Prophet said to 'Ali, 'I swear by God that if God leads a person towards salvation through you, it will be more valuable and beneficial to you than the value of all the beings in the whole world upon which the sun casts its rays'.[161]

Chapter 16

Muhammad, the Last Prophet

All Muslims of the world, no matter what their sects are, hold in common that the Holy Prophet of Islam was the last prophet, and in fact, Muslims believe in divine prophecy having ended with him, just as they believe in the Unity of God.

Islam is always fresh, wonderful, and comprehensive, and the more extensive is one's insight, the more one comprehends the comprehensiveness of Islam. As a matter of fact, there is no end to Islam's wonders and miracles.

Now let us survey the truth of this belief. First we will explain the most effective reasons for a faith being eternal, and then we will consider Islam.

The most important factor causing a faith to persist and enjoy perpetuity is its being consistent with and based on human nature. A religion of which the instructions are in accordance with natural and innate human characteristics will continue to prevail forever, will never suffer annihilation as a result of the passing of time, nor will such a faith become out of date and useless.

Instructions and precepts that are not restricted to a certain place or period of time are compatible with any kind of progress and will stay as valid and powerful as they have always been no matter how many changes take place in the material aspects of human life and how much advance is made in technology and natural sciences.

On the contrary, instructions and rules that are limited to a particular period or a special group fail to fulfill all aspects of human needs at all times and under all circumstances. For example, if a rule is made that commands people are only allowed to use natural vehicles such as horses and camels for traveling and transportation, such a rule will obviously be discarded and outdated because new necessities make people utilize new means and equipment. One of the reasons why past faiths are not durable is that they have been meant for a certain group or a special period of time.

Comprehensiveness: An eternal faith must be all-embracing, comprehensive, and able to meet all human needs and wants. It is an already experienced fact that man's thirsty, stormy soul does not find peace and satisfaction with a series of empty ceremonies but is in great need of comprehensive precepts and rules that are capable of guiding him all through his life, of providing solutions to his various problems both in personal and social life, and of satisfying his spiritual demands and wants.

Giving guidance in deadlocks: There are certain occasions in human life when either due to the conflict of general rules or due to an unexpected emergency, man finds himself in a deadlock and starts wondering what to do and how to proceed.

Thus an eternal faith must, in addition to overall rules and instructions, provide man with other sets of rules and guidelines that explain the solutions to exceptional problems and emergency situations that general rules are incapable of handling.

And it is such a comprehensive faith that is in accord with all times and all conditions of life and can benefit all. In fact, it is only a perfect faith that serves the supreme purpose of leading human beings onto God's path. The foregoing factors are the most significant causes of the duration and perpetuity of a faith all of which are in Islam. Now let us find some explanations for these factors.

ISLAM: THE IMMORTAL FAITH

It is a reality that, in the legislative system of Islam, human nature, which is the same at all times and in all places, has been taken into consideration and positive answers have been given to natural human wants and needs. A careful study of Islamic precepts and programs reveals the fact that they have been so designed as to regulate all human instincts. For example, for the proper satisfaction of human sexual instincts, various simple plans and rules have been offered that properly satisfy and regulate this natural instinct at the same time that they prevent unrestrained sexual relations, so human societies may be immune from the corruption and decline that sexual freedom causes.

The fundamental rules and laws in Islam are meant not just for a particular time or a particular place needing modification and change as conditions change, they are compatible with all environments and all times and are capable of providing human beings with all the guidelines they need to live happily and prosperously and to find eternal salvation as well.

In the Islamic programs and teachings concerning jihad, for instance, no emphasis is placed upon weaponry and tactics of the time of the Prophet, such as fighting with swords. Rather, Islam has given this general command concerning jihad: Strengthen your fighting abilities, mobilize your forces, and acquire good arms and ammunition so you will be able to defend your vital rights against your enemies and overcome them. This is a general all-embracing rule that is in accordance with all conditions of life and all sorts of progress made in technology. And thus this comprehensive rule can invariably give guidance on the questions concerning war in Islam, and the same is the case with other Islamic rules and instructions.

To the deadlocks and emergencies that occur in human life, either individual or social, the faith of Islam has offered laws such as 'the law of emergency', 'the law of not guilty', 'the law of no loss',[162] and the like, which present suitable solutions to all problems, however complicated they might be. Moreover, the Imams, the successors of the Holy Prophet of Islam, and religious leaders whom Muslims follow can offer decisive solutions to social deadlocks and problems.

The programs and rules designed by Islam are far more extensive and elaborate than those presented by other schools of thought. In Islam, all legal, economic, military, moral, and other issues and points have been presented and surveyed in the most elaborate and perfect manner. The Islamic theologians have so far compiled thousands of books on the fore-going subject for which the sources are the Holy Qur'an, the sayings of the Holy Prophet of Islam, and the teachings of the offspring of Prophet.

Thus, taking into consideration these facts and proven realities, any knowledgeable person will admit that Islam is a perfect faith, capable of fulfilling human needs and of presenting solutions to all problems, and so there is no need for any other faith or any new school of thought.

THE END OF PROPHECY WITH THE PROPHET

The comprehensiveness of the rules and precepts of Islam and the end of prophecy with the Holy Prophet of Islam have been clearly expressed in the Qur'an: *'And the word of your Lord has been accomplished truly and justly; there is none who can change His words, and He is the Hearing, the Knowing'* (6:115).

'Muhammad is not the father of any of your men, but he is the Messenger of God and the Last of all Prophets, and God is

cognizant of all things' (33:40).

In the Arabic language, wherever the word *'khatam'* is attached to a word, it conveys the meaning of 'the last' and in this verse it refers to 'the last of the prophets'. *Nabi* means any type of divine messenger.[163]

Obviously, the word messenger can be applied to all prophets so by saying that Muhammad is the last of all prophets, God means that he is the last of all messengers and that after him there will come no prophet, nor any messenger from God, nor any person with a new holy book.

'Surely this Qur'an guides to that which is most upright and gives the good news to the believers who do good that they shall have a great reward' (17:9).

Therefore, human beings have no need for any other prophet, any other rules and regulations, or any other school of thought because all they need is to be found in the Qur'an.

There are so many documents and testimonies to the fact that the Prophet was the last of all prophets that in Islam this reality is considered one of the clearest points.

Now your attention is drawn to some narrations:

The Prophet has himself said, 'You must know that there will come no Prophet after me and no faith after my faith of Islam...'.[164]

Imam Baqir (peace be upon him) has said, 'God has ended Holy Books with your Book, the Qur'an, and prophets with your Prophet...'.[165]

Hazrat 'Ali (peace be upon him) has said, 'God assigned Muhammad, peace and the mercy of God be upon him and his descendants, to be a prophet after all other prophets and has ended revelation with him'.[166]

The Prophet said to Hazrat 'Ali, 'Your relation to me is like that of Aaron to Moses, peace be upon him, with the difference that there will come no prophet after me'.[167]

Imam Riza (peace be upon him) has said, 'The faith of Muhammad (peace and the mercy of God be upon him and his descendants) will not be abolished until the Day of Resurrection, and no prophet will come after him until that day'.[168]

These and many other traditions and narrations are perpetual proclamations of the Prophet as the last of all prophets and Islam as the only comprehensive faith.

The splendour of the purport of this faith as well as its profound precepts and comprehensive rules ensure its perpetuity till the Day of Judgment.

Now that God has endowed us with such a matchless magnificent faith, surely it is our duty to communicate it to all other people so all will benefit from this holy faith.

Chapter 17

Ghadir and the Prophet's Successor

It was in 10 A.H. and the time for Hajj. The Hijazi deserts witnessed large crowds of Muslims who unitedly chanted the same slogans and proceeded towards the same holy end.

That year the sight of the Hajj pilgrimage was much more exciting and moving than ever before. Muslims most hurriedly and eagerly traversed the way and went to Makkah — this holy city.

The celestial melody of *'Labayka'*, 'Yes, I have come', resounded through Makkah. Caravans reached the city one after the other. The *hajjis* unitedly and harmoniously in pilgrim's garb, while shedding tears of joy and love for God, hurried to the sacred threshold of God and circumambulated the Ka'aba — the Holy House built by the champion of monotheism — Abraham, the Friend of God.

Farid Vajdi has calculated the number of *hajjis* to have been 90,000[169] in the year 10 A.H., but there are some who hold that

115

the number was 124,000.[170]

The Holy Prophet of Islam watched that splendid scene with the utmost affection and eagerness. He was pleased to observe that the Masjid al-Haram was overflowing with Muslims who had gathered together in conformity with the holy precept, '*Truly the faithful are brothers*', and were worshipping God like brothers and angels.

The Holy Prophet was clearly happy with his great achievement — with having fulfilled his divine mission in the best manner possible.

Nevertheless, his resplendent face was sometimes covered with a halo of sorrow and anxiety, and his pure heart filled with sadness and worry.

He was in fact worried about the fate of the Muslims after his leaving this world for heaven. He feared lest after him the society of Muslims should break apart; Muslims should disperse, the spirit of unity and fraternity should vanish among them, and consequently they regress.

Obviously, the Holy Prophet of Islam was well aware of the fact that the *Ummah* of Islam was in great need of honest, knowledgeable leaders, or otherwise the fruits of his years of efforts would all be wasted.

For this reason, whenever he was going to leave Medina either for war or for other purposes, even if his trip was short, he would assign a competent, trustworthy person to supervise their affairs and would never leave the people of Medina without any guardian and supervisor.[171]

Thus, how is it possible to imagine that such a compassionate, sympathetic prophet might have left the momentous affairs of his beloved *Ummah* of Islam to chance and not have designated any reliable administrator for them.

And no doubt he knew very well who deserved the position of the caliphate of the Muslims and for whose mature stature the garb of the caliphate had been sewn.

That celebrated man was the same who, in the presence of the chiefs of the Quraysh and the relatives of the Prophet who had been invited to the House of the Prophet of Islam at the beginning of his prophetic mission, had been acknowledged as the successor of the Holy Prophet of Islam by the Prophet himself.[172]

He was a pious, God-fearing man who did not associate anything with God and did not prostrate before idols even for a single moment.

He was a sacrificial soldier of Islam. His knowledge originated in the knowledge of the Prophet of God and his judgment was the best.[173]

He was well-known. He was 'Ali, son of Abu Talib.

The Hajj ceremonies were over, and the Muslims were preparing to move towards their own towns when suddenly the call of the herald of the Holy Prophet of Islam resounded in the Hijaz desert and made the Muslims stop. His heralds called on the people to gather together again.

The Muslims, of course, did not know why they had been given this command, but the fact was that the Angel of Revelation had descended and conveyed this verse to the Prophet, *'O Prophet! Deliver what has been revealed to you from your Lord; and if you do it not, then you have not delivered His message, and God will protect you from the people; surely God will not guide the unbelieving people'* (5:67).

The issue about which God spoke to His Prophet in such a serious tone was nothing other than the formal announcement of the caliphate of 'Ali, the significant subject that the Prophet hesitated to declare, for he feared lest this announcement should cause dissension and discord among the Muslims and was thus waiting for a favourable occasion to make clear the matter to them.

Upon receiving this revelation, he knew that the time had come for the crucial purpose. So he immediately assembled the Muslims at Ghadir Khum, which was a hot, arid desert, to clarify the vital issue in Islam — the issue of the caliphate.

The people started wondering why that command had been issued, but before long the congregational ritual prayers was announced and after saying the noon ritual prayers, the crowd of Muslims witnessed the celestial, enchanting countenance of the Prophet over a pulpit made of saddles of camels.

A profound silence prevailed. Then the divine, meaningful words of the Prophet broke the silence of the Hijaz desert. After praising Almighty God, he announced the heart-rending news of his oncoming death and then asked the Muslims, 'O people! What kind of a prophet have I been for you?'

All exclaimed unitedly, 'O Prophet of God! You did your best to admonish and rectify us and never neglected to train us and led us onto the path of piety. May God reward you best'.

The Holy Prophet of Islam said, 'After me, God's Book and the sinless leaders are side by side your leader and guide. You should perfectly follow them, so you will not go astray'.

Then he took 'Ali by the hand, lifted him so that all would see him and exclaimed, 'O people! Who is the guardian and supervisor of the faithful?'

The Muslims answered, 'God and His Prophet know best'.

The Holy Prophet of Islam said, 'God is my Master and I am the Master of the faithful'. Then he added without any pause, "Ali is the Master of those whose Master I am. Almighty God be the friend of his friend and be the foe of his foe. Help those who help him and frustrate the hope of those who betray him...'.

The Prophet repeated the sentence, "Ali is the Master of those whose Master I am', three times. At the end of the speech he said, 'Those present should convey this truth to those who are absent'.

The crowd of Muslims had hardly dispersed when this verse was revealed to the Prophet, *'This day have I perfected for you your religion and completed My favour on you and chosen for you Islam as a religion'* (5:3).

After the magnificent ceremonies of designating the successor of the Holy Prophet of Islam were over, the Muslims hurried to congratulate 'Ali for being appointed as the Prophet's successor and Caliph.

Abu Bakr was the first to congratulate 'Ali and 'Umar was the second. They parted with 'Ali while saying the following words, 'Blessed are you, son of Abu Talib, who have become my Master and every believer's Master'.[174]

THE NARRATORS OF GHADIR

As a matter of fact, there are more than 120,000 narrators of Ghadir. According to the command of the Prophet, the Muslims present at Ghadir regarded the incident of Ghadir and the issue of appointing 'Ali as the successor of the Prophet as most significant and narrated it to the others.[175] And it was for this reason that in public gatherings of Muslims, the reminiscence of Ghadir was renewed repeatedly.

About 25 years after the day of Ghadir, when most of the faithful companions and followers of the Holy Prophet of Islam had passed away, and just a few were still alive, 'Ali asked the people to bear witness if they had been present in Ghadir and heard the Ghadir tradition from the blessed mouth of the Prophet. Immediately 30 people stood up and narrated the Ghadir tradition.[176]

In 58 or 59 A.H., a year before the death of Mu'awiyah, Imam Husayn, peace be upon him, assembled the Bani Hashim and Ansar and other *hajjis* at Mana and, during an extremely moving speech, asked them, 'I swear to you by God to speak out if you know that on the day of Ghadir, God's Prophet appointed 'Ali as the Master and Leader of the *Ummah* of Islam and commanded the audience to convey this message to the others'. All said that they knew this fact.[177]

Sunni scholars have mentioned in their reliable books the names of 110 companions of the Prophet who had heard this tradition from the Holy Prophet of Islam and had narrated it to others.[178] Even a number of scholars and Islamic theologians wrote special books on Ghadir.[179]

THE PURPORT OF THE DISCOURSE ON GHADIR

The available documents reveal that the words *mawla* (master) and *vali* (guardian) refer to the successor of the Holy Prophet of Islam and the Guardian of the *Ummah* of Islam, and that no other meaning can be applied to these two words.

Now, take notice of the following points:

We have realized that the Holy Prophet of Islam was hesitant to propound the Ghadir tradition and that he did not declare it until God openly and seriously commanded him to do so.

It is totally wrong to hold that by the Ghadir tradition the Prophet meant to remind the people of the position of 'Ali as a friend of the Holy Prophet of Islam and the Muslims. If that were the case, the Holy Prophet of Islam would never have hesitated to announce it, for obviously such an announcement would cause no discord or dissension among the Muslims.

Thus the Holy Prophet of Islam surely had reference to the issue of the caliphate and the assignment of his own successor, which was clearly likely to elicit the mutiny and mischief of ambitious opportunists.

Before uttering the well-known sentence, "Ali is the Master of those whose Master I am', the Prophet asked the audience to admit that he himself was their guardian and leader and that he was to be obeyed by them, and after the people present in Ghadir Khum had admitted this fact, the Holy Prophet of Islam attributed the same position to 'Ali immediately, saying "Ali is the Master and Leader of anybody whose Master and Leader I am'.

With the permission of the Prophet, Hissan ibn Sabit composed a poem about Ghadir Khum and circulated it. In this poem, the position of the Caliphate and Imamate of 'Ali have been openly expressed and specified. No one among that great crowd of Muslims protested that Hissan had misapplied the word *mawla* (master). Rather, Hissan was confirmed and applauded for this poem.

The poem, in effect, said, 'After the Holy Prophet of Islam had the people admit that he was their divine Master and religious leader, he said to 'Ali, "Stand up, 'Ali. I assent to your Leadership and Imamate after myself. Then, "Ali is the Master and Leader of anybody whose Master and Leader I am. You should all be loyal followers and sincere friends of 'Ali"'.[180]

After the Ghadir ceremonies were over, the Prophet, together with 'Ali, sat in a tent and ordered all the Muslims, even the women of his own family, to congratulate 'Ali, to swear allegiance to him, and to greet him as the Commander of the Faithful.[181] It is obvious that all these ceremonies and orders testify to nothing other than the designation of 'Ali as the Caliph and Imam of the Muslims by the Holy Prophet of Islam.

Twice the Prophet said to the people, 'Congratulate me, for God specifically appointed me Prophet and my family Imams'.[182]

These testimonies and documents leave no doubt about the Ghadir Khum tradition and the caliphate of 'Ali.

Chapter 18

The Morals and Behaviour of the Holy Prophet

The more science and technology advances, the greater is the need for the observance and practice of the teachings and instructions of divine prophets in human societies. This is because science and technology provide only machines and instruments and by no means prevent their misuse by human beings.

The terrible rise in murder, other felonies, corruption, suicide and so forth clearly points to this very fact. If morality, which is a significant part of the teachings of divine prophets, does not prevail and govern in human societies, surely not only will advanced science and technology fail to ensure human peace and prosperity, but they will add to our problems and miseries. For the exploiters and colonialists utilize advanced technology and sciences for their own satanic purposes. They murder or make homeless millions of human beings as they have always done and trample upon the rights of the weak and the defenseless.

As a matter of fact, the only factor that can halter man's restive soul and control his stormy instincts and passions and thus utilize science and technology for human prosperity and pacific life is true morality, which originates in faith in God.

The moral teachings and precepts of the divine prophets and their moral behaviour are the best means of leading man to his ideal life. It goes without saying that both in personal and in social life the observance of moral principles is required of all. However, for those who must lead societies and guide the people, this requirement is much greater, because, first, the one who is the instructor of society must himself be a model of supreme moral behaviour and excellent human characteristics, so he will be able to wipe moral decay out of people's hearts and minds. Obviously if he himself is lacking in morality, he will fail to lead the people onto the path of humanity and virtue.

Second, the responsibility of leading human societies is so great and crucial that no one can successfully perform it unless he has perfect morals. For this reason, God selected his prophets from among those who possessed exalted spirits, great tolerance, extraordinary patience, and other excellent moral characteristics. It was with this weapon of morality that divine prophets overturned the debased societies that were plunged in corruption and led the ignorant people who had gone astray onto the path of virtue and salvation.

In the holy Qur'an, God has addressed the Prophet Muhammad: *'Thus it is due to mercy from God that you deal with them gently, and had you been rough, hard-hearted, they would certainly have dispersed from around you'* (3:159).

The sublime celestial morals of the Prophet brought about the waves of the revolution of Islam first in Arabian society and afterwards all over the world. In the light of this all-embracing spiritual and intellectual resurrection, dispersion turned into unity, unchastity into chastity and virtue, idleness into hard work and industry, selfishness to altruism, and Arab arrogance to modesty and affection. Men and women were thus trained to become models of good moral behaviour and have altruistic manners forever. The morals of the Prophet were so sublime and praiseworthy that God has regarded them as great. '*And truly you (Muhammad) possess great morals*' (52:4).

THE PROPHET AMONG THE PEOPLE

The Holy Prophet of Islam possessed the magnificent status of prophecy and divine leadership, but his manners in dealing with the people and his way of life were so simple and gentle that when he was among the people and a newcomer wanted to know about him, he had to ask, 'Which one of you is the Prophet'?[183]

He had no love for luxuries or the illusions of this mortal world. He was never enchanted by any worldly things, and he invariably looked upon this world's life as a passing one.[184]

The Holy Prophet of Islam spoke in short, meaningful sentences and was never seen or heard to interrupt anybody's speech.[185]

He never spoke with a morose face, nor did he ever apply rough, awkward words. Unlike tyrants and despotic rulers, the Holy Prophet of Islam never looked at those who were addressing him with half-closed eyes.[186]

The Holy Prophet of Islam did not care to sit down in the seat of honour in gatherings, and on entering any place would sit down in the first empty seat available.[187]

He did not let anybody stand up before him and treated others most respectfully. Of course, the virtuous people were most revered by him.[188]

The Holy Prophet was justly angered when he observed a violation of God's commands and of Islam and was most pleased at the good deeds. Both his pleasure and displeasure were for God. He would never allow anybody to accompany him on foot when he himself was riding. He would pick him up beside himself if he was able, and if not, the Holy Prophet of Islam gave him a time for an appointment in a given place and would ride alone.

On group journeys, the Prophet would work like the others and would never let anybody work instead of him. Once on a journey, his companion asked him to allow him to do the work. In answer to this request, the Holy Prophet of Islam said, 'I do not like to be treated as if I were privileged because God does not like any of His creatures to consider himself privileged or to be treated as if he were privileged over others'. And he got up and collected firewood.[189]

He invariably stood by his words and pledges. He paid affectionate visits to his relatives and friends but would never take their side unduly. The Holy Prophet of Islam would never permit anybody to backbite others and said, 'I want to meet people with a loving heart'.

His modesty was peerless. He was extremely patient, tolerant, and forgiving.[190]

Anas ibn Malik, who was the servant of the Holy Prophet of Islam, has narrated, 'I used to prepare milk for the Prophet to break his fast with. One night he was home late. Thinking that he had been a guest at somebody's house and thus had broken his fast there, I drank the milk. Before long he returned home. I asked his companions if he had broken his fast and they said that he had not.

'When the Holy Prophet of Islam was informed of the matter, he made no remark about it and behaved as if he were not hungry at all and went without supper with a cheerful face. The next day he also fasted.'[191]

The Holy Prophet of Islam immensely loved the ritual prayers, but on occasions when people demanded to talk to him about something, he would say his ritual prayers briefly and instead, pay attention to the demands and needs of the people. He would spare no efforts to fulfill the people's needs.

The Prophet treated everyone with great respect and considered nobility and honour to be owing to faith, piety, and good behaviour. He was not interested in wealth or status, nor did he revere anybody for his riches or position.

His behaviour towards slaves was amazingly affectionate, and he would do his best to remove the troubles and sufferings of the slaves and the poor.[192]

THE PROPHET'S TOLERANCE AND FORGIVENESS

The Holy Prophet of Islam never attempted to retaliate against the insults and disrespect of anybody, and forgave people's mistakes or their misconduct. His reaction to the torment and disregard of the ignorant people was forgiveness and tolerance.[193]

In spite of all the tortures and torments that the Quraysh had inflicted upon the Holy Prophet of Islam, on conquering Makkah, he forgave them and set them free.[194]

In the war of Uhud, a man named Wahshi killed Hamzah, the beloved uncle of the Holy Prophet of Islam. However, he forgave his sin. Also, he forgave the many torments and troubles that Abu Sufyan and his wife, Hind, had caused for him and he did not take revenge.[195] However, for all his tolerance and mercifulness, he did not take pity on those who violated God's threshold and sacred precepts and would punish the violator in accordance with divine rules. In affecting God's orders, he would take no notice of anybody's intercession.

When the Prophet was informed that Fatima Mukhzumiyah had committed theft, he punished her according to the laws of Islam concerning theft and did not regard the intercession of Asamata ibn Zayd in this respect, saying, 'The ruin and downfall of the preceding peoples was due to the fact that they did not enforce the laws of punishment in the case of the aristocrats and the people of status. I swear by the One in

Whose hands is my life that even if Fatima (his daughter) had committed such a sin, I would cut off her hand'.[196]

THE PROPHET'S CLEANLINESS AND ORDERLINESS

The Holy Prophet of Islam was fond of scent[197] and spent more on buying perfumes than on food.[198] His pleasant smell filled the air of any place he passed, so that whosoever passed there knew that the Holy Prophet of Islam had passed that way.[199]

He used to brush his teeth frequently[200] and washed his blessed hands both before and after meals.[201] Whenever the Holy Prophet of Islam was about to leave his house, he would look into a mirror or into water; he always left home with a clean, pleasant appearance.[202]

THE PROPHET WAS A PIOUS AND SINCERE WORSHIPPER OF GOD

The Holy Prophet of Islam had great love for ritual prayers so that during the night he would get up several times, brush his teeth, and then offer the most devoted prayers.[203] He would stand worshipping God and talking sincerely to the Almighty Creator for so long that as a result of so much standing in prayer, his legs were swollen.[204]

The Holy Prophet of Islam took lessons from watching the sky, the moon, the sun, and every other thing in nature, and these phenomena attracted him to their Creator more than to themselves.

He was so devout and pious that not even for a single moment was he enchanted by any luxury or pleasure of this mortal world. In short, the Holy Prophet of Islam was a perfect model of all excellent virtues and sublime human qualities.

In such a small book it is not possible to describe all his praiseworthy manners and morals. In fact, we have just presented a pale reflection of his celestial, resplendent portrait so that all over the world Muslims who regard themselves as the followers of Islam can make his morals and conduct their own model of behaviour and learn divine morality and correct programs for life from him.

As the Holy Qur'an says, '*Certainly you have in the Apostle of God an excellent exemplar for he who hopes in God and the latter day, and remembers God much*' (33:21).

May God's greetings be upon him who was the selected superior and the best of pious human beings. And the greetings of the angels upon the faithful.

We too greet him most cordially and sincerely. May he accept our respectful greetings as well as the greetings of you, our sisters and brothers in Islam. May Almighty God help all of us to follow exactly the blessed footsteps of the Holy Prophet, whose path is sure to lead us into eternal salvation and paradise.

To end this book, we narrate an invaluable tradition of the Holy Prophet of Islam and his honoured family. In the Holy Qur'an there is a verse closely related with the Tradition of the Cloak: '*And stay in your houses and do not display your finery like the displaying of the ignorance of yore; and keep up prayer, and pay the poor-due (zakat) and obey God and His Apostle. God only desires to keep away the uncleanliness from you, O people of the House! and to purify you a thorough purifying*' (33:33).

This verse is famous as the *ayat-i-tathir* and is closely related with the Tradition of the Cloak. The following is the tradition:

One day the Holy Prophet of Islam came to the house of his daughter, Fatima, and told her that he was very tired and asked her to cover him with his cloak. As she was covering the Apostle of God, his face lit up and shone like the full moon. After a while Imam Hasan came to the house and said that he could smell the fragrance of his grandfather. Fatima said that he was resting under the cloak. Hasan greeted the Holy Prophet and asked his permission to come under the cloak. The permission was granted. Similarly, Husayn, 'Ali, and Fatima, after greeting him and receiving permission from the Apostle, went under the cloak. Fatima, peace be upon her, said that when they, the *ahl al-bayt*, gathered under the cloak, Almighty God said, 'Let it be known to you, my angels and those who are in the heavens, that I swear by my honour and might that I have not created the heavens and the earth and what are in them, but only out of love for the five honourable ones who are under the cloak'.

Gabriel asked God who was under the cloak. God informed him that they were the people of the house of the Apostle. Gabriel requested permission from God to be the sixth under the cloak. Gabriel greeted the Prophet and received permission to enter under the cloak. Gabriel said that God has created the universe because of them and out of love for them. And *'God only desires to keep that which is ritually unclean away from you, O people of the House, and to purify you a thorough purifying'*.

'Ali asked the Holy Prophet to explain the significance of their gathering under the cloak. The Prophet said, 'I swear by God that whenever this tradition will be recited among our friends and lovers, God's mercy will descend upon them and the angels will surround them and ask forgiveness for them until they disperse. God will also remove the sorrow and answer the prayers of those who had come to ask'. 'Ali swore by the Lord of the Ka'aba that the *ahl al-bayt* and their friends had profitted both in this world and the next.

'Surely God and His angels bless the Prophet. O you who believe! Call for blessings on him and salute him with a good salutation' (33:56).

NOTES

1. Will Durant, *History of Western Civilization*, Vol. 1, pp.95, 301; Vol. 4, p.304; Vol. 7, p.95.

2. See the *Nahj ul-Balaghah* of Khuie, Vol. 2, p.173; *History of World Religions* (Persian translation), p.479.

3. The Persian translation of *Jahiliyat ul-qarn ul-'asharin* compiled by Muhammad Qutb.

4. *Nahj ul-Balaghah*, the first part printed in Damascus, p.66; *Fiyd ul-Islam*, Vol. 1, p.83, the 26th sermon.

5. The third edition of the Encyclopedia, p.255.

6. *Bihar ul-Anwar*, Vol. 15, p.325.

7. *Ibid.*, p.250.

8. *Kamil ul-Tawarikh*, second section, p.10; *Tabaqat*, Vol. L, p.61; *Bihar ul-Anwar*, Vol. 15, p.125.

9. *Bihar ul-Anwar*, Vol. 15, p.257.

10. *Ibid.*, pp.258-263.

11. *Ibid.*

12. *Sirihi Halabiyih*, Vol. 1, p.99.

13. *Bihar ul-Anwar*, Vol. 15, pp.331-395; *Sirihi ibn Hisham*, printed in 1375 A.H.L., Vol. 1. pp.159-60; *Halabiyih*, printed in 1382 A.H.L., Vol. 1, p.99.

14. *Bihar ul-Anwar*, Vol. 15, pp.402, 406.

15. *Sirihi ibn Hisham*, Vol. 1, p.168.

16. *Bihar ul-Anwar*, Vol. 15, pp.382, 402, 366.

17. *Ibid.*

18. *Ibid.*, p.336.

19. *Ibid.*, p.142; *Sirihi ibn Hisham*, Vol. 1, p.168.

20. *Sirihi ibn Hisham*, Vol. 1, p.180.

21. Basra was a small town near Damascus.

22. Lat and Uzza were two of the famous idols that the Arabs worshipped and swore by on various occasions.

23. *Sirihi ibn Hisham*, Vol. 1, p.181; *A'lam Alwari*, published in Najaf, 1390 A.H.L., p.26; and *Bihar ul-Anwar*, Vol. 15, pp.193-204.

24. *Sirihi ibn Hisham*, Vol. 1, p.167 (footnote).

25. *Ibid.*, p.183.

26. *Bihar ul-Anwar*, Vol. 16, p.3; *Tarikh Ya'aqubi*, Vol. 2, p.15.

27. *Ibid.*, p.74.

28. *Bihar ul-Anwar*, Vol. 16, p.3; *Tarikh Ya'aqubi*, Vol. 2, p.15.

29. *A'yan ul-Shi'ah*, Vol. 2, p.8; *Sirihi Halabiyih*, Vol. 1, p.152.

30. *Sirihi ibn Hisham*, Vol. 1, p.188; *Bihar ul-Anwar*, Vol. 16, p.22.

31. *Bihar ul-Anwar*, Vol. 16, p.12; *Tarikh Tabari*, Vol. 3, p.1127.

32. *Sirihi ibn Hisham*, Vol. 1, p.188. This monk was not the monk who met the Prophet in his childhood.

33. *Kamil ibn Athir*, Vol. 2, p.39. Printed in Beirut, 1385 A.H.L.

34. *Bihar ul-Anwar*, Vol. 16, pp.20-21.

35. *Ibid.*

36. *Sirihi Halabiyih*, Vol. 1, p.152; *A'yan ul-Shi'ah*, Vol. 2, p.8.

37. *Bihar ul-Anwar*, Vol. 16, pp.56-73.

38. *Ibid.*, pp.7, 10; *A'lam Alwari*, p.146.

39. *Ibid.*, pp.10-71; *A'yan ul-Shi'ah*, Vol. 2, p.8.

40. *Ibid.*, p.3; *A'yan*, p.18; *A'lam*, p.146.

41. *Bihar ul-Anwar*, Vol. 16, pp.8, 13.

42. *Ibid.*

43. *Islam from the viewpoint of Voltaire*, second edition, p.5.

44. *Ibid.*, p.6.

45. *The Book of Samuel*, 2, section II.

46. *The Life of Muhammad*, compiled by Dr. Heykal, p.315.

47. *Muruj ul-Dhahab*, Vol. 2, p.287.

48. *Udhri Taqsir Bih Pishgahi Muhammad wa Qur'an*, p.35.

49. *Bihar ul-Anwar*, Vol. 22, pp.200-204.

50. *The Life of Muhammad*, compiled by Dr. Heykal, p.319.

51. *Ibid.*, p.320; *Bihar ul-Anwar*, Vol. 22, p.203.

52. *The Life of Muhammad*, compiled by Dr. Heykal, p.321.

53. *Bihar ul-Anwar*, Vol. 22, pp.214-218.

54. See *The Holy Qur'an*, Sura Ahzab, Ayah 37.

55. *Sirihi ibn Hisham*, Vol. 3, p.295.

56. *Isabih wa Isti'ab*, p.305; *Musu'ati Alenabi*, p.369; *Sirihi ibn Hisham*, Vol. 1, p.223; and *A'lam Alwari*, p.141.

57. *Ibid.*; *Musu'ati*, p.345, *A'lam*, p.142.

58. *Bihar ul-Anwar*, Vol. 22, p.203; *Sirihi ibn Hisham*, p.372; *Musu'ati Alenabi*, p.404.

59. *Rahbarani Buzurg va Masuliathayih Buzurgtar*, second edition, p.37.

60. Will Durant, Persian translation, Vol. 11, pp.1-10; *Al-Durrat ul-biyda fi Sharhi Khutbati Fatimati 'l-Zahra*, pp.27, 54.

61. *Da'irat ul-Ma'arif Farid Vajdi*, Vol. 6, p.250.

62. *Majma' ul-Bayan*, Vol. 10, p.534, new edition.

63. *Al-'Asr ul-Jahili*, Dr. Sufi Diyf, fifth edition in Egypt, p.70.

64. *Sharh ul-Mu'allaqat ul-Saba'a* by Alz-Zuzani, p.3.

65. *Bihar ul-Anwar*, Vol. 18, p.280.

66. *Ibid.*, pp.277-281; *Nahj ul-Balaghah* of Fiydul-Islam, p.802.

67. *A'lam Alwari*, pp.17-18; *Bihar ul-Anwar*, Vol. 15, p.410.

68. *Bihar ul-Anwar*, Vol. 16, p.224.

69. *Sirihi ibn Hisham*, Vol. 1, pp.192-197; *Bihar ul-Anwar*, Vol. 15, pp.337, 412.

70. *Bihar ul-Anwar*, Vol. 18, p.206.

71. *Manaqib*, Vol. 1, p.40

72. *Kamil*, Vol. 2, p.48; *Tarikhi Tabari*, Vol. 3, p.1148.

73. *Udhri Taqsir*, p.19.

74. *Ibid.*, p.18.

75. Hysteria is a mental disease.

76. *Udhri Taqsir*, p.20.

77. *Sirihi ibn Hisham*, Vol. 1, p.237.

78. *The Life of Muhammad*, compiled by Dr. Heykal, p.134.

79. *A'lam Alwari*, p.47.

80. *Sirihi ibn Hisham*, Vol. 1, p.238.

81. *Manaqib*, Vol. 1, p.42.

82. *Sirihi ibn Hisham*, Vol. 1, p.246; *Bihar ul-Anwar*, Vol. 18, p.208.

83. *Ibid.*, *Sirihi*, p.245; *Bihar*, p.188; *Al-Ghadir*, Vol. 3, pp.219-241; *Tarikhi Tabari*, Vol. 3, p.1160.

84. *Wasa'il ul-Shi'a*, second edition, 1384 A.H.L., Vol. 3, pp.16, 17.

85. *Ibid*.

86. *A'lam Alwari*, p.37; *Jami' ul-Ahadithi Shi'a*, Vol. 2, p.31. It is to be noted that at that time each of the prayers was two cycles (*rak'at*).

87. *Tarikhi Tabari*, Vol. 3, p.1122.

88. *A'lam Alwari*, p.38, printed in 1390; *Tarikhi Tabari*, Vol. 3, p.1162.

89. *Tarikhi Tabari*, Vol. 3, pp.1171-1173; *Tafsiri Majma' ul-Bayan*, Vol. 7, p.206; *Bihar ul-Anwar*, Vol. 18, p.192. This point is confirmed by all Islamic as well as non-Islamic historians and is among the confirmed facts of history. *Al-Ghadir*, Vol. 2, p.278.

90. *Tarikhi Ya'qubi*, Vol. 2, p.22.

91. *Sirihi ibn Hisham*, Vol. 1, p.262; *Tarikhi Ya'qubi*, Vol. 2, p.19.

92. This phrase was used by the Arabs whenever they wanted to draw the attention of the people to an important issue.

93. *Tarikhi Tabari*, Vol. 3, p.1170.

94. *Sirihi Halabiyih*, Vol. 1, p.311.

95. *Tarikhi Tabari*, Vol. 3, p.1170; *Manaqib*, Vol.1, pp.43-44.

96. *Sirihi ibn Hisham*, Vol. 1, pp.265-266.

97. *Ibid.*, pp.266-267.

98. *Sirihi ibn Hisham*, Vol. 1, pp.295-1296.

99. *Tarikhi Tabari*, Vol. 3, p.1176.

100. *A'lam Alwari*, new edition, p.57.

101. *Manaqib* Vol. 1, p.51.

102. *A'lam Alwari*, p.58.

103. *Kamil*, Vol. 2, pp.66-67.

104. *Ibid.*

105. *Ibid.*, p.108.

106. *A'lam Alwari*, pp.55-61.

107. *Tarikhi Tabari*, Vol. 3, p.1229; *A'lam Alwari*, pp.61-62.

108. *Tarikhi Tabari*, Vol. 3, p.1231; *Bihar ul-Anwar*, Vol. 19, p.60.

109. *Sirihi ibn Hishim*, Vol. 1; p.481; *Tarikhi Tabari*, Vol. 3, p.1232.

110. *Bihar ul-Anwar*, *Vol. 19, p.78.*

111. Tarikhi Tabari, Vol. 3, p.1234.

112. *A'lam Alwari*, p.63.

113. *Sirihi ibn Hisham*, Vol. 1, p.486; *Bihar ul-Anwar*, Vol. 19, p.69.

114. *Ibid.*, p.489; p.88.

115. *Kamil*, p.106. Quba is a place near Medina.

116. *Tarikhi Tabari*, Vol. 3, p.1245.

117. *Bihar ul-Anwar*, Vol. 19, p.116.

118. *Kamil*, Vol. 2, p.106.

119. *Sirihi ibn Hisham*, Vol. 1, p.494; *Bihar ul-Anwar*, Vol. 9, p.122.

120. *Mu'jim ul-Buldan maddihi Yathrib* and *Majma' ul-Bahrin Maddihi Tharb*.

121. *Bihar ul-Anwar*, Vol. 73, p.293; *Rudih Kafi*, p.246.

122. *Sirihi ibn Hisham*, Vol. 2, pp.504-505.

123. *Usul ul-Kafi*, Vol. 2, pp.166-167.

124. *Ibid.*, p.169.

125. *A'lam Alwari*, p.69.

126. *Tarikhi Tabari*, Vol. 5, p.2271.

127. *Bihar ul-Anwar*, Vol. 20, p.350.

128. *Ibid.*, p.362.

129. *A'lam Alwari*, p.110.

130. *Kamil*, Vol. 2, pp.248-249.

131. *Usud ul-Ghabih*, Vol. 1, p.206.

132. *Tamadduni Islam wa Arab*, p.807.

133. *Jang wa sulh dar Islam*, translated by Sayyid Ghulam Riza Sa'idi, p.345.

134. *Bihar ul-Anwar*, Vol. 19, p.143.

135. *Muhammad sitari kih dar maccih dirrakhshid*, p.92.

136. *Bihar ul-Anwar*, Vol. 19, pp.265-266.

137. *Kamil*, Vol. 2, p.118; *A'lam Alwari*, p.76.

138. *Tabaqat*, pp.27-29.

139. *Tarikhi Tabari*, Vol. 3, pp.1463-1476.

140. A Jewish tribe residing near Medina.

141. *Bihar ul-Anwar*, Vol. 20, p.191; *Tarikhi Tabari*, Vol. 3, p.1472.

142. *Tarikhi Tabari*, Vol. 3, pp.1487-1493.

143. *Kamil*, Vol. 2, p.192; *Tarikhi Tabari*, Vol. 3, p.1511.

144. *Kamil*, Vol. 2, p.216; *Tabaqat*, Vol. 2, pp.77-78; *Tarikhi Tabari*, Vol. 3, pp.1575-1584.

145. A place near Damascus.

146. *Tabaqat*, Vol. 2, pp.92-94.

147. *A'lam Alwari*, pp.104-112; *Bihar ul-Anwar*, Vol. 21, p.106.

148. *Kamil*, Vol. 2, pp.247-250.

149. *Bihar ul-Anwar*, Vol. 21, p.149.

150. *Sirihi ibn Hisham*, p.482.

151. *Tamaddun*, p.148.

152. *Kamil*, Vol. 2, p.61.

153. *Safinat ul-Bihar*, Vol. 2, p.413.

154. *Kamil*, Vol. 2, p.210; *Makatib ul-Rasul*, Vol. 1, pp.30-31.

155. *Makatib ul-Rasul*, Vol. 1, pp.35-41, 60-182.

156. *Ibid.*, p.90; *Sirihi Halabiyih*, Vol. 3, p.277.

157. *Muhammad wa zamamdaran*, p.162.

158. *Sirihi Halabiyih*, Vol. 3, p.285.

159. *Makatib ul-Rasul*, Vol. 1, p.172.

160. *Al-bidayah wal Nahayah*, Vol. 5, p.53.

161. *Bihar ul-Anwar*, Vol. 21, p.361.

162. The law of emergency is applied in emergency situations. The law of non-guilt is applied in cases of severe trouble. The law of no loss is applied when a loss may occur. The conditions and qualifications of these laws have been explained in detail in the books on theology and jurisprudence.

163. *Jami' ul-Javami'*, p.275; *Tafsir al-Mizan*, Vol. 2, p.144; *Tafsir ul-Kashif*, Vol. 3, p.164; *Tafsir ul-Biyadwi*, p.477; *al-Bayan*, Vol. 7, p.91; *Ruh ul-Ma'ani*, Vol. 22, p.32.

164. *Mustadrak*, Vol. 2, p.262.

165. *Usul ul-Kafi*, Vol. 1, p.177.

166. *Najh ul-Balaghah*, Fiyd ul-Islam, sermonn 133, p.403.

167. *Kamil*, Vol. 2, p. 278.

168. *Uyun akhbar ul-Reza*, Vol. 2, p.80.

169. Encyclopedia of *Farid Vadji*, Vol. 3, p.542.

170. *Al-Ghadir*, Vol. 1, p.9.

171. *Kamil*, pol.p.216, 278, 242.

172. *Tarikhi Tabari*, Vol. 3, pp.1171-1173.

173. *Fadail ul-Khamsih*, printed by Dar ul-Khutub ul-Islamiyah, Vol. 1, pp.178-186.

174. *Al-Ghadir*, Vol. 1, pp.9-11.

175. *Ibid.*, pp.60-61.

176. *Al-Ghadir*, Vol. 1, pp.166-174.

177. *Ibid.*, pp.198-199.

178. *Ibid.*, pp.14-61.

179. Twenty-six have been mentioned in the first volume of *Al-Ghadir*, pp.152-157.

180. *Al-Ghadir*, Vol. 2, pp.34-41.

181. *Ibid.*, Vol. 1, pp.270-271.

182. *Ibid.*, pp.274.

183. *Bihar ul-Anwar*, Vol. 16, pp.220-229.

184. *Ibid.*

185. *Kohl ul-basar*, p.69.

186. *Bihar ul-Anwar*, Vol. 16, pp.226-228.

187. *Ibid.*, p.240.

188. *Ibid.*, pp.229, 281, 182.

189. *Kohl*, pp.67-68.

190. *Bihar ul-Anwar*, Vol. 16, pp.226-232.

191. *Kohl*, pp.67-68.

192. *Bihar ul-Anwar*, Vol. 16, pp.228-229.

193. *Ibid.*, pp.264-265.

194. *Kamil*, Vol. 2, p.252.

195. *Ibid.*, pp.248-252.

196. *Irshad us-Sari Lisharhi Sahih Bukhari*, Vol. 9, p.456.

197. *Wasa'il*, new edition, Vol. 1, p.442.

198. *Ibid.*, Vol. 1, p.443.

199. *Safinat*, Vol. 1, p.419.

200. *Wasa'il*, new edition, Vol. 1, p.349.

201. *Ibid.*, Vol. 16, p.472.

202. *Ibid.*, Vol. 3, p.344.

203. *Ibid.*, Vol. 1, p.365.

204. *Kohl*, p.78.

Index

E

Ethiopia, 40, 41, 72, 83, 91

F

Fakh pasturage, 45
Fatima, 34, 128-130
Fatima Makhzumiyah, 127

G

Gabriel, 50, 52, 55-57, 117, 130
Ghadir Khum, 115-121
God *see* Allah
God's House *see* Ka'aba, *also* Masjid ul-Haram

H

Hafsa, 39, 41
Hajj, 76, 115, 117
hajjis, 115, 119
Halima, 21
Harith, 21, 41
Harith ibn 'Umar, 97
Harqal, King, 105
Hasan, Imam, 129
Havazin, 98
Hawzah, 105
Hayy ibn Akhtab, 42
Hijaz, the, 19, 28, 103, 115, 117, 118
hijra, 75-80, 88, 95, 96
 beginning of, 79, 80
Hind, 127

145

K

L

M

N

Nabi, 113
Nafisa, 34
Nahj al-Balaghah, 16
Najashi, 104
Najran, Bishop, 106
nationalism, 15
New Testament, 50, 51

O

Old Testament, 50, 51

P

paganism, 58
Persia, 20, 83, 104
pilgrimage, 97, 115
prayers, ritual, 57, 58, 118, 126, 128, 129
prophecy, 75, 104, 109, 112, 125
prophets, 52, 55, 56, 63, 94, 102, 113, 124

Q

Qasim, 34
Quba, 78
Qur'an, the, 38, 51, 75, 77, 82, 83, 88, 93, 104, 112, 113, 118, 124, 129
Quraysh, the, 23, 26, 27, 29, 32-34, 40, 46, 47, 64-73, 76-79, 81, 90, 94-97, 103, 117, 127

R

S

T

U

Uhud, the war of, 95, 99
'Umar, 119
Ummah, 56, 116, 119, 120
Umm Habiba, 39, 41
Umm Kulsum, 34
Umm Salma, 39, 40
'Utbah, 70
'Uzza, 26

V

Vajdi, Farid, 115
vali, 120

W

Walid, 46
Walid ibn Maghirah, 70
Warqa ibn Nawfal, 33, 56

Y

Yamamah, 105
Yasir, 72
Yathrib, 26, 76

Z